TIM

The Price Paid

PAINE

TIM
The Price Paid
PAINE

A STORY OF LIFE, CRICKET
AND LESSONS LEARNED

MACMILLAN
Pan Macmillan Australia

Pan Macmillan acknowledges the Traditional Custodians of country throughout Australia and their connections to lands, waters and communities. We pay our respect to Elders past and present and extend that respect to all Aboriginal and Torres Strait Islander peoples today. We honour more than sixty thousand years of storytelling, art and culture.

First published 2022 in Macmillan by Pan Macmillan Australia Pty Ltd
1 Market Street, Sydney, New South Wales, Australia, 2000

A catalogue record for this book is available from the National Library of Australia

Typeset in 13.5/18pt Bembo Std by Midland Typesetters, Australia
Printed by IVE

The author and the publisher have made every effort to contact copyright holders for material used in this book. Any person or organisation that may have been overlooked should contact the publisher.

The paper in this book is FSC® certified. FSC® promotes environmentally responsible, socially beneficial and economically viable management of the world's forests.

To Bonnie, Milla and Charlie. You are my life.

CONTENTS

PROLOGUE

One day you are living the dream. It's a cliché but this was the complete cliché. The dream with a capital D. Captain of your country, about to play an Ashes series with a team that's as good as any going around, playing cricket with mates, travelling the world, living out the fantasy.

The next you're sitting at home with nothing but shame. Then there's despair.

Your wife is leaving you, your name is mud, you hate yourself and you hate what you have done and you hate the thoughts tormenting your every waking moment. The kids are looking at you with no idea what's going on, and you can't sleep, you can't eat, you can't function, you can't go outside or answer the phone or look yourself in the eye.

The darkest of thoughts keep coming and you want to bargain, you'd give up everything to have your wife back, but you'd given up everything for a game and now you don't even have that.

You want to know what that was like? What it was like to see everything go up in flames? What it's like to live among the ashes? Come into this place for a while then, but be advised that it's not pretty. I hope you don't think I feel sorry for myself, no doubt there are times when I did, but mostly I hate myself for what I'd done and I'm not just talking about those few minutes of stupidity on a mobile phone on the eve of the Brisbane Ashes Test four years before.

I don't want to make excuses or beg for your pity. Don't read it and weep, I've shed enough tears. Read it and learn and thank whoever that you never lived it.

Good days you can frame like memorabilia and assign an individual number, bad ones just run into each other, they find the lowest ground and just pool there.

Most days I'm broken, sometimes I'm angry and one day in the middle of all this I see my Australian kit all packed up in the Cricket Australia bag on the shelf in the garage and ready for the first Test in Brisbane and I stuff everything into the rubbish bin. Then I pick up the Cricket Tasmania bag and I do the same. Pads, bats, gloves, helmets, everything.

This spiral started almost four years to the date it finished. November 2017, Brisbane, at the team hotel in Southbank. On a high, about to re-ignite a cricket career I'd thought had passed me by. The Ashes are on, the first Test a few days away, the tension exquisite, but excruciating too.

A text exchange from an employee at Cricket Tasmania turns flirtatious and the exchange goes too far. I was an idiot, but it was consensual and . . . it was unspeakably, unforgivably stupid.

I knew I'd done something really, really dumb. I was a dickhead.

I worry about it constantly but life goes on. Until it doesn't.

June 2018, Hobart, and that dream I'm living has gone up a notch. I'm no longer the recycled wicketkeeper whose selection they say highlights how desperate Australian cricket is. Seven months after those stories were written, I'm the Australian captain. Maybe they did turn to me in desperation, but they turned to me and I'm ready to go to Brisbane to meet the new coach Justin Langer and lead the team to England for a one-day series. I'm at home, the phone rings and I see Nick Cummins's name come up on the screen. He is the chief executive of Cricket Tasmania, he's the reason I'm still playing cricket for the Tigers, the reason I had to ring Kookaburra Sport 18 months before and say I wasn't going to take that job as a sales rep. It was a good opportunity, but Tassie, who'd just employed Nick and made a few other changes, were willing to give me another shot. Then Cricket Australia followed and gave me a second chance and now I'm here about to lead the team on my first tour as Australian captain.

Cummins says he has an issue. He says the employee has left but she's told them she has sexual messages and a picture I sent her. She makes allegations about other men working there too.

My heart's in my mouth. My pulse rate's gone through the roof. I know I'm trying to keep calm but I'm not doing very well at it.

'Yeah, they're from me,' I admit. There's no denying the exchange.

I don't remember much more of the phone call because I am thrown into a world of fear and panic. I could see instantly how bad this was going to look when my wife Bonnie found out. This is going to break her, we have a child, a home, a relationship that's going better than it has been. At this point cricket's a secondary thought. I've told everyone since I got back into the game that every day has been a bonus. Don't get me wrong, cricket matters, I've devoted every minute of my life since I was a boy in shorts to the game, for most of my life it mattered too much, but right now I can only think about Bonnie.

I ring my manager, James Henderson, he's a good mate too, a good man, another Tasmanian who has looked after Ricky Ponting and Phil Hughes and who knows his way around. He's been guiding me since I was recalled in November. Things have gone to another level now I'm the captain. I can hear in his voice that this is serious, but nobody needs to tell me that.

Nick or James rings Cricket Australia and I suppose they're briefed. I don't know. I try and carry on with my pre-tour routine, but I can't concentrate.

Somehow I get to Brisbane where the team is all gathered, ready to meet Justin Langer as our coach for the first time and prepare for the trip over to England. We're having meetings, we're talking about a new start for Australian cricket, JL's telling us his vision, there's the pall of the sandpaper incident in South Africa sitting over the group like a dark cloud, but I've got my own personal storm that's keeping me distracted.

The dream has become a nightmare, and it is horrendous.

The worst part of it was agonising over what it would do to Bonnie, but the other part was wondering when it would all come out. Would I wake up today and see it all over the papers, turn on the radio and hear the breaking news? That would be so hard for my mum and dad. I was just in a totally anxious state. I couldn't think about anything else, there were waves of anxiety and anguish crashing over me the whole time.

Everyone in Brisbane was nervous and excited about a new start. Australian cricket was in a strange place. No one was really sure what would happen. Steve Smith and David Warner, the captain and vice-captain, had been suspended for a year. Cameron Bancroft got banned for nine months. The game was at a loss about where to go and what to do. The media and the public had been vicious. It felt like we'd been attacked by an angry mob.

In the middle of it all, I'd been appointed as captain and JL as coach and we were supposed to find a way back into people's hearts, but it was going to be a long journey. The one-day series in England was going to be the first time we'd played since the scandal broke over us in South Africa. Brisbane was the first time we'd all got together and so there was a lot to talk about, a lot to be anxious about.

One day between the meetings and training sessions, I was picked up at the team hotel in Southbank and spirited away to a secret meeting at another hotel in the city. I was met in the foyer by a lawyer who James had found to represent me. I talked through it with her and then we went upstairs to a meeting room where Cricket Australia's integrity officer, their lawyer and maybe one other person was there. I think there was a public relations person in the room, but to be honest I haven't exactly dwelt on those sorts of details since.

They questioned me like they believed the worst version of this story – it was intense but I understood that they wanted to be thorough. I had deleted the text exchange soon after it happened and told them that. I offered them my phone and they sent it away to somebody who could take a forensic footprint of it. It had been a consensual exchange, there was no doubt about it, and if they could find the messages at least they would see that.

James and Nick Cummins had both said I needed to tell Bonnie, and the representatives for Cricket Australia said the same thing, and they were right.

You can understand why it was a conversation I was not all that keen to have. I'd been stewing on it for days, but I knew I had to do it. It didn't go down well, as you can imagine. It was a rough few days for us but if I'm going to be selfish I have to admit I felt better for having told her.

Some time after that meeting Cricket Australia confirmed it was not a breach of the code of conduct, that it was a private matter and I could get on with my job.

Had I sexually harassed that woman I would have deserved to be dumped, but I knew I hadn't, it was a private conversation between two adults. It was shameful on a personal level, the real victim in this was Bonnie, but professionally I was cleared.

Cricket Australia were going to back me in public if anything came out and my manager worked with then chief executive James Sutherland to prepare a statement if needed.

There was no confidence it was going to end there, however, and I was the least confident of that happening.

I don't reckon I was ever naive enough to hope that this would pass, but I don't know what I would have done if you'd told me how long I would have to live like this. Sure, it hasn't been with me every minute like it was then, or now, but it was always there to some degree and there were going to be plenty of other stressful weeks just like this one.

Over the years I've wondered why I did what I did and I don't want to make any excuses – it was dumb, it was wrong, it was a breach of trust with my wife – but how was I so thoughtless, so self-indulgent? Why would I take such a stupid risk? I think maybe it was just a way of escaping from all the pressure I was under, it wasn't that I was on a high about getting a second chance at Test cricket, it was a way to escape the reality of that, the stress of it.

I'd have given up that second chance if I could have my time over again.

There were moments in that week or so in Brisbane when I was training or on the field where I was momentarily free of anxiety, but it came screaming back every time I paused. Between deliveries in a game or at training it would just hit me again and not allow me to think about anything else. It was all-consuming.

Over the years, there'd be a week or a month or so where I'd get a break from it, but it would always lurk in the background. It seemed every time Australia was about to play a series someone would ring Cricket Australia or Cricket Tasmania or my manager and start asking questions and it would trigger the stress again.

So I kept living the same nightmare over and over again.

At times I behaved poorly and I treated people poorly. I was doubling down and I am as ashamed of that as I am of that text exchange. More ashamed of it, actually. Looking back I was so anxious it made me grumpy and agitated and I was awful to be around. I was like a man who just needed to escape the crowd to find some space but I couldn't find any.

I think I was highly, highly stressed. I'd get home from cricket tours and I would be snappy or not talking at all. Poor Bonnie had no idea what was going on in those periods. When the issue would flare up because of a phone call, I would hide it from her and just descend into the pit again. I didn't want to worry her, but I was treating her really poorly.

Bonnie was the one who copped it the most and that kills me.

For a lot of that period the smiling, carefree captain was the public persona, but at home I was a mess. We'd go out and people would say to Bonnie, 'He is such a good guy,' and later she would say to me, 'How come everyone else gets this good guy and I get this shitty, grumpy you?' After we had dealt with it initially in 2018, I never really spoke to her about it again so she had no idea how it was consuming me. She just thought I was being a prick.

To be honest I wasn't aware of this myself at the time. I thought I was normal, that I was entitled to some peace and quiet. When I was home I just wanted to sit in front of the television and veg out, Bonnie would be talking to me and I couldn't hear her. I didn't want to. I was a selfish prick.

I went into a bit of a hole when I was first made Australian captain. I used to be a really social guy but I became the opposite and I stopped wanting to see anybody. All my life I was always going out to catch up with mates, having a beer, then when I met Bonnie we had a great social life, we loved going out.

I think that changed when I became captain because wherever I went I was recognised. For the first few weeks I thought that was really cool, but then it became an absolute punish. Nobody spoke to me about anything other than cricket: at Bonnie's work functions, at the pub, anywhere, anytime, all the time. Nobody ever wanted to just talk about other shit. They wanted to know what Cummins was like, or Warner, or this or that. People wanted to take photos. Even my friends became like that.

I told Bonnie that I couldn't go to these social things anymore, it was no fun for me, and then I started to withdraw. When I was home I didn't want to go out and see people. In those dark periods I would stop eating and I'd lose energy.

For nearly four years I lived like a condemned man. Would the story come out? It was going to be a shitstorm if it did. I was terrified but when it did come out, it was worse than I ever imagined.

Something had set me off the day I threw my cricket gear out, in December 2021, the day of the first Test match in Brisbane. I don't know what it was, it could have been a phone call or a story in the news. I was angry but it was hard to say why

Maybe it was the awful vacuum I was in.

Maybe because I'd always thought family could wait, that I would devote myself to cricket and then I'd be a great husband and a great dad when my career was out of the way. Everyone in my family saw that as me being selfish, but I was rationalising it by saying that I would put everything into cricket to help them. I would make up for not being there physically or emotionally with what I earned financially. I would buy them houses and cars or whatever to make up for my absence.

When I had time off from the game, I saw that as time to chill out, rest, reset myself. I didn't have the energy to throw myself into family life to compensate for the time I'd been absent. I just needed to sit in a chair and say nothing. In my day job, I was constantly having to talk to people, deal with people, talk to JL, talk to players, talk to team managers, deal with this problem and that problem. I was training as hard as everyone else, but because I was captain I had to be available to anyone for any little thing that was going on.

When I came home, the last thing I wanted to do was talk. That's all I'd done all day. Talk and listen. Talk and listen. I just needed some silence at home.

On a Saturday in winter, when there was no cricket, I would sit in front of the television and watch every game of football from 1 pm until 11 pm. Then I would get up on Sunday, go to the coffee shop by myself and read the papers for an hour and a half. I'd go home, open my laptop, get on the phone, and then the footy would start again and I'd be glued to the telly.

If Bonnie wasn't there, I spent time with the kids, but it was never for very long.

Now cricket had thrown me out on the streets. when they told me I should stand down as captain they had taken away my purpose. I was broken and so was my marriage. I couldn't see any way back to the game if they weren't going to support me and at this point I couldn't see how I was going to repair the damage done to my family.

When I was at rock bottom, my great mate Peter Siddle told me that things would get better and he was right. I'm getting there and so is my family. I've found a new way to live, and I'll get to that.

But there's a whole lot of other stuff to talk about first.

1

A BOY FROM HOBART

I t started innocently enough.

Still, cricket was always serious for the kids of Bambra Street, Lauderdale, in the 1980s. There was no point if you weren't playing to win, weren't trying to be the best you could be. Of course it was fun, but there was no fun if you were beaten. Cricket was our currency. The measure of our worth. Our language. Our thing. We were just kids, we didn't have anything much but on the cricket field we were kings. It was our space, we owned it and we loved it.

Aussie rules football was serious too, but not like cricket was.

If they'd had drones then, you'd start a movie about our lives with a shot rising above a quiet street in a secluded

Hobart suburb where the waters lapped at the shore and the past was hanging on for a bit longer than it was in other parts of the world. We were still living the innocent childhood. Push bikes to everywhere. Backyard cricket on long summer evenings. Footy when the days got shorter. Short pants all year round.

Me, my older brother Nick, Jared Watkins, Andy Matthews, Ryan Downie and Matthew Wade – or a combination of those kids – were the Lauderdale gang. Not in any official sense, rather we were the ones most obsessed by cricket and footy. Little else mattered in those days.

The shortest of us, Wadey, was my neighbour, my mate, and – many years later – a man I would take the field with for Tasmania and then Australia. Sometimes he would also be my rival for the wicketkeeping gloves in the Test team. Even when we were kids, despite his relative youth and diminutive stature, he was a gun cricketer and that's why he was part of our gang. Didn't matter how young or small he was because he could hold his own. He couldn't hit the ball off the square but, the way I remember it, there wasn't a bowler in junior cricket who could get him out. Tenacious and tiny. Like me, I guess, but the short span of years that divided us back then gave me seniority – three years is a big deal when you're a kid.

In the years that followed, if Matty and I were competing for a spot in the state or national team, there was never any tension between us and I guess that is because we went way back.

It's hard to forget where you came from and who came with you.

Scott Wade, Matty's dad, was a legend, one of the best footballers on the island and one of the many who'd made a name for themselves on the mainland when he was chosen for Hawthorn. He was still a big name around the game in those days.

I don't know when we started these backyard matches but I know by the time I was in the later years at primary school they had their own rhythm and intensity. It was a ritual, almost a religion. Everybody lived within a few minutes of each other and calls would go out in the morning and the games would be on at an arranged time.

Wadey's granddad had a roller. I don't know why he had a roller but he did and when you take cricket as seriously as we did, you want to roll the wicket like the professionals do. I remember knocking on Wadey's granddad's door and being led around to the garden shed and then the sound it made on the road as we pushed it down the street to his cousin Andy's house, which had the best backyard for cricket.

Everything had to be perfect or as close to it as we could get. Pitch, outfield, stumps, score sheets. We'd mow the lawn down, roll the pitch and then get to work on the finer details. We'd carefully paint the crease and then do our best to paint sponsors' logos in the grass. I remember somebody got the idea to cut the logo out of a beer carton and tape it to the stumps at either end so that we'd have the same local beer sponsor as the state team. Andy's dad would have a few beers while umpiring the matches so we were right if we ever needed to replace the sponsor's logo. Every time you bowled someone, you had to stick the cardboard back on before the game could continue.

Even then we put a lot of effort into the craft of backyard ball maintenance. My brother and Jared were masters of getting it just right. They'd put in twisted rubber bands on the tennis ball for the seam which was taped on first to make it a bit wobbly, then you'd do the taping for the swinging part.

Nick and Jared were a couple of years older than most of us and set the standard. If you didn't meet it, you got no sympathy. They played hard, like the men we looked up to. You didn't give a sucker an even break and you most certainly did not give your little brother or his mates one.

There was a grim determination about Nick and I, we played to beat the other side, the other bloke. There was fun in the game but the only real joy came with a win and the bragging rights.

Nick never gave me a second chance or went easy on me from an early age. I remember bowling at him for hours on end if the others weren't there. I'd bowl and bowl and bowl until I was just about on my knees from exhaustion, but he'd defend the occasional good ball, slog the bad ones as I wearied. When I'd finally get him out and it was my turn to bat, I'd be so tired he'd knock me over easily, sometimes with the first ball. He'd celebrate the wicket and then walk towards me, take the bat and we'd start all over again. No mercy.

I think our whole family was like that, well, the men at least. The old blokes came at you hard and made you earn it. Dad would sometimes join in our games and very occasionally he would give us a break and hit a catch. Not an easy catch, mind you, he'd drill it and you had to hang on. You had to earn your victories.

The sport possessed us and our games were an obsession. It was all-consuming to the point that I would sit in the classroom at school, thinking, 'How am I going to get Nick out?' or 'How am I going to score runs against Jared this afternoon?' You can't concentrate on school when you've got *that* on your mind!

Jared was a bit bigger than us, he was quicker too and he was a handful at times. Us younger ones had to learn to hold our own and we soon did. There was no slack for anyone who didn't cut it and I'm ashamed to say we didn't really rate anyone who was not up to standard – it was a pretty exclusive little cricket arrangement we had.

Early school reports said both Nick and I were intolerant of anyone who wasn't at our level and I cringe now when I think about it. I reckon it held me back when I was captain later in life – I had to learn empathy. I had to mature emotionally and realise not everyone was going to play at the same standard and it wasn't their fault.

The drive to be the best demands a certain level of selfishness, I guess . . .

Along with learning your skills you had to learn how to hold your own in a verbal contest with the older boys. From early days we learned not to take a backward step when somebody confronted us, not to flinch, to never give an inch even if it was someone bigger and older lording it over you. And you learned how to give a bit of lip back if you were on the receiving end.

For a long time to come, older and more experienced opponents would be surprised that we'd answer back if they tried anything on. You can imagine what a shock it was for a big sweaty fast bowler in club cricket – twice our size and twice our age – to be told to 'get back and bowl' when standing mid pitch trying to intimidate me or Wadey or any of us boys. But I'm getting ahead of myself.

Later, the game will put me back in my place, but for now it's all summer days and good times.

I was a 'fast' bowler then. Eventually, after bowling for what seemed like years on end without success, I worked out Nick's weakness. He used to fall across his front pad a little bit and I got really good at hiding the ball when I ran in so he couldn't see the seam. I think I might have picked it up from a Waqar Younis or someone like that. I would get a few to go away then turn the ball around, duck one in and hit him on the pads – as I've said, we took it seriously, we watched our heroes and we learned their tricks.

Years later Nick told the newspapers that he reckons he got a bad back from bowling to me in the backyard. He clearly has a selective memory.

As a bowler Jared was really hard to get a handle on because he would turn his hand around and you'd think the seam was going this way but then he'd turn it back in the delivery and it would go that way. It was obvious once you worked it out, but it was another lesson. You had to watch the bowler's hand all the time, look for changes and adjustments.

We were living and breathing cricket and we were fascinated by its complexities. As we got older it got a bit more complicated because life started to get in the way of the game. Jared went to a school in town instead of the local school and we'd have to wait for his bus to make its way over the bridge that connected us to town. Waiting for him drove us mad, we thought it was pretty selfish of him to go to a school so far away that it delayed our start times by 30 minutes.

Most of the time we had fixtures and tables running which we drew up with a set number of rounds and set teams. Ryan Downie, the younger of the Downie brothers from down the road, was on my side. It was two players a side, there could be six or eight people there, but if it was a rostered match it was two on two and the others would score or umpire. Games weren't quick because it was hard to score runs. We had automatic keeper so you didn't need a person, but if the ball was swinging a lot the batsmen would take block out of their crease and we'd have to change and put in a real wicketkeeper to bring the stumping into play. We were all developing our cricket smarts.

The slips cordon was half ferns and half a shed and we made it that if the ball slipped out of the ferns it was considered a dropped catch and you batted on. It didn't happen often, but occasionally one fell out. It would bring the house down if you got a nick and the slips dropped it. If you got dropped you knew you were having a good spell and you'd be in all day. I reckon it was the equivalent of getting out on a no ball.

Not all the matches followed such strict protocols. Occasionally we'd play in the street or even at the end of the street on the beach, and while we were still having a crack it wasn't as intense as those backyard games became over the years.

We'd watch cricket on the television regularly, but were probably more committed to our own matches. If someone was nearing a hundred, our game would stop – well, not stop, just pause while we went inside and watched until the player got his century and then we'd head straight back out.

If, say, Warney was putting on a clinic or something, we would watch for a bit, but never if we were at Andy's place, because if we were at Andy's it was full competition, game on. They were the big games. Very serious, lots of arguing, lots of fights, though none bad enough to derail a game. Nobody in our lot would take their bat or ball and go home. Nobody ever ran to mum or dad. I reckon if I'd have done that, my reputation would have been shot, no matter how young I was or how hard Nick and his mates were going at me. The game mattered more than hurt feelings. And the best way to come out on top in that situation – in fact, the only way – was to win.

I think I took that attitude later to state cricket. Interestingly, the Tasmanian state sides turned the corner and started to win Shields when we stopped considering ourselves underdogs or the little brothers. Tim Coyle banished any notion that Tassie was punching above our weight and demanded we consider ourselves the equal of the big states.

There's no doubt we are different down here.

Anyone who has been to Tasmania outside of summer will be well aware of the fact we have more than one season. Winters down on the island are bitterly cold and they seemed to last forever but it never bothered us. I don't reckon we ever got out of our shorts and t-shirts. To this day, it is a matter of pride to wear shorts no matter how cold it gets.

By the time the first cold winds started blowing up from Antarctica, we'd have migrated from the cricket pitch to the footy field which was a spare block about 200 metres down the road. The pre-season ritual was just as obsessive: we'd put up goal posts, paint the boundaries and 50-metre arcs (which were nowhere near 50 metres from the goals) and paint sponsors' logos. We even had a scoreboard. We called our field Hadlow Park because it was on Hadlow Road. No, we weren't creative. It's still there if you want to go and have a look.

In Tasmania, if you don't know, we play Australian rules football. Always have. We pride ourselves on the number of champions from down here who have gone up and made it in the Australian Football League over the decades. The names of Tasmanian players who crossed Bass Strait to make it in the big league were known to all of us. They were giants.

Even in winter we spent as little time inside as possible. We had computer games but we weren't that interested in them. If it rained we might wander in, but it took a bit of persuasion – it had to be bucketing down for us not to play cricket, and nothing stopped the footy. If it got wet at Andy or Jared's backyard, which were our grass pitches, we'd pause and move the game to our place because we had concrete. As lenient as their parents were, they didn't like us wrecking their lawns. Our dads loved their lawns.

★

The Paines were a pretty normal family in a pretty normal suburb. There were six of us: Mum, Dad, Nick, Meagan, me and Madeline.

Lauderdale is a village of about 2000 people across the bay from Hobart, but most of us live on the Roches Beach side. Basically, you drive left out of town, swing over the arch of the bridge as if you are heading to Bellerive Oval and track southeast of there. It's a 20-kilometre trip that takes about 25 minutes on a good day. We were on Bambra Street which ran down from the main road towards the north end of the beach. It was quiet, comfortable and a cauldron of sports. There were plenty of kids around the same age.

My whole family was sports mad so it was no surprise we turned out the way we did. Sally, my mum, loved sport like the rest of us, she played softball at state level and was a catcher – of course. She was also very good at hockey and basketball, but did her knee and had a family and you know that story.

My dad, John, played footy and we'd spend Saturday afternoons when we were little watching him play. He was alright, a pretty tidy amateur sportsman. Dad and Nick are similar size, both a bit shorter than me – I got the height and the good looks. He was a good cricketer and was a wicketkeeper, so with Mum and Dad both in that line of work it was obvious which way I was going to go.

Our grandfather on Mum's side, Albert Shaw, was one of the best club footballers in the state and his son Robert played AFL and later coached, which was always a buzz for us when we got to visit them and hang around at the footy. We'd get to be team mascots and watch the action up close, but Robert always had us escorted from the change rooms when he gave his warm-up address.

The highlight of my experiences with Uncle Robert was when I got to sit on the coach's bench when he coached Tasmania to a famous victory over David Parkin's Victorians in 1990. There's a picture somewhere of me and Uncle Rob on the bench. It was always special for a team from our parts to beat anyone from the mainland, but especially nice to beat the Victorians at footy. The Vics thought they owned the game and their clubs have been stealing our best players for years.

My brother Nick was a pretty good footballer, I wouldn't tell him that but he was. He was captain of Clarence footy club here and he won six premierships, they were the powerhouse club in that time.

Nan lived in a house about a block from Bellerive Oval where they play all the first-class cricket. She loved our sports – her little car would be parked near the fence at every game us kids played over the years. When Dad played footy Nan's car was our base; when we played cricket or footy, we'd look up and see her there and it was kind of cool. Even later when I was playing first grade, I'd sit in the front seat with her during breaks, or when I wasn't batting, to eat her sandwiches and biscuits and watch the game through the windscreen. It gave me the greatest buzz years later to have her at a couple of Test matches.

Our house wasn't fancy but it wasn't small either. Nick and I shared a massive room upstairs. It was a converted attic space and it was perfect for us. There was enough room so we weren't living on top of each other, but it probably didn't matter because we had similar interests – any sport – and we got on fine. We had some big fights, but nothing so serious it intruded on our games.

Our sister Meagan was in between the two of us, a year above me at school, but younger than Nick. We always got on well. She's quite sporty, played a lot of hockey and married Shannon Tubb who played cricket for Tasmania and South Australia where they live now. It was only natural that my brother-in-law would be a cricketer.

Then came Madeline. We are pretty similar, but the one thing she's got over me is intelligence. She's the smart one. She's a nurse, and quite sporty of course, plays netball, loves her footy. Actually, she loves her footy too much. We both barrack for Essendon, but I can't sit and watch a game with her; she's one of those people who gets so uptight and one-eyed that every decision from an umpire against the Bombers is wrong. It drives me mad.

I'm a neat freak, maybe even a bit obsessive with it, and I've got a reputation for being tight with money:

Madeline's the same on both of those things. All of my
gear is always clean and I spend a fair bit of time keeping
it that way. I'll clean my pads between innings. I've got
rows of old sneakers in my wardrobe but you can't tell
they're old because they're all perfectly clean and looked
after. People sometimes ask if trainers I'm wearing have
been re-released when actually they're a vintage model in
perfect nick. As for being tight with money, well, there is
some truth to it, but not as much as people make out. I like
to think I'm careful with money. When I started earning
money from cricket when I was quite young, I wanted to
make it last. I've never been wasteful. I only like spending
big amounts when I know it is going to make me money,
I like to invest; if there's no upside I'm not interested.

If you ask anyone around the team they'll tell you I'm
a tight-arse, but I play up to it a bit and it works. People
assume I won't buy the coffees so they don't ask. That's
their bad luck. I pay but I just groan about it first. Put on
a bit of an act. People would be disappointed if I didn't.
I reckon I'm generous enough around my mates, but this
has become a game within the game.

Dad works in the furniture business. There isn't a stain
John Paine couldn't get out of any fabric (maybe I got
a bit of my neatness from him). He is quiet at home, but
I reckon when he played footy he was a bit of a mouth
and I reckon that's where Nick got it from. It was obvious
that opposition teams didn't like them, but everyone

who played with them rated them highly as teammates. It was better to have them on your side than be playing against them. They're both quite hard and don't mind a bit of a barney if it comes their way. Neither would take a backward step.

I don't remember Dad fighting (they were just scraps really, a lot of pushing and pulling, not much else), but I remember heaps of blues with Nick on the field because he was tough and lippy and opposition teams would go hard at him. I'd get really nervous for him, especially when Clarence played Glenorchy because I knew that he would get belted at some point, but if you watched closely he usually started it by giving someone a sneaky hit under a pack.

Nick had no fear. He let me do the worrying, he loved that. He was a bit similar to Wadey but like Wadey he mellowed as he got older.

Like I said, Nick won six premierships with Clarence and when he retired, aged 31, the local paper, *The Mercury*, called him 'one of the State League's greatest warriors'. He was a good cricketer too – a keeper–batsman like the rest of the family.

Our dad and mum were a classic local couple. They went to different schools but their fathers knew each other because they were both wicketkeepers and both played footy.

Mum worked in Parliament House and then for the police in clerical roles. At home she was the boss. If I wanted to do anything that pushed the boundaries of the house rules, I would ask Dad because he would let me, but with Mum it was no chance, rules were rules. Dad would take us to the footy club and give us ten bucks so we would disappear and he could have a few beers. He'd say, 'Don't tell your mother,' and there was no way we would do that and blow the whistle on that lark.

Dad is very quiet, but Mum is opinionated and passionate, she doesn't hold back when she is in a mood. She can be diplomatic enough most of the time, but not at home. If I visit now she tells me what she thinks in no uncertain terms about somebody or something, but Dad never will and never did when I played junior sport either. I got my diplomatic side from Dad, but it took a while to arrive.

We didn't miss out on too much as kids, our parents worked hard to get us what we wanted, we had a very good upbringing in that sense. I look back now and I can't believe how much driving Mum and Dad did for the four of us. They would finish work, pick us up and drive us round for hours after that. Any parent of sporting kids will know what it's like.

Sometimes we'd catch the bus up to Nan and Grand-dad's house after school to wait for our parents to finish work and that was good. I can't remember any Test matches at Bellerive but Nick and I would often walk over to watch Tassie play Shield cricket. The ground was only about 100 metres from our grandparents' house. Looking back now, I realise just how lucky we were to be brought up in a community of people who played and loved sport. Our parents understood us because we were just like they'd been as kids and they encouraged us.

Jared's dad, David, was a handy local cricketer and always hard to get out when he decided to join in one of our games. He was another adult who wouldn't go easy just because you were kids. He came up to the Sydney Test after my recall which gave me a chance to make amends for something that happened many years before when we were – this won't surprise you – playing cricket in the backyard.

David had a Dynadrive bat which was just about the most precious thing any of us could imagine. He kept it in the cupboard with his kit, but sometimes we'd sneak it out when he wasn't home and have a hit. I broke it. Of course I didn't mean to, I just tapped it onto the ground when I got out. It wasn't a dummy spit, we didn't do them, it was just a minor show of frustration. Honest. Anyway, the handle snapped. I was horrified. We all were because we knew that bat was his pride and joy.

We didn't tell him what happened, thinking we could fix it before he found out. We tried for weeks. At least it felt like weeks. My dad had a vice and we tried to glue the bat back together, but it wouldn't take. Desperate by now, we looked in the Greg Chappell Cricket Centre catalogue and it was like $75 with postage to buy another one and there was no way we could afford that.

Eventually we mustered up the courage to go over and tell him. We were sweating bullets. I was the most nervous, but he just laughed and said, 'That's alright, that bat was no good.'

Anyway, when he came to the Sydney Test I pulled out one of my old bats and wrote 'Sorry about the Dyna-drive' on it and signed it. I walked over to the stands one morning when we were warming up and passed the bat to him in front of the old gang. That felt good. One debt paid off. It got a laugh too.

Before we leave the backyards and school grounds, it is worth recording that my brother Nick and Preston Downie, Ryan's older brother, decided they would be our cricket coaches at Lauderdale Primary School. Even after they moved on to high school, they would still catch the bus back with us so they could keep an eye on our outfit.

Naturally we were ruthlessly competitive, we were the only team that got a pre-game rev-up from the coaches and the only one who took it seriously. On reflection we probably took it too seriously. For everyone else it was about participation, but for us it was about winning. Nick and Preston really cracked it with me and Ryan if our side lost because they expected us to win everything.

We were pretty good at Lauderdale Primary and even better when we got to Rokeby High School. I don't think our team ever lost a game of cricket at high school. We tried to keep the gang together and I can remember recruiting Wadey when he was in his last year at primary school to come and make up the numbers for our high school team. He ended up at a different high school, but we still snuck him over for games.

In Years 7 and 8 we smashed everyone. I remember bowling one team out for 5 one week and another for 7 the next week. If we batted first I would open the batting and I'd get 50 almost every week. Nobody else was getting much of a chance, so in the back half of Year 9 and Year 10 we reversed the order, just for the fun of it. I would open the bowling and our opening bowler Andy Matthews became our wicketkeeper.

Playing junior cricket meant I was always about half an hour late for the senior game. Dad would drive me to the junior game in the morning on the way to work and usually Mum or Nan would pick me up and get me to the next one. Nan was always at the club games, as I said, and she'd bring me some lunch too.

I started to get a reputation at both footy and cricket. Mum reckons the other parents would talk about the 'little blond kid from Lauderdale'. The hair and my height – or lack of it – made me hard to miss and easy to underestimate.

I played third grade against the grown-ups when I was 12 and well shy of puberty. I was tiny. I remember playing against Glenorchy at Olinda Grove, Mount Nelson, and I still remember this bowler, his name was Matt Farrow, a fit, strong bloke who was good enough to play a bit of first grade but for some reason he was playing thirds on the Sunday instead.

We had men in our side and this Matt Farrow was hitting them in the head and around the body and I remember sitting there feeling pretty nervous because he was seriously fast and you could see our batters weren't enjoying it. To make things worse, it was a synthetic pitch and they're always quicker than the turf ones we played on. Some of the parents there were grumbling about this bloke playing in a grade where there were always a few kids making up the numbers.

I was batting at about No. 7 and I had no real protection: I had a helmet but I had thin junior pads and gloves. I remember Nick was so worried he took his vest off and gave it to me so I had a bit more protection around my ribs. I don't think Dad was there that day, but Nan was and she acted like it wasn't a big deal. For Nick to give me the vest meant it was serious because normally he would just tell me to 'get on with it'.

Strangely enough I wasn't that scared when I got out there. Matt pitched a few up at the start because he probably thought he could knock this 12-year-old's stumps over, and I remember I actually enjoyed the contest.

The wicketkeeper for Glenorchy was a bloke called Brett Smith who later became their president. He was a pretty big fella. I don't remember this, but apparently he said something when I walked out to bat and I turned around and came back with something like, 'Shut up Father Christmas'. Apparently you were meant to keep your mouth shut at that age. I think the other team were a bit shocked, imagine a short-arse 12-year-old mouthing off back at the adults. I didn't get heaps but I top-scored in both innings. We were out for about 50 both times and I scored 20-odd not out.

I don't think things like that happen now. I don't think 12-year-old kids would be allowed to face men and, if they did, I have a feeling it would play out differently, but it was just the done thing then. It didn't matter if you were 12 or 20, they were just at you, it was the way cricket was and I wasn't used to any different in the backyard, so it didn't bother me.

I earned a reputation as the kid who wouldn't take a backward step. The only thing that changed as I got older, I think, was that I learned to stop talking back, particularly when batting. Enrico Di Venuto, father of Michael, was one of the coaches at the University of Tasmania Cricket Club where I played my senior cricket and he was one of the big influences on me in my early teens. He told me it was pointless trying to win an argument when you were batting. He added that there was plenty of time for that when you were keeping. And there was.

There's a story behind me going to Rokeby High which isn't great. It was the local high school, it was where Nick and his mates went, where all my mates from primary school would go and it was obviously the school where I would go, but I had to fight to get there.

When I was in Year 6 I had already started playing a bit of club cricket for the University of Tasmania. The dad of one my teammates was Barrie Irons, a local legend and the deputy headmaster and the First XI cricket coach at Hutchins School. Barrie wanted me to go to Hutchins, which was one of the best private schools in Tasmania. It was one of those old-world institutions with a reputation for turning out fine young men. Hutchins was offering me a scholarship, but I had no interest in that sort of thing. I did reasonably well at school and I wanted to be with my mates. Looking back I understand how much that would have frustrated my parents, but they let me tag along with the gang rather than making the most of this extraordinary opportunity.

Later, when I was washed up and considering a job selling sports gear, I would regret that decision. I wasted my years at high school hanging around doing subjects I had no interest in because all I was interested in was being with my mates and playing cricket. I turned my back on an opportunity that would have given me further options later in life. It placed more pressure on me in the middle of my career because I had nothing else to fall back on. I was often jealous of the players who had finished school or uni, and now I think that having the best possible education would ease a bit of pressure on professional sportsmen. To be honest, I still have some regrets about that choice.

I still see Barrie walking his dog around the suburbs and often he grins and says, 'I should have got you over to Hutchins.'

2

TEEN CAPTAIN

I was blessed. Maybe I knew it, probably I didn't, but life was being handed to me on a platter. Cricket and football came easily to me, and 'the little blond-haired kid from Lauderdale' seemed to make every under-age representative team well before he should have. He made runs, he made an impression with his keeping, he made people sit up and take notice.

If I'd learned one thing in the backyards of Lauderdale, it was that sport was only fun if you won and you only won if you took it seriously. I wasn't grim faced about it, it wasn't a chore like swimming 100 laps at 5 am before school, or torturing your body on gym mats from the time you are a toddler. I loved playing sport, loved

39

the camaraderie of team sport and I was naturally talented. Sport was serious fun.

Tasmanian cricket threw an arm around me. At the University of Tasmania Cricket Club there was a group of men who identified my skills and set out to nurture them. Naturally, they were all old-school, they loved the game and they wanted others to love it too. They put in the hours with me.

Back then you could still play football in the winter and cricket in the summer, these days it seems to be a lot harder because everyone wants to identify talent early and isolate it from the other sport. Cricket pre-season camps cut across the end of the footy season, footy pre-season starts in the middle of the cricket season. There was a time when you could do both even at the elite level. Max Walker, who was a Hobart boy, succeeded at the top in both sports. Alex Carey might have been the last bloke to do both at a serious level. He captained Greater Western Sydney the year before they entered the AFL.

Most cricketers are frustrated footballers and I think it works both ways. If you watch the Australian team before play, you will notice the footy comes out and everyone fancies themselves. If you watch footballers at a summer barbecue, they're all keen to play cricket.

By all reports – mostly his – Ricky Ponting was as good at footy as he was at cricket, but a broken elbow in a state carnival put an end to his winter pursuits. He still loves the game and was notorious for taking 'hangers' over teammates in kick to kick.

Later on, when I first went to the Cricket Academy in Brisbane, we talked such a good game that we actually found ourselves playing for a local club, which was one of the dumbest things you could do. For a start, we weren't allowed to do it. Once you reach those talent streams, they want to guard you from injuring yourself as much as possible and footy is a pretty rough game.

We were staying at Griffith University and were living with the students and one night we were watching them play footy and must have got talking to the team who asked us if we'd ever played. Cricketers being cricketers we talked ourselves up, told them how we would have been playing in the AFL if not for cricket. None of us had played for a few years and the longer you haven't played the better you get. They called our bluff, telling us that if we were that good we could play that Saturday with them. We couldn't back out and so about ten of us had to sneak out the next weekend with footy gear hidden in our bags, pretending we were off to watch a match.

Truth was, not all of us were footballers. Doug Bollinger was from New South Wales and they don't really have much of an Australian rules culture there, or they didn't, but Doug was huge and scary and they decided he would be the ruckman. Poor Doug had no idea what he was doing at the first bounce. He ran in and jumped, but instead of punching the ball like you should, he gave it a little fairy tap. I'll give him his due, though, because once he realised what he was supposed to do, he came charging in like a raging bull and scared the you-know-what out of the poor bloke on the other side.

We went pretty well. The Griffith Gladiators won the first six games straight and the cricket boys dominated. It got to the point where we would even try to play the ball the length of the ground with only academy cricketers touching the ball.

I remember the first game because I had kicked 3–2 at the break. It was going beautifully until about ten seconds into the second quarter when someone tackled Doug and his head came flying back into my nose and smashed it. It was a pretty bad break and left me with nightmares about Doug's bloody great head smashing into my face. I was obviously in trouble at the academy, so we had to make up a story that we'd been playing kick to kick and I copped one going for a mark. I went in for surgery on the Monday and missed five or six weeks training.

A few more injuries followed mine. I remember Adam Voges couldn't bowl his left-arm spin because he copped a knock in the bicep, and a few blokes wouldn't train early in the week because they had a corked thigh or pulled a hamstring. George Bailey missed a few days with a sore neck from footy. Doug got blisters from his football boots, the injury list went on and on. Jason Krejza was a classic.

He was always on the physio's table at the academy during the week and unable to train because he had bad hips or something, but he never once missed a game of footy on the weekend.

It's a testament to our group that the story never got out. We managed to keep that a secret for many years from our coaches David Moore and Bennett King.

I played for Lauderdale footy club and had clocked up about 150 first-class games by the time I was 15, which goes to show you how many times I'd double up and play in a higher division and with my own age group. I made most of the rep teams, including the Tasmanian Under 16 side, and transferred to Clarence at that stage because they played in the state competition. They were the outfit my brother Nick did so well for over the years, and they were a powerhouse team in those days. I started on the bench in my first senior game for them and went okay. We won that day by a truckload of goals and Clarence went on to win the premiership, but my first game was to be my last.

On the Monday after the game I got a call from Cricket Tasmania. Rookie contracts had just come in and they wanted to give me one despite the fact I was only 16. So that was the end of the career of one of Tassie's finest young footballers (if we ever run in to each other, I'll be happy to fill you in further on how good I would have been).

★

My education in cricket was moving at a fast pace by that stage. University of Tasmania was just the right club for me. Enrico Di Venuto, father of Michael and Peter, took me under his wing; the club president Murray Macdonald was a close friend of my dad's and he kept an eye on me. The club was loaded with serious, seasoned cricketers who all taught me little things along the way. I might not have been too keen on learning lessons at school but in cricket I lapped them up.

Dene Hills was coming to the end of his Sheffield Shield career around that time and so I got to see a bit of him. Dene played more than 100 games for Tasmania, he opened the batting with my hero Jamie Cox and had scored 21 first-class centuries before he finished in state cricket. The number 21 rolls off the tongue, but it is more than a fair achievement and takes a lot of application to raise the bat 21 times. These days Dene is the performance analyst with the Australian cricket team and Michael Di Venuto is an assistant coach.

Michael Di Venuto played nine one-day internationals for Australia, but never got a crack in the Test team and he was achingly unlucky. Divva played 336 first-class matches and scored 60 centuries among his 25,000 runs.

One of the quicks at University, Josh Marquet, had played for Tassie; Brad Thomas, our all-rounder, had played a few; and so had Tony Daly. These were hard, established cricketers and for the first few years at the club I kept quiet and watched how it was done. I was lucky that a couple of the younger blokes, Josh Bean and Shannon Bakes, adopted me. They were about six years older than me and I think I got to know them because they were always keen to kick the footy before training while the old hands were more intent on saving their energy. Josh went on to play 300 games for University and is now their coach, while Shannon was in my bridal party when I got married.

It would have been easy to get led astray in my early teens and I'd often tag along to the pub after training or a game, but I never drank. Enrico and Murray kept a close eye on me and I didn't really want to drink anyway.

There was, however, one time and it's a story I don't mind telling around the Australian team to embarrass Dene. He was just coming towards the end of his state career then and we were playing New Town who were an extremely good cricket team at that stage. They'd basically rolled our whole top order by lunch, Dene was out and he asked me, Josh Bean and James Kingston if we wanted to jump in his car to find something to eat. He was a legend and we weren't going to say no, but we did look at each other when he went down the road and pulled up outside the Cooley Hotel.

We followed him in and he walked to the bar and returned with a jug and three glasses. He was, as I said, a state legend so we just did as he did. At the same time Andrew Downton, New Town's fast bowler and another

Tasmanian player, walked in to place some bets. Downton's eyes lit up when he spied us having a beer in the corner. Josh still had to bat that afternoon and when he walked out to bat he copped a fair old spray.

As I grew I got more confident in my cricket. I'd play in the age competitions and hold my own, but wonder about how much harder it would be at the next level. Every time I took the step up, it seemed to come pretty naturally. After making the Tasmanian team in the Under 15s, I knew I could compete with anyone my age on the island and when we played teams from the mainland I knew I could hold my own against anyone my age in Australia.

Representing your state was serious stuff but we'd always been serious, as I said. I captained Tasmania in those rep games once I came of age, but was often playing when I was three years younger than the cut-off so I'd have a couple of years just playing and then lead the side in my last season. I led the Under 15s team, the Under 17s and the Under 19s, gaining confidence with each milestone. I was in the system, I guess, and I was enjoying every minute of it. Back then I didn't have to think about my batting or keeping, it all came naturally and there have been many years since when I wished that was still true when it came to my batting.

I was still playing in the Under 15s – and Under 17s – when Tasmania decided to recruit me. The season before they approached me, Tasmania coach Greg Shipperd had rung and asked if I would be a substitute fielder for Tasmania in the game against South Australia.

Would I ever.

I guess it was Greg's way of giving me a taste of what was to come and a way of seeing how I'd go in that environment – even if it was doing the most menial tasks.

I felt like an intruder that day, I sat in the change rooms as quiet as a kitten, I was pretty intimidated by the quality of players around me. The Tasmanian side was packed with guns including my hero Jamie Cox, who got a hundred batting with Dene Hills, who got a half-century. Coxy scored 51 first-class hundreds and was one of the better players never to get a chance at Test level. He represented the state in 161 Sheffield Shield games and I reckon everyone in Tasmania was pissed off he never got a Test match. I know I was but looking back those things all fed into the whole 'us against them' attitude we had.

Michael Di Venuto was batting at No. 3 that day, and Dan Marsh, David Saker and Shaun Young were all in the side. Youngy was called up to play the last Test of the 1997 Ashes when Australia had a run of injuries and Paul Reiffel went home for the birth of his child. Saker, like Dene Hills, was another guy who would become an assistant coach in the Test team when I was there.

Andrew Downton must have spied how nervous I was that day because in the rain delay he sat me down and told me that he wanted me to read a magazine cover to cover and not miss anything because the team would test me on the contents later. It was an adult mag, but I was wet behind the ears and did as I was told. I was sitting in a corner reading articles about things I never imagined could happen when Tim Coyle, the development manager, came in and took it off me. I think Mark Ridgway was involved in that incident too.

Things were going well for me in the summer of 2000–01 and I was having a fair bit to do with Tim Coyle in the state under-age sides and that worked out great for me because it was always good to have a wicketkeeper of his class and a coach of his abilities around.

That summer I was still young enough to play in the Under 17s, but got picked to play for the Tasmanian Under 19s in the National Championships, which was held in Tasmania early in the summer. George Bailey, Xavier Doherty, Brett Geeves and Ben Hilfenhaus were all in that side. All would go on to play Test cricket and it was an indication of the talent we had coming through. A fortnight after the Under 19s I hooked up again with the Under 17s for that championship in Brisbane and must have been finely tuned because I knocked up a century in the first game against the Northern Territory and one in the last against the Victorians.

In April I was picked for a three-day game against the

England Under 17s at St Peter's College in Adelaide and held my own. It was that June, after that first senior footy game for Clarence, I got a call asking me to head down to Bellerive on Monday morning because Cricket Tasmania wanted to sign me up on a rookie contract, which was a good thing because I had all but given up on school where things were, well, not going great.

I'd finished Year 10 at Rokeby and all my mates, including the guys from Clarence High, were heading over to Rosny College which specialised in preparing kids for a trade. I had no interest at all in that stuff, but signed up to do a building and construction course so I could hang around with my friends. It was another decision made to advance my social life, not my education. Before the first half of the year was done, it was obvious I was wasting my time and everyone else's.

Looking back, I wonder if I would have bitten my tongue the way Mum and Dad did when I opted for this path. First, I turned down the opportunity to go to a really good school and now I was staring out the window at a school which taught trades I had no interest in pursuing. Mum says she just knew I'd make it as a cricketer and I was obviously of the same mind. I remember a teacher in Year 10 having a go at me when I said I was going to play cricket when I finished school. She pointed out there were only 11 players in a cricket team. She was almost right. I was confident, that was true. Some might say cocky.

Or arrogant. What the teacher was wrong about was that there weren't 11 places for me because I only wanted to do one thing and that was to be the wicketkeeper.

Mum reckons that she was getting feedback from Rosny that I was a distraction and that I was holding my mates back. They wanted to get an apprenticeship and there was a bit more in it for them than me. I feel bad about that now. But going to that school meant I could keep playing club cricket till I graduated.

I went into Cricket Tasmania that June day with my parents who had to sign the contract because I was 16 and not old enough to sign anything. I think I was the youngest ever player contracted to a state, but I took it in my stride in a way. I was going to be paid $10,000 a year which was great money for someone who was still at school, but it was made clear that I was a long way off achieving my dream of playing for Tasmania in the Sheffield Shield.

To me, the money was proof I could make a career of cricket and the schoolteachers had been wasting their breath. It was the first year of the rookie program and Tasmania signed up George Bailey and Xavier Doherty who were older than me but had been my teammates in the Under 19s.

If you know Australian cricket, you would notice just how strong Tasmanian junior cricket was at that stage. I think it is fair to say that I didn't think too much about becoming an Australian player then, because what

I wanted most was to represent my state. Remember that Tasmania had never won the Sheffield Shield trophy at that point, but we were producing a long line of great cricketers. David Boon made his Test debut the summer I was born, Ricky Ponting made his when I was ten. His uncle Greg Campbell played four Tests and a dozen ODIs. These were landmark moments for Tasmanians.

A young Shane Watson had come down from Queensland to play for us halfway through that season. He was called in from the academy and I'd gotten to know him because he was a bit closer to my age – about three years older. Watto proved his class by scoring a century and we thrashed South Australia by an innings in what was the second-last game of the summer. He is one of the most talented cricketers you will ever see. He was a really fast bowler back then and he hit the ball so hard. He also had a great pair of hands. And he is one of the nicest blokes you'll ever meet.

There was a group of men who had taken me under their wings at club and state level in much the same way that my brother and Preston Downie did when I was a kid. As I said, Enrico Di Venuto, Michael's dad, was key at University and then there was Tim Coyle who guided me through the state programs and then Greg Shipperd who was in charge of the men's program. I would never have made it without them.

★

The summer of 2002–03 pretty much followed the course of those that came before and those that would come after. I didn't play a lot of cricket for University because I had to dash off to the Under 17 and Under 19 National Championships. Greg Shipperd elevated me for two Tasmania Second XI games at the start of the season and a few more towards the end. The first game against the ACT passed uneventfully then Shippy decided to slip me in for the second half of the game against the Victorians, our greatest rivals. There was no team Tasmanians resented more than that mob across Bass Strait. There was something in the Victorian cricketing DNA that made them unlikeable. It wasn't just a Tassie thing either, most states had the same attitude to them. They were bullies back in those days, especially to us younger players.

I was still more boy than man when they elevated me for that Second XI game against Victoria. I wasn't shaving. I looked like I was about 12. I hadn't completely grown and I was wearing what were essentially kids' pads. I can only imagine what I looked like to the other side.

Unfortunately for me, Shane Harwood from Ballarat was bowling for the Bushrangers and he trapped me in front for a duck in the second innings. He bowled faster than anyone I'd ever faced. He basically blew my pad off. I'd never been hit so hard and limped off slowly like my leg was broken. Shannon Tubb, who is now my brother-in-law, was batting below me and he was laughing so hard that tears were running down his face as I made my long, slow, painful exit. We still laugh about it. It's worth pointing out that Harwood got Tubby for a duck soon after.

The Second XI's games were a great learning curve. You played against people on their way up, on their way down, and some who were at the top and just blowing off some cobwebs. At the start of 2002–03 we turned out against a New South Wales side that included Michael Slater, Shane Lee, Corey Richards (he got two hundreds), Greg Mail, Phil Jaques, Jason Krejza and young Doug Bollinger.

I first ran into Mitchell Johnson around this stage in an institute challenge match in Mackay. I don't think I'd ever faced a left-arm quick before, but I wasn't too worried before he bowled because watching from the boundary he just seemed to walk in off a short run as if he was not really having a crack. He was coming back from some stress fractures at the time and looked like he was at half rat power.

Never judge a book by its cover or a bowler by his run up! Mitch was just so powerful, so athletic and so balanced he didn't need to run up like other bowlers. The first or second ball he bowled changed course halfway down the wicket and just curved in at me. You know the one. You've seen it in all the highlight reels. It brought plenty of batsmen better than me undone in the years that followed. Basically it was a repeat of the Harwood incident except Mitch's yorker nearly ripped my foot off the end of my leg. My sandshoes were no protection. I wasn't too worried about being given out because I was in shock from the pain. I limped off. Again. I think there was a lesson learned, but deliveries like that are hard to play even when you are awake to what a bowler can do. Sometimes a bowler just comes up with something that is going to take you down no matter how good you are. Especially a bowler as unique – and fast – as Mitch.

Some people make an impression on you from the start. A week after I turned 17 Tasmania played Western Australia in the Under 19 Championships in Newcastle. It was a game to decide third place but what stands out most strongly for me from that game was my first sighting of an 18-year-old Shaun Marsh. From behind the stumps you get a fair view of a batsman and while he didn't make a lot of runs he hit the ball so hard and played these elegant cover drives that left me thinking he was the best player I have ever seen. Shaun in full flight, as the world got to see later on, is next level cricket. I knew I would be seeing more of him in the future. Same as I would with Mitch.

Peter Siddle was one of quicker bowlers going around in those days at that level: a broad-shouldered boy from the Victorian bush with a big smile and a different set of chompers to the ones he sports today. He was bloody good, fit and strong, and he rattled a few line-ups, but things didn't go his way in the tournament. He's a great bloke Sidds, and I was delighted when we got him to come down to Tasmania in 2020–21 after Victoria let him go.

The first hundred against the Vics set me up and was an important innings for me in a lot of ways. I'd just been to the Cricket Academy in Adelaide that year. It hadn't gone that well at first. Bennett King was the head coach and he was a hard taskmaster. I think in Tassie everybody had looked after me because I was always the smallest and the youngest and I'd got along with the older blokes, but Bennett was not falling for my boyish charm. He had higher expectations and he'd sought me out for some serious criticism. It was the first time I got whacked between the eyes with that complete honesty approach. Nothing was excused and nothing sugar-coated. I was quite intimidated by him, a bit scared to be honest.

It was probably the first time I was treated like a man, when I did something wrong he really let me know. I have so much respect for him now, but I would have told you something different at the time. He was the first one to hold me accountable. It was at the right time too because I reckon I could have become a bit lazy or a bit too much of a smart-arse if I was let go. Bennett demanded more from me, not from a performance point of view, but more about how you train, act, be professional, treat other people.

Going well early settled things a bit between me and the boss and we developed a great relationship.

★

The Australian Cricket Academy was my first extended time away from home and it was a bit of a shock. I was lucky that David Moore and Troy Cooley were assistant coaches. Troy, or Truck, was part of what some might call the Tasmanian mafia and was well respected in cricket circles. David's a great bloke and part of the wicketkeeping union which meant we spent a lot of time together. I could be myself around him but with Bennett King I was a little more guarded because I knew he was watching me carefully, but that was only because I think he knew that a bit of tough love was appropriate. He did me a favour to be honest.

Tim Nielsen also coached at the academy, and he would later be my first coach in the Australian team. I loved him – he was a wicketkeeper too, and he's bloody fun, he loved to wind people up. But at the same time, he was an awesome coach, very passionate, no frills, an unbelievable thrower, and he really cared about his players.

I was also lucky I had George Bailey and Xavier Doherty there at the same time. We all fronted up together and looked out for each other while everyone else tried their best to make life uncomfortable. Sport was a bit different then, players tested us, bowlers were bouncing George and me in the first net training sessions just to let us know how things were. For a whole week I didn't get one pitched up from certain individuals. Some guys wouldn't talk to us and it wasn't great when some did talk to us. Damien

Wright had moved down from Sydney and was going through some similar stuff so we teamed up.

I understood it, I was a young guy with blond tips who thought he was pretty hot. It was nerve-racking because I had gone from the top of the group to the bottom and was being tested like I never had before.

After a while, things settled down. If you stood your ground, everyone respected that and got on with it. I guess they just wanted to make sure the new boys were up to it, especially the little kid from Tassie who still looked like he hadn't reached puberty.

Apart from that introduction and my little issue with Bennett King, academy life was fantastic. Having George and Xavier with me was good – we had a great group that included Dan Christian, Jason Krejza, Adam Voges and Shane Watson for a while. Rhett Lockyear was there and we became best mates, still are. I got on really well with Callum Ferguson too.

You can imagine what life was like for a group of young men at that age, living at the Del Monte Palace Hotel on Henley Beach, playing the game they love and heading out on the weekend with the $50 allowance we got for our work around the academy. Even then that didn't get you too far so we'd ration our money by spending Friday nights at the local pub then hitting the nightclubs of Adelaide on Saturday. Money being tight, the boys would load up with a few takeaway drinks in the cab so we didn't have to pay bar prices in town. By this stage I had graduated from having a soft drink in the corner like I was the team mascot or the coach's son to being part of the gang.

It was a good year to be one of the 'senior' players as there was an Under 19 World Cup in 2003–04 in Bangladesh which sounded like an adventure and definitely one I wanted to be part of.

I captained Tasmania Under 19s in the National Championships in Brisbane that summer, as I had done in my last year with the 15s and 17s, and we had a good carnival. We lost the first match against Victoria, but I was happy with my own game. I got a century opening the batting and five dismissals, including a pair of stumpings off our leggie Jason Shelton. We beat Queensland, got done by a New South Wales side that had Stephen O'Keefe batting up the top of the order and a nuggety little left-hander by the name of David Warner batting further down. I got another 80-odd at the top of our order and was starting to enjoy batting up high. Or at least I did when it went well. We beat the ACT and NT, got beaten up by Queensland, then picked ourselves up again only to put in a pathetic effort against the ACT in the final four-day match.

After the championships they have a dinner where they read out who has made the Under 19 Australian team. Most of the time, it is a bit like being chosen in the All Australian footy team because you get named and don't get to play, but as I said that year was a World Cup year and so it was important to make the team. And they made me captain too, which was a surprise and absolute bonus. I think that was the stand-out moment of my career to that point. Under 19s aren't the be all and end all, but being captain of that side tends to indicate you have the inside running at that point of your career.

Bennett King was one of the selectors at the championships who made me Australian Under 19 captain, so I guess that was proof that he was being hard on me because he saw something he liked. Adam Crosthwaite, Theo Doropoulos, Callum Ferguson and Steve O'Keefe had all captained their various state sides in the tournament and I guess they were my rivals for the Australian job.

It's one of the curious things about cricket that your rivals in the state game become your teammates in the national one. Maybe it keeps a lid on things during the year. The Sheffield Shield used to get pretty willing and sometimes you'd hear stories about blokes who probably didn't get along but you couldn't carry a grudge into the national dressing room. Just as you had to let them go in your own side. Blokes like a Matty Wade or Dave Warner could maybe seem like an enemy when you played against them and if you were silly you'd think they were awful people, but it only took a brief taste of playing with them to understand how team-oriented they are. And good blokes. I love both of them but I understand how you could get a different opinion playing against them.

People just seem easier to like when you share a purpose rather than being at odds, and we had a good time in that Under 19s team. Being made captain seemed another natural progression for me and I was being groomed for it and the responsibilities that came with it. Tim Coyle was head of our state program and we'd been pretty scrappy in one Under 19s game. The coaches were dirty on us and Tim sat me down outside the team hotel and said he wanted me to talk to the group because the message would be better coming from me than from the coaches.

We'd let the ACT beat us and the coaches were fuming. We'd got tired as the carnival went on, we'd got slack. I remember Patrick Doherty, Xavier's brother, was a pretty laidback guy and he'd been asleep in the dressing room before he went out to bat. We didn't warm up well, all those little things that you don't think seem like much but they add up. The coaches thought we didn't take things seriously enough. We got beaten in a game against South Australia and afterwards we were all having dinner in the sports club. The players finished early and went out to the car park and were yahooing about and playing handball while the coaches finished eating. They were far from impressed when they came out and took the opportunity to let us know. Ali de Winter and Tim Coyle absolutely fried us over that. They were drumming lessons into us. You could have fun but you had more fun if you won.

When I was playing club cricket or school cricket I was always captain, I don't know why, maybe because of my footy background. I reckon if you played footy you are more prepared to be vocal on the field because that's what you are brought up with and you have to use your voice. I was never one for holding back or keeping my thoughts to myself anyway. I captained at primary school and then when I went into Year 7 at Rokeby where we had kids coming in from a few other schools. I remember John Barley, who was our coach, coming over to me in the nets in one of our first training sessions asking me to do the job at the big school. I was pretty happy about that.

Being captain of junior teams didn't mean that much. The coach told you what to do and you went out there and did it. In senior teams things were supposed to be different.

Cricket Australia today announced the 14-man squad to travel to Bangladesh for the 2004 ICC Under 19 World Cup, played from 15 February to 5 March 2004.

The squad is:

Tim Paine (Captain)	Tasmania	RHB, WKT
Ahillen Beadle	New South Wales	LHB, SLA
Scott Coyte	New South Wales	LHB, RMF
Adam Crosthwaite	Victoria	RHB, WKT
Theo Doropoulos	Western Australia	RHB, RM
Callum Ferguson	South Australia	RHB, RM
Moises Henriques	New South Wales	RHB, RMF
Cameron Huckett	Victoria	RHB, RMF
Josh Mangan	Victoria	RHB, LB
Stephen O'Keefe	New South Wales	RHB, SLA
Lachlan Oswald-Jacobs	South Australia	RHB, RM
Gary Putland	South Australia	RHB, LMF
Ken Skewes	Northern Territory	RHB, LM
Shane Wallace	New South Wales	RHB, OB

Team management – Bennett King (Coach), David Moore (Assistant Coach), Brian Freedman (Manager), Max Pfitzner (Physiotherapist).

And so I headed off to Bangladesh as the captain of the Australian Under 19s with high hopes as we'd won the previous tournament, which George Bailey and Xavier Doherty played, and were the defending world champions. But the tournament went dreadfully, absolutely dreadfully.

We were awful and we had a horrible time. I don't want to make excuses, but I can't stop myself here. Australia won the 2002 event in New Zealand and we could always hold our own in places like that and in England and South Africa, but take us to the subcontinent and we were so out of our depth it wasn't funny. For young Australians the subcontinent is one of the biggest challenges you face. And I reckon even when you do find your feet, it remains the most difficult place to bat – and sometimes to bowl.

We landed in India for a series of practice games in early February. The first was in Cuttack which is well off the beaten track and then we went to Eden Gardens – a very empty Eden Gardens – for two more. Calcutta, or Kolkata as it is known now, was something else, especially for a boy from Lauderdale. If you stood still, I reckon the population of Hobart would drive by every two minutes. The place is just so full of people and life, but as cricketers it was the grounds we were more interested in. Even an empty Eden Gardens blows your mind. I had visions of that Test Australia lost in 2001, and of David Boon scoring runs at the top of the order when we won the 1987 World Cup there. It was one of those magical, slightly out of focus and mysterious grounds.

India beat us in the games. They were very, very good and had blokes who could spin it both ways which was a huge shock to kids from Australia who'd never played on pitches like that or against bowlers like them. You can't prepare for that stuff, you have to experience it and learn from experience. They figured us out really quickly, they'd bowl a couple of overs, maybe five or six at the most, with their seamers and then just bowl spin until we were out. It was a good lesson for us and our first sighting of a few names who became familiar over the next decade. Ambati Rayadu, who went on to be a decent ODI batsman, got a good hundred in the first game. Shikhar Dhawan made a century for them in the second game and Suresh Raina got me out.

We did manage to hold our own to win the last two practice matches against a local side.

Bangladesh was, if anything, more crowded than Calcutta, but we were shunted off to a place called Rajshahi to start the tournament. It felt like the end of the world.

Our hotel rooms had no glass in the windows. They did have metal bars to stop us climbing out if there was a fire – which was a distinct possibility. We'd all brought our PlayStations but it was a farce because once a third person started playing on the floor, the power went off and the whole place was plunged into an alarming darkness. I can still remember how dark it would get and how brave we pretended to be about it. There were mosquito nets on the beds to keep out the ones small enough to fit between the bars on the windows and the bathrooms were a challenge, especially for a clean freak like me.

We played Canada in the first game and had no trouble there, and we were having no trouble at 0–37 in the second match against Zimbabwe. Theo Doropoulos had flown out of the blocks, but was then knocked over by a skinny tall bloke by the name of Tinashe Panyangara who was a fair bowler. We weren't in trouble when I was gone a few overs later, with the score 2–51, but we soon were as Panyangara went through us and we were all out for a shameful 73.

Naturally we got beaten and from then on we were behind in the tournament. It turned out pretty good for Panyangara, however, as he made his Test debut that year after the local board sacked most of their senior players. He went on to play about a dozen Tests over the years and last I heard of him he was in the Latrobe Valley playing for one of the local sides.

We beat the other teams in our group, Canada and Sri Lanka, but were already out of finals contention because of our net run rate. We just wanted to go home, but we were sent through to the other side of the draw to play out the Plate Final – the consolation cup. By now a few of us were sick and not many of us were having any fun. It was humiliating, we'd won the previous World Cup, our men's cricket was so strong but we'd failed and were now in the bottom half of the comp.

I didn't keep in that series, we used Adam Crosthwaite because, believe it or not, I was expected to bowl. I was no longer the tearaway I imagined I was back in Lauderdale, now I bowled little medium pace cutters. I didn't get to roll the arm over in our game against Scotland, in fact I didn't get to do much at all in that game as I was 2 not out when we hauled in their total of 22. Their score was the lowest in the history of the tournament and 10 of their runs came from extras. Six of their batsmen made ducks. I think the game started at 8.30 am and was finished just after 9 am.

In relative terms their day was as dirty as ours had been against Zimbabwe.

One consolation in playing the Plate Final was that it was against the home team and there were about 15,000 very enthusiastic supporters. It was bloody loud, they were climbing fences and literally hanging from the rafters – the atmosphere was fully charged.

The other bonus was we were in Chittagong in a better hotel. This one had glass in the windows and enough electricity to support our PlayStations. Bathrooms weren't too shocking either.

Bangladesh batted first and got off to a good start, with their opener Naeem Islam smacking us around. Then I got him out and we were in the game. I had bowled eight overs so I knew I was going alright, but I must have been a bit too enthusiastic because my whole body started to cramp after a while and I had to leave the field. I had to drop down to No. 7 when we batted. We almost chased down the total, too, thanks to Steve O'Keefe hitting 66 off 65 balls, but he was run out and we fell nine runs short.

Aside from the heat, the thing that made fielding so challenging was that people in the crowd were breaking chunks of concrete off the stands and pinging them at us. We thought it was pretty funny, but looking back it was not great and I reckon if it happened now there'd be a walk off. Maybe we didn't deserve anything more.

Our coaches certainly lined us up for a stoning of sorts after the match. We went home with our tails between our legs.

I'd played my last game of under-age cricket. It was March 2004 and I would turn 20 that December.

3

LEARNING THE TRADE

Tassie gave me my first chance in the senior side after that disappointing experience in Bangladesh at the Under 19 World Cup. No more under-age cricket for me. I was playing with and against the big boys now.

My first game was in a domestic one-day against Western Australia and I played as a batsman because Dave Dawson was our keeper. I opened and did okay, I guess, scoring 28. We won that match and I was picked for the 50-over game against South Australia at Bellerive two days after turning 21. I scored 45 before Dan Cullen bowled me. We lost the match. I was thinking this cricket thing was pretty easy and after the game we got among it to celebrate my birthday. Then Tim Coyle came up to me and said, 'Oh, by the way Divva's got a sore back, you're on standby for the Shield game so take it easy tonight.' Michael Di Venuto was a hundred years old and always had a sore back. We thought he used it as an excuse to get out of training and so I just kept drinking and I had a monster of a night.

Hell, it was Saturday night and you only turn 21 once. I turned up Sunday for training feeling pretty shabby. Divva wasn't looking too flash either, which concerned me, but I went through the drills and went home and had a better night's sleep. I still wasn't feeling great on Monday – I don't ever pull up well after drinking and I had really put in an effort that Saturday night. I wasn't up to playing cricket.

When I got to the ground Divva was in the indoor centre hitting balls and I thought, 'Thank god for that.' A bit later he walked into the change rooms, threw his bat into his kit, and said, 'Good luck youngster.' *Oh shit!* The weekend wasn't the greatest preparation for my first Shield game and I walked out onto the ground two hours later to face South Australia's Jason Gillespie and Paul Rofe.

Nine balls later I nicked Rofe off for a debut duck. Then I had to sit there and watch Travis Birt and George Bailey cash in and put on the best part of 300 runs together while I reflected on my disappointing start to Sheffield Shield.

Nine balls was enough, however, to make an impression on me. I'll never forget walking out and having to face Jason Gillespie. I have a clear memory of the first delivery, I played a backward defence and the force of the ball nearly knocked the bat out of my hand. It was so different to anything I'd ever experienced. Sure, it was quick but I'd faced guys who were quick. This delivery seemed to have weight and speed. I understood for the first time the expression, 'He bowls a heavy ball.' The ball felt like a brick and I remember the bat being knocked back and almost hitting me.

I also remember sitting there after taking my pads off, thinking, 'I will never ever let myself prepare like that again.' I really didn't think I would play, I convinced myself Divva would be fine, but that was a lesson learnt straight away. You always have to be ready to play. I was really disappointed in myself, I had grown up dreaming about how I would get my first game for Tassie and I would score runs, but when the time came I didn't even give myself the best opportunity to do well. I was so dirty on myself.

I'm one of those people, I always pull up poorly after a few drinks. I just can't have beers and play cricket. I don't think I ever drank before a game again after that experience and people in those days did a fair bit of that. How that all played out still annoys me, I hate the fact I got a duck in my first game of Sheffield Shield cricket. I really hate it.

Every game at that stage of my life was part of a sharp learning curve. Darren Lehmann was captain of the South Australians and he got me out in the second innings with his cunning. I'd made a few runs and been batting almost an hour and their offie Dan Cullen was bowling. At one point Boof brought up the deep square fielder and said, 'Let's have a look at this kid's sweep shot.' I thought, 'I'll show him,' and swept at a ball that beat me and had me trapped lbw. I walked off thinking, 'You idiot, you've never played a sweep shot in your life.' Cullen was a very clever bowler and I was just blocking them up to that point. Boof had this way of talking you into things, he wouldn't have a go at you, but he'd say, 'This bloke can't hit it off the square, bring the field up', or 'He can't hit it over the top', and stuff like that. You'd think, 'I'll show you,' and then you'd be out, exactly as Boof had predicted.

I had a bit of time to think about what I'd learned in my first Sheffield Shield as Divva's back came good and I was not needed in the Shield side again until later that year when I got called up for the game against New South Wales at Bellerive in March. We beat them by an innings and did the same to Queensland in the last game of the year which was also at home. I didn't do anything special in those matches but I held my own. We'd gone alright that year and won four of the ten matches which would have been enough to put us into the final, but the Victorians had more points than us from the same number of wins.

Tim Coyle, the development coach when I came through the ranks, had taken over the side that season and we were building some momentum. He brought in a crew of young blokes: Ben Hilfenhaus, George Bailey, Travis Birt and I were all getting a crack at it. We all had a bit of attitude. I remember Birty taking on Stuart MacGill in the game against New South Wales. Other sides bristled at these cocky kids and in a way so did our older teammates, but it was a good thing. It turned out the veterans like Michael Di Venuto, Dan Marsh, Sean Clingeleffer, Damien Wright and Michael Dighton got a lift from having us around. They liked our energy. I spoke to Wrighty about it years later when he took over as coach and he said it really changed the dynamic of the team.

I brought my Lauderdale attitude to the Shield side and so did the other young players. Wrighty said he remembered in one of those early games that I was at short leg when he was bowling. He gave some batsman a spray and the bloke bit back. I chipped in with something intellectual like, 'Shut up and bat mate.' Wrighty liked the way we had his back and were willing to chirp; it probably wasn't the way the team had been before. He told me later he remembered thinking in that moment that the next generation of players might make a difference.

Birty would field at covers and he was the same. Bails would field in front of the batsman too and while he didn't say much, he brought real energy to the game. Hilf was bowling fast in those days, so the character of the team changed.

Winning three in a row at the back end of 2005–06 gave us belief. So the next year we were ready to go and the old guys trained a bit harder because they could smell success.

We were on to something in the summer of 2006–07 and we had some history to sort out. The Sheffield Shield started back in the 1890s with New South Wales, South Australia and Victoria. The big three let Queensland join them in the 1920s and Western Australia in the 1940s. They didn't get around to letting us in until 1977 and we spent a lot of the following years around the bottom of the table. The little island state was never really considered serious competition by the big boys on the mainland, but we were starting to get our act together.

Part of what improved us was a change of attitude. No more of this sense that we were punching above our weight when we won, we had a mindset that we were in the right weight division and equal to anyone else going around – the dressing rooms at Bellerive might not have had the history or grandeur of an SCG, MCG or Adelaide Oval, our wicket might not be as intimidating as Perth or as tropical as Brisbane, but it was XI against XI and we believed we could play cricket as good as any of them. Better, in fact. We were young and cocky with it, but we also had some serious talent among the veterans.

We went up to the Gabba for the first round and took
the points. I opened with Divva and I was flying when
I nicked off Andy Bichel on 34, but Divva kept going.
Travis Birt got a half-century, even Brett Geeves slapped
one up. Ben Hilfenhaus had big Matty Hayden's number
and Adam Griffith was up and about. They'd won the
Shield the season before so we were pretty happy with that
effort. It is fair to say Tasmanian teams had not fared well
there in the past.

The next week we headed across Bass Strait then
turned left and didn't stop until we got to the WACA –
another place we'd never done well at. You get a sense of
just how big and how diverse our country and cricket is
on the Shield circuit. We can be playing with snow on the
mountain at home, then gasping for a breath in Brisbane's
humidity or sweating in the face of the sharp heat and pace
at the WACA.

Most batsmen go to Perth and worry about the bounce
but it suited me. I wasn't big and strong, and I was more of
a back foot player, so I could handle the pace and bounce.
An added bonus was that the outfield was lightning fast
so where I'd have to turn myself inside out to hit through
the field on the lush grass at home, here the ball would
race away even with my skinny arms. I still remember
cracking a few fours there in an earlier one-day game and
feeling like a bit of a power hitter. The other thing was
that, throughout my whole career, I've been vulnerable

when you bowl at the stumps, but in Perth those balls I could let go and they went over the top. Anything hitting the stumps had to be pitched up in the scoring zone so it was a lot easier to bat.

Western Australia won the toss and sent us in and when I was on 12, I had a flashback to the games in the backyard. I nicked one off Steve Magoffin and it sailed straight to Adam Voges in the slips, but somehow it spilled out again. It was one of those magic moments when the taped-up tennis ball miraculously fell out of the ferns and you got another chance. After that it went really well, I wouldn't say I smacked it, but I timed the ball nicely. It was just one of those days, I got in the groove a bit. I was leaving well, and whenever they gave me a boundary ball I put it away.

I reckon I got into the zone for the first time at that level, I was really relaxed in the middle and in control. Divva was out fairly early, but Michael Bevan and I put on 132 then Birty joined me and we were having some fun. I got through the anxious 80s and the nervous 90s and eventually brought up my maiden first-class century.

It was a huge moment but I kept a lid on it. I was determined not to be one of those roosters who has a big celebration when they hit their hundred and then gets out. I wanted to at least get into the 110s, anything up to and including 109 was not enough.

They took the new ball soon after I raised the bat and then the umpires said they couldn't bowl the quicks because it was pretty dark so they walked off with plenty of time left on the clock. I was about 118 and happy to call it a day.

I got to go back to the hotel, rest up and come back the next morning. I remember being bloody sore, I'd never batted that long before. If they had kept playing, they'd have been a fair chance of knocking me over.

The next day Travis and I put together another hundred partnership, then I did the same with George and when Dan Marsh came out I stuck around and we notched up another hundred stand. None of the others converted, but we were having a great time.

So I had a double century in my fifth Shield game and things were looking pretty good. If somebody told me then that I wouldn't bring up another first-class hundred in the next 13 years, I don't know what I'd have thought or done. How was that going to happen? A long jail sentence? An iron lung? I was 21, I'd scored a century in the 50-over comp and a double in the Shield. What have you been smoking?

When I was on 201, I was up at the bowler's end as Justin Langer was setting the field with his bowler and he walked past and said, 'Well done, young fella, but when you get off the field today get yourself a journal and write down exactly what you were thinking today and don't ever forget it.' I remember that moment clear as day. I took his advice and I kept a journal for a bit then stopped because I didn't feel like I needed it: that was just the way I played my cricket, I relied on my talent and didn't hold with thinking too much. When I did use the journal, I'd write something about being relaxed at the crease and not in any rush, that I was in control of time and the game, rather than the other way around. What I should have written down was what I was thinking to get to that stage, I should have noted my mentality that allowed me to settle in quickly and be relaxed.

Back then I just batted and I didn't think about it and I reckon now that is why my batting never went to the levels that it should have. I just don't think I understood the batting side of the game like I did with wicketkeeping, which I had control of and could fix if something was going wrong, but with batting I never mastered it. I need to consult people about my batting when things get out of whack, but with keeping it is easy because I know. That's my area. I know what I do well and it always works. With batting I just watched the ball and hit it, that's what I did when I was young. Then over the years I chopped and changed and doubted, but without really thinking about it. Later, when I had the injury, I lost my confidence and flair and that's what it took to make me start thinking about the mental aspect of batting. I got better at that, but I wish I had the mentality and understanding I developed later with the talent and flair and confidence of that kid who got 200 in Perth. That would be the perfect marriage but those two elements never did get to be in the same room.

I didn't quite understand what JL meant at the time, I was like, 'Who would have a batting diary?' Well, I have one now and I say the same thing that he said to me to the Tassie young blokes; write down what you are thinking. I watched a kid bat at training the other day, smashing them in the nets, I sent him a note from my phone later: 'I watched you bat in the nets today, just want to let you know you look excellent, keep doing whatever you are doing technically with the coaches because it is working, however, I don't know if you have got a batting diary, but it might be worth writing down what you are thinking and what is going through your mind so you know what you are thinking when you are going well and this is what you have to do.'

I didn't quite grasp that when I was in my 20s, I wrote down what I felt, not what I was thinking.

That was my first encounter with Justin Langer, a man who was going to have a profound influence on my life some time down the track. JL was 14 years older than me, a legendary Test player, and he was so scary, so intimidating. He didn't say much, it was just the way he'd look at you and still does now, he gets that look in his eye sometimes. I studied him up close, because I was at short leg for a lot of the time during that game when he made

188 not out in their first innings. I remember how hard he hit the ball for a little fella, but he was at the peak of his powers, he was an absolute gun. I hadn't played with Ricky Ponting at that stage, so JL was the first I'd seen at that top, top level. He was smacking it.

He was a hard bastard too.

He was sweeping our spinners with so much force that I was petrified, so in a drinks break I put my one-day keeping pads on under the creams. They were green and my pants didn't quite cover them so there was a little bit of green poking out from the bottom of my pants. I remember squatting for the first ball and JL looking at me, looking at the pads and looking away, shaking his head in disgust at how soft I was. For the next hour I was trying to cover them up between every ball. I was embarrassed by what I'd done and intimidated big time. JL was like that when he was a coach, too. Little things mattered to him.

Years later I got young Nathan Ellis onto one of the early SEN radio shows I did with Jack Riewoldt and got him to tell the story about his lucky Casio watch – he wasn't keen to go there for fear of JL's response, but it had to be told.

Nathan wasn't in the XI but had gone onto the field to substitute for one over and taken a good catch. Later he was sitting down and he saw JL coming over and naturally thought he was going to get a bit of a pat on the back for his effort, but he got an absolute baking. JL hates anyone wearing any bling on field. Even an old watch.

Back in the game in Perth 15 years earlier, I wasn't watching JL because I wanted to be an opener like him; I had no interest in opening. Even after I got the 200, I just thought about how much easier it would be to get there batting at No. 7 against the old ball, or even against the new ball but with tired bowlers.

We won that game. They declared behind, I scored 56 off 77 balls, but was out to a stinking lbw decision before we declared and then we strapped ourselves in as they reined in our total. They kept getting runs but we kept getting wickets. Hilfy took five, and with three balls left in the last over they needed six to win with one wicket in hand. We won with a direct hit run-out in the last over when Divva, who had never fielded on the boundary in his life, got lucky.

We also beat Western Australia in the one-day match. I was disappointed to be run out for 84, but picked up the Man of the Match in that game too. How good was I going? How bright was this kid's future? What could possibly go wrong?

During this time I also got a call to front up and play in the Prime Minister's XI match against England in early November. It was a buzz to play against the Poms, they had so many good players in that team and had shaken the foundations of Australian cricket when they beat our mob at home in the 2005 series. They played a full strength side for the PM's game while our main players rested. Mugs like me got a go in their absence.

I caught both their openers, Andrew Strauss and Marcus Trescothick, off the bowling of Shaun Tait. God, he was quick in those days, the ball hit your gloves so hard and you really did have to keep your wits about you. But stumping Sajid Mahmood off Cam White's bowling was the highlight for me.

I opened our batting but was gone pretty quickly thanks to Andrew Flintoff who was not the bowler he'd been two years earlier at home, but he was still too good for me. My opening partner, Phil Jaques, hit a brilliant hundred at the top of the order, Shaun Marsh belted it around in the middle order, and we absolutely pumped them – which was exactly what would happen in the Ashes that followed.

I guess it was a sign of the depth in Australian cricket at the time that Tait, who took 3–21 from eight overs, could not get a look-in with a bowling attack that included Glenn McGrath, Brett Lee and Stuart Clark. I distinctly remember him beating Freddy Flintoff with pace and spreading his wickets. He was a fearsome bowler with his tail up. Jaques, in the meantime, was waiting until Langer or Hayden threw it in. The rest of us were well back in the queue.

★

While it was exciting to get a chance to play against England, when I got home it was straight back to the Sheffield Shield. As I said earlier, Tassie were starting to make people take notice. I remember we were getting under the skin of other teams a bit. I was young and had 200, blond tips and a puffed-out chest, thinking I was pretty good. Travis, George and Ben were quite confident too. Playing well only made us chirpier on the field. We didn't sledge much but we were smart-arses. If I was at short leg and Trav was at point, we'd be having conversations across the batsman.

Trav even took on JL in that Shield match. JL had this thing of slowing games to his own pace by waiting until everyone was in position. If they weren't in place after he'd marked centre, he'd walk away, come back and mark centre again so that things were always on his terms. Birty saw this and decided to mess with him. He was fielding at point but would move backward of point between balls and just as JL got set up he'd move back to point. That would mean JL would have to set up again. This went on for a while before JL stopped and said, 'Are you right, smart-arse? Just stand where you are.' Birty replied, 'Shut the fuck up and bat.' JL hated that.

We weren't going to be pushed around by senior players or intimidated by other states even when their batsmen were legends of the Test arena. Hilf had it over Matthew Hayden. When he came to the crease, Birt and I would say to each other that he was sure to nick off to slip so we wouldn't be needed and could sit this one out. Cheeky little buggers we were. I remember one time Birty was eating something on the field and Matty had a crack at him about it. Birt said something about the food he was eating being better than the stuff in Haydos' cookbook.

We rarely ever talked to them, though, we would talk about them, or take the piss a bit, but if they spoke back we'd look away. I remember Tim Coyle said later that I looked like Jane but carried on like I was Tarzan. I think it was a compliment.

We were having a great time and it was clearly pissing people off. Okay, it might be childish, but I'm afraid they're the sort of mind games that get played out there and there's a degree of seriousness. If you could rile up your opponent, that was great. You never want to concede an inch to the other side, you want to show you belong, maybe even that you own the space.

A few games later Tassie dropped Sean Clingeleffer and asked me to take the gloves and open so they could shore up the bowling. I was a kid who was unaware of my limitations so I said, 'Yeah yeah', but I should have said, 'Sure, but it would be better if I don't open.' Looking back I think the selectors would have listened, but I never said anything to anyone even though I really didn't want to open and keep – it was bred into me to do the team thing.

I think my plan was to do it well enough to be able to say, 'How about I go down the order?' I wanted the gloves because I didn't think I'd ever bat well enough to play cricket for Australia but I thought as a wicketkeeper I could. I kept and opened for three games and it was bloody hard work. I probably underestimated how hard it was going to be mentally and physically.

I learned a big lesson in the January game against New South Wales at the SCG. They batted first and they batted into the second afternoon, notching up 540 thanks to a 192 from Phil Jaques, a hundred by a future Tassie teammate, Ed Cowan, and a real good innings by Brad Haddin who was clearly my main rival for Australian keeping duties. I was knackered when they declared five wickets down and I had ten minutes to turn around and bat. My legs were stiff and heavy and Doug Bollinger had me lbw first ball I faced. I got a bit of a rest before they asked us to follow on and that made zero difference – I got a duck off the second delivery to the same bowler.

At least that seemed to convince the selectors they were making a mistake.

We were going to finish the season at Bellerive which was seam-friendly so we didn't need the extra bowler (Jason Krejza) and we brought Sean Clingeleffer back in as wicketkeeper and it worked a treat. Sean was good fun, a good teammate, and there was no rivalry between us as I was never really in direct competition with him. He was a keeper, I was a batter, and I loved fielding – we were a good team.

I played one game with Ricky Ponting that year, it was at the MCG in November and he was warming up for the Ashes. When I was batting in the nets, Rick said, 'Bloody hell, how many videos have you watched of Coxy?' He clocked on to that pretty quickly. I'd modelled my batting on Tasmania's own Jamie Cox who he knew well. I had the same stance, the same gear. I was kind of happy he noticed. I didn't get to bat with Punter that game, but it was almost better to sit and watch him, it was like watching JL. He was the best player I had ever seen and he'd been absolutely smashing it. At the time he was hitting Shane Warne wherever he wanted, that was as good as he had been. In the game he hit a six, a pull shot that went 15 rows back, it was huge. We were sitting in the change rooms and we were all giggling – you know what it's like when you've got someone on your side that is so much better than everyone else? Like he's doing it for fun. The six was off Andrew McDonald who was slow so the power was all generated by that big lunge forward, that rock back, the crack off his bat was unbelievable in an empty MCG. It was power, finesse, it was phenomenal to watch.

Punter got out chopping a delivery from Cameron White onto his stumps. It was a bad ball but it drew a worse shot. He went berserk. The heat his anger generated at such a lapse was a lesson about how much he valued his wicket and demanded of himself.

It was such a buzz to have him at training and we were all hanging off him, trying to get him to give us some of his bats – all the usual stuff that goes on around a legend. We weren't intimidated because Rick's so welcoming, particularly with young Tassie kids, he would talk to you like you were equals.

There's some star players who like to set themselves apart, hold themselves aloof from their playing group and peers. I always felt Rick had that gap between himself and others because he was Ricky Ponting, but he did everything he could to bridge the distance in cricket teams and make people comfortable around him. That blew me away about him, he was a superstar but he always went out of his way to include others. He was such a normal bloke. At first I thought he was good to us because we were from Tassie, but when I got to the Australian set-up I could see he was that way with everyone – particularly with the younger players. He knew people would be intimidated, nobody was going to roll up to him and say 'G'day mate', so he would reach out to everybody who came into the group.

He put in, too. He'd bowl to you in the nets long after everyone else had given up on training. I thought he was doing that because it was a Shield game and he wasn't taking it too seriously. Later I saw him the day before a big game in the World Cup and, even though he was batting at No. 3 the next day, he stayed back 45 minutes after training to throw balls for me or anyone who needed them.

If Punter was at training for Tassie, it was like Christmas. It was too good to be true. There was more media, more attention, more staff – it was just amped up and he would light up the training group. You felt like you'd had six energy drinks and you were floating above the grass, no matter how cold or tired you were. You didn't want training to finish, you wanted it to go all day, you were running around with Punter, you were his mate, you were having a laugh and you so wanted to impress him. Training became as important as the game when he was around because you wanted his approval, you wanted him to say, 'He's a good player'. He led by example, too – he was ultra competitive in the drills.

Rick raises the energy levels without doing anything big, it's the respect he commands without demanding it. I think everyone he ever played with had that feeling. He wasn't over the top about it, he never asked anything of anyone else that he wouldn't do himself, but every time he spoke before a match or a series you could see the passion, you could see how much he loved it, and it rubbed off on you. Some leaders can make you nervous about big games but it was almost the opposite with Rick. He was ready for the fight and he wanted to win but he was going to lead us there with his actions as well as his words.

I'm not Ricky Ponting, not even close, but I tried to be that sort of leader, give energy and banter and have fun and be just another part of the team at state and Test level. If a GOAT like Punter could do that, everyone should.

It all came together for us in 2006–07 and in the last game of the season we faced New South Wales at the SCG in a game to see who would host the final. It had been a whole team effort but the old man, Michael Di Venuto, had a great season knocking up three centuries including a massive one to kick in the last match. Divva scored 181 in our total of 370 in the first innings then we tore through the Blues to have them all out for 53 in about 30 overs. Hilf was having a hell of a year and would finish the competition's leading wicket taker with 60 at an average of 25. My contribution in that game was modest (18 and 0) but we secured ourselves a home final.

There was a great feeling in Tassie on the eve of the final. We had the batsmen and bowlers to win our first ever Sheffield Shield and were pretty sure we'd account for the Blues in our backyard having just smashed them in theirs.

Going into the last innings, we had a huge lead thanks to a couple of centuries from Sean Clingeleffer and Luke Butterworth, and we just got to enjoy the cricket.

New South Wales had no hope and when Simon Katich hit one off Hilf straight down my throat at square leg, we were home and hosed.

I kissed the ball!

Crowds had been strong the first few days, but come the final day there would have been about 6000 in the ground, maybe more. They opened the gates and people just started rolling in as we closed in on victory. Nan was there, Mum and Dad, all our parents, all our friends. It seemed like everyone in Hobart came and watched. We'd started preparing for the celebration the evening before the last day. We had all the sponsors' gear signed and that afternoon we could almost taste the beer that was waiting on ice in the rooms.

You've got to remember this was Tasmania's first Sheffield Shield win. And it was against New South Wales. We'd made history. You could tell from the old blokes how much it meant. Michael Di Venuto had been part of the teams when we'd been beaten in 1993–94, 1997–98 and 2001–02, and he'd say later that winning this game was the highlight of a career that spanned 17 first-class seasons with the Tigers. How blessed was I to have landed one in my second season?

We stayed in the change rooms that night and lapped it up while members, the committee and fans whooped it up on the two levels above us. Friends and family were everywhere, but at the core of it were the eleven of us who got the job done: Michael Di Venuto, Michael Dighton, Travis Birt, George Bailey, Dan Marsh, Sean Clingeleffer, Luke Butterworth, Damien Wright, Adam Griffith and Ben Hilfenhaus. And it was appropriate that Tim Coyle was our coach, he was grassroots Tassie cricket. Then there were blokes like David Boon, Ricky Ponting, Jamie Cox and Roger Woolley who'd contributed along the way. We didn't need to be told what this meant to cricket on the island. It was unbelievable, it was huge, we had government receptions, all sorts of things.

I said earlier that when I was signed by Tasmania I didn't think about playing for Australia all that much – my biggest goal was to be on the field when we won that first Sheffield Shield final. That was always what I aspired to do. It was something never done before. I still get goosebumps thinking about it.

We partied until the morning, went home and got our whites and then met again at the Shamrock Hotel at about 10 am when it opened, but some of us went via the Customs House and had a few while we waited. We walked up to the Shamrock with the trophy, Dan Marsh was carrying it. People were tooting their horns on their way to work, yelling out the window of their cars. That day just got bigger and bigger.

Sunday was a bit slower, more of a recovery day, before we got on a bus and did a tour of the state on Monday. We took the Cup around Tasmania, stopping at every pub we could, and it felt like the whole island joined in. We went to Barnbougle, up to Ulverstone where Hilfy came from, drove back to the casino for a function there. I remember getting back to Launceston on Tuesday night and I was done. But the celebrations were far from over and for some of us the party kicked on for weeks.

My skin folds were always in the 40s, sometimes in the low 50s, but when I headed back to the academy after that season they were up to 86. I had not missed too many nights out and I was eating whatever I wanted. I reckon I deserved it. Winning the first Sheffield Shield for Tasmania was a once-in-a-lifetime experience and a dream come true.

4

THE ART OF KEEPING

Adam Gilchrist was the incumbent wicketkeeper when I started playing first-class cricket, but I'd grown up watching Ian Healy and he was the player I modelled my keeping game on. Gilly was very good, but Heals was a keeper's keeper, one of the finest glove men going around.

When Gilly came along, keepers were judged by how many runs they made and how fast they made them. It's like judging a singer on how well they dance.

I always wanted to keep as a kid because it gave me more time in the game. You bat until you are out. You bowl from one end and only for a limited time, but if you're behind the stumps with the gloves on, you're involved in every ball.

Keepers know other keepers, there's a lot of inside knowledge, things only other keepers see. The thing that drew me to Heals was he looked really elegant at his craft, he had a beautiful style and I enjoyed watching him do it, particularly when Shane Warne was bowling. Others may have been as effective, but weren't easy on the eye. As I've said, I'm a neat freak and it bothers me if everything is not in place. Style counts. Keepers can be great at their job, but if they aren't easy on the eye to me then I mark them down. Great keepers are stylish like, say, Damien Martyn when he was batting. They make it look easy, they look like artists. Brad Haddin was another I loved watching, he was an excellent keeper and he looked good doing it. Gilly was good too, but he was tall, he was left-handed and just didn't have that elegance behind the stumps. Sure, he changed the game and was an incredible player, but I'm talking about keeping exclusively and in my book Heals and Hadds were the men I'd rather watch.

Gilly was a unique batsman, everyone wanted someone like him in their side, but good luck finding a batter who can score 17 Test centuries at an average of 48, or 16 ODI centuries at the top of the order and an average of 36. He was just too bloody good with the bat, he was so good that he redefined wicketkeeping to the point that every conversation about glove men started with how many runs you could score with the bat. It distorted perceptions of the craft and it makes me cringe to think of some of the people who were given roles as keeper in different forms of cricket over the years that followed when they were basically batsmen who could take a catch and not let too many through their legs.

Wicketkeepers shouldn't be judged by their batting, at least not in the first instance. If everything is equal, let the batting decide the count back. Still, there was no getting around how good Gilly was at the top of the order in 50-over cricket and how damaging at the lower end of it in Test matches. If you could find another one like him, you'd be laughing and you can't blame teams for looking. I was aggressive with the bat but not on his level, I was more in the Brad Haddin mould.

I had a way to go before I got anywhere near these elite keepers and, in fact, I found myself dumped from the Tassie side at the start of the 2007–08 season. I opened the batting with Michael Di Venuto in the first game against Queensland at the Gabba. Batting second they made 544 from 165 overs and I got a duck when we were sent in to bat ten minutes after the conclusion of their innings. I was dropped from the team and replaced by Michael Dighton, which was something of a setback to the inevitable momentum my cricket had gained over the years, but to be honest I wasn't too disappointed at being told to have a break.

Peter Faulkner, James's dad and another legend of Tasmanian cricket, was selector then and I liked him.

He spoke his mind, he wasn't one for sugar-coating things and he told me, 'This isn't a bad thing, this is a greater opportunity for you to develop and get better. You are part of our future plans, just go back and enjoy yourself.' Because he was a straight talker, I believed him.

Things had happened pretty fast to that point and there hadn't been a lot of time for anything but cricket. I'd been contracted early and played through my late teens and even made my first-class debut in that week of my 21st birthday. Pete said it was time to go back and just be a young man, go out to nightclubs, enjoy myself and refocus. Looking back, it helped. It gave me a chance to step back and get a bit of perspective, have a bit of fun and work out what I really wanted to do.

Still, I wanted to be the best wicketkeeper I could be.

I felt that was where opportunity lay and that playing as an opening batter was affecting my reputation. I'd come out of junior cricket and everyone was impressed, but in first-class my batting was not that good. Opening just wasn't right for me, it got to the point where I realised it was better to wait outside the team for the spot I wanted, which was behind the stumps and batting in the middle order.

I made the most of the downtime and let my hair down. It was good to have a taste of how other people live on the weekend but bleary Mondays aren't for me and the novelty wore off pretty quick.

★

Tassie played the next four games without me and when they did call me up they asked me to keep but bat in the middle order, which was alright by me. No facing the new ball. No fresh quicks. No early morning juice in the deck. How hard could it be? I made a duck in the first innings, but gathered my thoughts and collected a half-century in the second before being caught behind by my old neighbour Matty Wade who'd defected to Victoria by then.

I enjoyed cricket a little more after the enforced break, my keeping was under control and because there was less pressure on my batting, I was able to enjoy having a hit. I scored half-centuries in the next game but we missed the finals that year and had to regroup for another summer, aware that some of our senior players were moving on, prime among them Michael Di Venuto. He'd thought about bowing out after the Shield final victory the year before, but he hung in for one more just to see if he could get a second trophy before leaving. Divva had been a Tiger for 17 years but was going to pick up a contract to play for Durham for three years. He said he couldn't play more than six months a year anymore and the green fields of England were a nice place to see out his final years – and make some good money. He was, behind Jamie Cox, the second-highest run scorer for Tasmania.

So there were some big boots to fill but I wasn't going to be the guy that filled them. The next summer Alex Doolan made his debut for Tasmania as an opener, and a year later Ed Cowan came down. Both would open for Australia at some point in the following years. I was focused on that keeper's spot, but needed to be patient. When Gilchrist stood down in 2008, the obvious replacement was Brad Haddin. I just bided my time, keeping my skills sharp and hoping to noodle a few runs here and there while I waited.

There was a bit of a bottleneck of keepers around. The year before, my old mate Matty Wade had accepted a deal from Victoria who guaranteed him a start in the team. In Tassie he'd been behind me in the one-day matches and behind me and Sean Clingeleffer in first-class cricket. He was just 19 and a very talented cricketer so he crossed the Bass Strait for a chance. You couldn't hold that against him.

Wadey went well in that first season, too. He hit 80-odd in the first game and a 95 in the match against Tassie at the MCG when I was out of the team. He went the distance when he came back to Bellerive in that next summer and scored his debut first class century not far from the backyards where we'd played so much cricket as boys. He might have been batting for the Vics, but I was happy to see someone from my old neighbourhood finding his own way. There were only six wicketkeepers getting a start in the Sheffield Shield so you had to take your chances where they arose.

The summer of 2008–09 was an interesting one for Australian cricket, but not a great one for Tassie. We got off to a bad start by losing to Queensland and Western Australia, did a bit better after that and could have made the finals but missed by a couple of points. At the end of January we played New South Wales at the No. 1 Sportsground in Newcastle in a game that attracted a lot of interest. Things were moving in Australian cricket that year and places were opening up in the Test team. Simon Katich, the Blues captain, had established himself as opener in the Test team but in that game he let Phil Jaques and Phil Hughes walk out to bat first. Matthew Hayden had just retired and this was going to be an old-fashioned bat off to see who would be Kat's partner in the three Test matches to be played in South Africa soon after.

Jaques was the senior partner and to some degree the incumbent. He'd played 11 matches for Australia since 2005, averaged close to 50 and had scored a century in his last innings in June against the West Indies before Hayden came back for what proved to be his final summer. There was a lot riding on that game, but it wasn't a fair contest. I could tell from the moment Jaquesy walked out to bat that he wasn't right. He had chronic back problems and wasn't moving well.

We'd already got a taste of what Hughes could do when he played us at Bellerive in early December. We won that game, but he did everything in his power to ensure we didn't. The little left-hander hit 93 and 108 which doesn't seem that extraordinary until you look at the context.

We had won the toss and sent them in on a wicket that looked like a jungle and by lunch they were 4–75, having lost Usman Khawaja, Peter Forrest, Ed Cowan and Dom Thornely. Hughes had hit 51 of the 75 and was throwing his bat at everything. Brett Geeves hit him in the helmet with one and the next delivery Hughes smoked him through the cover for four. It was spectacular hitting. His 93 stood out in a team total of 127 and his 108 was a big part of their 173 in the second. He'd scored 201 out of the team's total of 345 which broke a record set by Don Bradman. After the game George Bailey was so impressed he talked to us about changing the way we approached batting on a green top, but none of us had the skill Hughesy did. He had an incredible eye and just backed himself.

Jaques was out cheaply at the return match in Newcastle, while Hughes went on to score 151 and lock in his place in the Test team for the series in South Africa. I managed a respectable 63, which kind of demonstrated the difference in talent between me and young Hughesy who would go on to score two centuries in his second game for Australia. Alex Doolan made his debut for us in that match and not too long down the road would actually take Hughes's place as opener.

Meanwhile, I was biding my time and in June was pumped to be invited to play for Australia A against Pakistan A.

We had two four-day matches at Tony Ireland Stadium in Townsville and three 50-over games in Brisbane at Allan Border Field.

Things kept advancing for me the way everyone assumed they would, which is not to say they came easy. I worked hard for the opportunities I was presented and made the most of them when they came along. I'd been dropped from the Shield team once, briefly, but it hadn't been too traumatic. I'd never really known what it was like to try and fail, to go back and try harder and then fail again. That was ahead of me, but right now the sun was shining and the cricket was good.

Pakistan arrived with a handy side that included Azhar Ali, Mohammad Hafeez, Umar Akmal, Wahab Riaz and the like. We had some likely types with Michael Klinger, Callum Ferguson, Adam Voges, Jason Krejza, Doug Bollinger and big Cameron White as skipper. I was on 54 not out in the second innings in Townsville when we declared in the first game and was four runs short of another half-century when I got out in the second game.

We got smacked in the first 50-over match of the series at Allan Border Field, but I knocked up another 40 opening the batting. Dave Warner was made my opening partner in the next game which we won easily. Neither of us reached 30 in that game but while we were at the crease he was scoring at twice the rate I was.

I was pretty chuffed to bring up a 134 from 136 balls in the third and last game of the series. If you are checking the scores on Cricket Archive (which is what I did), you might want to note this sentence in the accompanying match report: 'Paine's knock was studded with 13 fours and five huge sixes'. I might get that framed.

Dave Warner was showing some serious talent himself then but couldn't get a start in the New South Wales Shield side which already had a young Phil Hughes and Usman Khawaja at the top of the order. Not to mention Katich, Jaques, Thornely, Steve Smith and Ed Cowan. Davey made his debut for Australia in a T20 match at the MCG that January and he absolutely slaughtered the South African attack. Two months later he finally got to make his debut.

Jamie Cox took me aside after the last A game and said to prepare myself to fly over to England next week because Brad Haddin looked like he would miss that last Test and would not be up for the ODI series.

I was excited, then nervousness and doubt set in, but I did my best to push that aside and concentrate. Hadds had come in for Gilly and had the job in the 2009 Ashes, but he broke his finger before the game at Edgbaston and had to be replaced at the last minute by Graham Manou. Hadds came back for the last two Tests of the series, but they were so worried about his finger I got the call-up to join the Test squad as cover for the last match at The Oval. Manou had injured his hand covering in the third Test.

It sounded pretty exciting, but in all reality there was no chance of me playing in the Test and that was made clear to everyone. I was there as back-up only and unless something terrible happened Hadds was not going to miss another game.

I was only going over a few days early as I'd been picked in the one-day squad for the 50-over series that followed which was pretty exciting in itself. Okay, it was more than pretty exciting.

It was a pretty cool experience to fly to London and stay at the Royal Garden Hotel with the team. Everyone loves London and staying next to Kensington Palace was a real buzz. Hadds told me at training that he was alright and I wouldn't be playing and I was kind of relieved. It was such a big Test as it was the Ashes decider with the series tied one-all and it would have been nerve-racking. The feeling around that game was incredible. It was almost intimidating being in the vicinity of it.

I did get to have a bit of fun, though. On the Saturday of the Test I was sitting on the bench with Phil Hughes when Warney, who was commentating, came over and started chatting to Hughesy. I kept quiet, but he asked us what we were doing and said we should come out that night. We were going into the last day of the match and so we decided, why not?

I didn't have a driver's licence and knew from bitter experience that because I looked so young I needed some ID. I had to go and ask our security guy Frank Dimasi for my passport and he was very stern, telling me not to lose it. Me, Hughesy and Brett Lee, who wasn't playing either, went to the Goat Tavern across the road from the team hotel and had a beer or two and waited for Warney to text us the nightclub address. He eventually did and we headed to this fancy place in Mayfair and he was waiting outside the club for us. I will never forget the sight of him. He had a cigarette behind his ear, maybe even two ciggies behind his ears, and a fake sleeve tattoo. He said to Brett, 'What do you reckon, Binga, pretty cool, eh?' Warney led us in and he had this roped off area and all these people with him. I think one of them had something to do with the Rolling Stones and one was the boss of Advanced Hair. We didn't know them but we didn't mind.

We had a monster night, of course. The sun was coming up as we got home. I think Binga might have left early. I didn't go to the cricket but they did. Turns out I'd lost my passport somewhere which didn't go down well. I had just arrived in the Australian team and was already in Frankie's bad books.

I think that might have been the only night I ever went out with Warney but I will never forget it. What I can remember of it. He bunged it on for us that night.

★

After that game we went to Edinburgh to play a one-off 50-over game against Scotland. Greg Blewett presented my first Australian cap, he was there commentating and I'm sure whatever he said was great but I can't remember a word of it. I was so bloody nervous, it was an off Broadway start, it wasn't Lord's or the SCG, it was Edinburgh, but playing for my country was still a magic moment in my life. The lead-up was grim, it rained all the time and we couldn't train outdoors which wasn't ideal. Michael Clarke was captain in Ricky's absence, and Shane Watson and Dave Warner opened. I got to keep to Brett Lee and Mitchell Johnson. Dirk Nannes, who was to be central to one of the twists in my life story, also played. He was really quick then, but I'd had my exposure to really fast bowlers keeping to Shaun Tait in Australia A. The game went okay, I held my own, got 29 not out, but when we got on the bus and drove to London that's when it got serious. I was playing for Australia in England!

I'd heard so much about all those venues, watched so many games played there. Getting to The Oval with your kit ready to go put it all into perspective, there is just something about those English grounds with all their history. Games went up a gear.

I had a shocking attack of nerves that weren't helped by being sent in to bat first. I faced a few balls in a state of panic and then got run out by Shane Watson. It was a nice bit of fielding from Paul Collingwood. Still, there wasn't a run in it, it was a bit disappointing, but I wasn't going to say no to the big fella. He was in some good touch then so I was the sacrificial lamb.

I can get annoyed when someone runs me out if I'm in good form, but other times it's like, 'Oh well, saved me the embarrassment of getting knocked over,' and this was one of those times. No one means to run somebody else out and everyone gets over it quickly. I remember players going berserk when they were run out but by the time the guilty party is out they've usually calmed down. I have never known for it to continue in the dressing rooms.

We put on 5–260 with zero contribution from me. England were starting to find their feet when they batted before I stumped Ravi Bopara off Nathan Hauritz's bowling. The ball didn't spin and beat the outside edge, he just overbalanced slightly and I took the opportunity. They were well placed at 2–124 before that but fell away soon after. I was pretty pumped to get a stumping for the Australian team. I got a run-out, too – Luke Wright tried to take a sneaky single off me on a no ball but got sent back and I underarmed it into the stumps like you would playing tenpin bowls. We won the game.

Brett Lee and Mitch Johnson generated some real heat in that match and I discovered that it's very difficult to see in England. The lights aren't that bright, the sight screens are small so when I'm crouched the crowd was in my eye line. People moving about in the stands made it hard to pick up the ball. I kept well for most of that series but never felt really comfortable. Nathan Hauritz, Mitch Johnson, Cam White, Nathan Bracken, James Hopes and I were all playing our first ODI in England so it was nice to get a win. Punter was having a bit of a rest and didn't come back until halfway through the series.

Next stop Lord's. Being a boy from Hobart I shouldn't love it, I should be cynical about its upper crust carry on, but you just can't help be seduced by it. Everyone goes on about the tradition at Lord's and I don't usually listen to that stuff or notice it, but I remember thinking it was really cool when I was there. At first you think it's just an old cricket ground, not that big or anything, but when you walk in it has something special. You can feel its history. You remember the big moments, the Ashes battles, the scenes on the balcony when Australia won the World Cup in 1999. It is just such an awesome place.

There's history dripping from the walls which are covered in cricket paintings. It's like being in a cricket museum and if you squint you can imagine the old codgers playing in their blazers and long beards. Walking through the committee room is a trip, then making your way to the centre on that sloping ground, checking out that Father Time weathervane, the members with their silly jackets, the room attendants in suits. And the lunch is next level . . .

At every other ground the food is there and you help yourself, but at Lord's you sit down in the lunch room and it's like you are in a restaurant. There's a menu, you order and they serve it to you. The waiters are dressed up, they call you 'sir', and the food is like Michelin restaurant standard. It's a long way from the Sandy Bay bakery which is my regular lunch place but I could get used to it.

There's a lot of talk about the sloping ground at Lord's – you see it on the telly – but you really notice it when you stand on it. You can feel it when you're keeping, you move better down the hill than up it, you feel it batting too. If you look back at the members' stand, you can see the slope of the ground against the line of the fence and it is significant. When Jofra Archer was coming down the slope at me in the 2019 Ashes, that was about as difficult as it gets. Ask Steve Smith about it. Or Marnus Labuschagne who got clocked on the head when called in to replace him.

When I went back for the Ashes years later, I lapped it up more than I did that first time. Maybe because the first time I was just pedalling as hard as I could to prove myself as a worthy member of the Australian cricket team. In 2019 I was more mature and more aware of my surroundings. I remember sitting on the balcony, thinking, 'Wow, I'm here.' It really hit me. It made me think of my family and my nan and I wished they could have all been there to experience it too. I took my uncle Robert, the football coach, there on one of the training days and he was blown away.

Ricky came back into the side when we returned to Lord's for the fourth match of the series. Now I got a chance to bat with one of the greats at one of the great games. I got my confidence up with a nice leg side stumping when I was keeping to Nathan Bracken in the England innings. Eoin Morgan just missed one, overbalanced and attempted to swap feet, but I got my timing perfect and knocked the bails off as he was in the act. Keeping to Nathan wasn't easy as he was pretty quick and he had some change-up balls that kept you on your toes. It felt good to show off my skills to the senior players in a game.

Brett Lee took five wickets and we had them all out for 220. I was feeling pretty comfortable going out to bat with Shane Watson. We knocked them around a bit and when he got out that was when I got nervous. I looked up to the pavilion and waited for Ricky to come out and I started to panic. I wasn't sure what to do. I was suddenly part of a scene I'd witnessed so many times on the television. I was batting with Ricky Ponting! My mind was racing as he walked out. I knew him, but he was still Ricky Ponting and it was still an international game, and at Lord's no less.

What am I going to say to him?

Rick just strolled out and said, 'You good?' and I said, 'Yeah,' and he said, 'Keep going,' and that was it. Then, after he'd had a stretch and took his mark, I had a little giggle. I couldn't help it, it was so cool being there with him. Same as with Michael Hussey and Michael Clarke, I knew all their little mannerisms, I used to imitate them when I was younger. I always used to kick stuff away from the crease like Ricky did even when there was nothing there.

There was a good reason behind that gardening, it was a way of slowing the game to your pace. The whole game waited for batsmen like Rick, it stopped until they were ready and they controlled it, it was quite a skill, you wanted to be able to do it yourself. I wrote about JL doing it earlier. All the greats do. Shane Warne did it when he stood at the top of his mark. He seemed to pause the action until he was ready. Young spinners, especially when they are struggling, can't get through an over quick enough. I think it's like that when you are batting without confidence. You are apologetic for being there and just want the game to keep going.

Someone who has got that straight away is Marnus, he takes control of the pace of the game before he faces a ball. He's more calculating than he seems. From the first innings in England 2019 when Marnus came in for Smithy, he took his time, he went through his routine at his own pace where most young players would be nervous and rushed. In his early games teams would get frustrated and say things, hurry up, blah blah blah, but they don't bother anymore because he doesn't do anything until he is ready. Smithy is the same. When he is at the crease, nothing happens until he is ready. Marnus has it, Davey Warner always had it. The best players do.

While Ricky did the hammy stretch, tended to his garden and then did the big scratch on the wicket, all I was thinking was, 'How good is this? I'm batting with Ricky Ponting!' Then we got down to business. I got my way to a half-century at a fair clip and got a little handshake from the legend. Rick wasn't going to hug me and they didn't fist bump in those days. I didn't want the innings to end. We won that game and I was on cloud nine. I'd proved I could hold my own at the very top level and I'd done it in front of Ricky Ponting.

We went down to Nottingham for the next few games and while I didn't get to bat with the great Tasmanian – I was out early – I got to sit on the balcony at Trent Bridge and watch him bring up a brilliant century which included a six onto the roof at the River Trent end.

I picked up another stumping when Nathan Hauritz got one to spin between Matt Prior's bat and pad, which was another one that I gave myself a tick for. He'd run down the track and in that situation you lose the ball for a moment and everything in your system is telling you to react, but you have to stay low, stay calm and be ready to finish the job. I'd rehearsed this moment so many times. Adil Rashid tried to steal a run off me later in the innings too, but I did him in with an underarm to the stumps just as I had against Scotland earlier.

It was good to establish my credentials as a keeper in the international game.

Notts was good fun too, it's not much of a town, but it has a great sporting history and you can have a lot of fun there. Trent Bridge is a cool ground, right next door to Nottingham Forest's home ground where the great Brian Clough made a name for himself. There's a statue of him in town (and one of Robin Hood). Both grounds are just over the river, not far from the city centre, and the cricket ground has a little pub in the corner with a beer garden that spills into it.

I must have been paying attention when Rick got his hundred because I got my own in the next game, this time making most of my runs with Michael Hussey as both Watto and Punter had abandoned me. We were 2–40 and in some strife, but when Huss came out he was really clear and reassuring. I think it was the first time I batted with him. He was a great guy around the rooms and the nets, just a no-nonsense sort of fella with good manners and a gentle side.

I liked batting with Huss because he was so normal out there, like Rick. He'd talk about where we could score and when I was struggling, he'd say, 'Relax, it will come.' I had a tendency at that age to do something silly if I got under pressure, but he kept saying, 'Plenty of time, plenty of time, we'll get there.' So we just knocked them round and ran hard and I remember looking at the scoreboard and he was 20-odd and I wondered how he got there. He just kept going, knock, knock, knock, he didn't hit a four but you couldn't keep him on strike, that's how good he was. He started so well, he took the pressure off me. He was calm and he stuck with me until I got my century.

It's time for me to put my elite humility aside and read to you from the cricinfo match report:

> Called in as a late replacement for the injured Brad Haddin, the wicketkeeper-batsman displayed temperament far beyond that of a man playing just his third week of one-day international cricket during a 148-ball innings of 111. He batted methodically in the tense early exchanges, relying on cover and square drives for the bulk of his runs before expanding his repertoire to include a deft reverse sweep off Graeme Swann and a series of well-struck cut shots. Patience and placement were his major weapons, although Paine did dip into the power reserves on occasion, most notably when he dispatched a Dimitri Mascarenhas slower ball over the long-off rope.

I'm available to talk further on the subject if anyone is having an event at their club.

We were in front 6–0 in the series and I had my first hundred for Australia. We lost the last match at Durham, but nobody seemed to mind too much.

After England we moved on to South Africa for the Champions Trophy which was a great experience. We went through the group stage undefeated and I managed a half-century in the washed-out game against India. Thanks to Shane Watson, my opening partner, scoring centuries in both finals – 136 not out against England in the semi-final and 105 not out against New Zealand in the final – we managed to raise the trophy.

From there it was on to India for a seven-match series but I only played two. I broke my finger in the second match which was in Nagpur. Peter Siddle bowled one that kind of wobbled and it smacked into my finger and ballooned up in the air. It was really early in the game and it hurt like buggery. I didn't look at it until the end of the over and then saw that it was bent at an angle. I knew I was in trouble, but I put my glove back on and got through to the drinks break and that's when I took the chance to run off and got all these injections in it. The finger went numb but then the numbness continued down into my palm and I couldn't feel much at all by the end of the next over. We topped it up again which meant I would open the batting but I could only grip the bat with my bottom hand.

It was one of the few times I broke a finger. I was desperate to stay on and play but David Boon, who was a selector, talked me out of it. It was disappointing but we'd been on the road for a while and wicketkeepers are going to get injuries so I disappeared back to Tassie and was ready to go again in the Sheffield Shield side in December.

We were set for a big year with Ed Cowan coming down from New South Wales so he could get a bit more of a chance and the extremely talented Sean Cosgrove joining us after he'd been cut by South Australia. If the Redbacks didn't want him, we sure did. Cozzie was one hell of a batsman. Tassie elevated me to the role of vice-captain below George Bailey after Dan Marsh stood down from the role.

We didn't get it together in the Sheffield Shield, but the 50-over competition which was going by the name of the Ford Ranger Cup at the time was a good one for us. We reached the finals and I had a day out knocking up a hundred, Michael Dighton got 80 and Ed Cowan 61, to give us 6–304. Gerard Denton took 5–45 as we steamrolled the Victorians for 110. It was the fourth consecutive year the Bushrangers lost the title and you'd almost feel sorry for them, except they were Victorians. They had a few players out, but when you factor in that Chris Rogers, Brad Hodge, Aaron Finch, Andrew McDonald, Matthew Wade and Glenn Maxwell all played for them, you can see why we were pretty proud of that victory.

★

At this point in my career I had made a hundred for Australia in an ODI, a first-class double hundred, a fist-ful of 50s in the same format and runs at most other levels, but I was essentially doing it by instinct. I saw the ball and I hit it, I knew where to put my feet, how to hold the bat, and what risks and rewards were associated with which shots.

It came naturally and while I worked on it I didn't really understand batting or think too much about it. As I said earlier, I was a wicketkeeper-batsman in my mind and it was wicketkeeping I prided myself on.

Maybe because I knew keeping was something I could really excel at, something where I could be better than anybody else. And I just loved it. Keeping was my thing.

I was blessed to have some very good keepers around me in the state set-up, with Tasmania's homegrown wicket-keeping guru Tim Coyle always somewhere close. Before Tim there was Enrico Di Venuto. His son Michael might be one of the legendary players but Enrico has a similar place among the coaching staff. He's just one of those blokes who is the soul of every cricket club and he looked after me when I was playing for the University of Tasmania. When I was a teen, Enrico devised a drill for me to do after training on Tuesday and Thursday nights that involved a bar stool. We'd place ourselves either side of it and he'd sling the ball through the legs towards me and he was unbelievably good at getting a nick on the way through. It got to the point where the one you had to watch was the one that went straight on. I loved doing that drill with him, it was a great challenge.

Later, when I had to keep to Nathan Lyon the thing that made him so difficult – apart from his bounce – was the ball he had that went straight on and caught the edge. I didn't know it at the time but I'd been training all my life for someone like Nathan and believe me he is far harder to keep to than he looks. If you aren't on your toes when he is bowling, you will be found out quicker than any batsman. Nathan is a real test of your technique when he gets edges because it is his bounce and drift, not spin, that will take you down.

I loved it when those drills I did as a 14-year-old paid off years later. Doing keeping drills after the main training session also taught me work ethic and endurance. We'd drill for an hour or so and then wind up as it got dark. Enrico devised a competition where if I got through without dropping one, he had to buy me a Coke at the pub; if I dropped one, my dad would have to buy him a Guinness. It was a good deal, but it's worth noting that it wasn't just me staying back that extra time, it was Enrico going the extra yards for a young bloke. People like him are essential at clubs and don't get enough credit. I reckon if you asked every international player, they would each have someone like that in their background – sometimes a parent or a sibling, but more often than not a club volunteer. I know Ricky Ponting always credited a bloke called Ian Young who would stay back long hours giving him throwdowns after he'd been at work all day.

Enrico put the work ethic into me but Tim Coyle refined me, taught me technique and got me thinking deeply about the fine art of wicketkeeping. Enrico made it fun for a teenager, but Tim made it a challenge for a young man who wanted to be the best in Australia at the craft. Tim, a burly bloke from Launceston, played a handful of first-class games but was a mainstay of cricket at that end of the island. After a long playing career, he coached in Launceston for a decade before being picked up by Tasmania as a game development manager.

From 2002 to 2005 he was our fielding and wicket-keeping coach and it was no coincidence that during his tenure we won our first and second Shield finals as well as a one-day trophy. He was key to the development of those teams and he just had a no-nonsense way about him that made us believe we could win anything.

Like Coyle, I've devoted myself to understanding how wicketkeeping works so that when it goes wrong I know exactly what is wrong. I distilled keeping down to a basic checklist.

When I'm standing back to the fast bowlers, I say to myself, 'Stay low, hands out in front, head to ball.' I know I have to make a small first step and push off from my inside leg.

When I'm standing up to the stumps for the slow bowlers, it is only slightly different: 'Stay low and still, hands out in front, head to the ball.' It's important to keep ground contact and not jump up.

If I'm not feeling good or something is not right, I've got the checklist which is basically just three things: body height (don't stand too high), seeing the ball into gloves, and energy in my legs. If I'm out of whack, it is usually one of these things that needs to be adjusted.

With batting I need help if things are going wrong, and I feel like I'm always after reassurance from someone else. But with keeping I can sort it out myself, then and there. I can tell myself that I need to change an angle or go a bit wider. I know what I need to do and I have the courage to do it.

It wasn't until I made it into the Test team the second time and I watched Steve Smith, David Warner and Marnus Labuschagne that I started to understand they were the same with batting as I was with wicketkeeping. They know what they have to do and how to do it and they never doubt it. It might change from bowler to bowler, but they have the courage to do it within their framework. Steve and Davey have been at it a lot longer, but I find Marnus is really good at seeing what's going wrong with my batting and knowing what to do to fix it. He'd make a good coach, our Marny, but he's got a bit to do before we get to that point.

Because I am clear on keeping and preparing, even if I have a bad day I accept they come along and it doesn't take me long to figure out why it was a bad day, but with batting it's hard for me to pinpoint what went wrong. With keeping, I just know what it is, I had a shit day because of this or that, and can be confident it won't happen tomorrow. It's like if Smithy gets out lbw, he says, 'I'll never miss one of those again.' Or Davey who comes back and says, 'I'll never nick that again.' They front up next innings totally confident. That's what I'm like with my keeping. I wish I was the same with my batting

Balancing keeping practice and batting practice is one thing, but being a keeper *and* a batsman is quite another. We do these psych tests to establish what sort of personality group we fall into and it's difficult for me because I'm two different people. One of the questions is, 'Do you get nervous through the game?' and I don't know the answer. If they are asking me if I am nervous when keeping or nervous when batting, then the answers are completely different. When it comes to batting, sometimes I'm crapping myself with fear, I'm full of doubt when I'm at my worst, but the moment that it's over and it comes time to keep, I am totally calm and confident. It's like having a split personality.

People ask why can't you bat like you keep, but it's not as easy as that. It was when I was younger, but after I broke my finger in 2010 my confidence went; the keeping came back quickly but the batting took a long, long time and I think it only improved late in 2019–20. I had people like JL and Darren Lehmann say, 'Who cares, just bat, if you get runs it's a bonus. We just want you to be the best keeper in the team and captain well, runs are nice but not necessary.' Boof, too, did a bit to free me up when I came into the Test team. Hadds was another who reinforced the 'bat like a keeper' message. So by the summer of 2020–21 I was feeling pretty good about my batting again and I started to play more freely, but I knew it had limitations.

I've got the skill set for batting, I have no doubt about that, but after that finger injury I just couldn't get my head right and I guess I never did completely. There's a difference between getting it right and not caring – not fretting is probably a better way of explaining it. I stopped worrying about my batting towards the end of my career and that freed me up. I had given up trying to sort it out. You can't do that when you are 21.

You hear batters or bowlers say they want to test themselves against the best players or in the worst conditions. With the gloves on, the harder it is, the more I like it, because that is my thing. I couldn't wait to tour England or to tour India because that is where average keepers look average and I wanted to test my skills in those conditions. But if it's batting I don't want to face a Dukes ball in England because it will swing and I'll miss it all day, or in India the SG ball will spin on those decks and I'll be beaten, but if it's swinging or spinning with keeping I want to get in there and test myself. That's what I did all the work for.

Keeping on a subcontinent wicket doesn't change the basics so much. If it is spinning square, I will open up slightly or I will stand a little bit deeper. If it is Nathan Lyon to a right-hander I will close off, I bring my right foot (outside foot to a right-hand batter) slightly forward of my back foot, because I know if it is spinning it is going to beat the inside edge more than the outside.

When it came to international keepers I loved watching Kumar Sangakkara, he was one of my favourites and very easy on the eye. Kumar was good anywhere, he had a technique he could adapt to any conditions. Hadds was the same. That's what I like and I aspired to being someone who could keep in any conditions and have a solid basic technique to adjust for whatever I faced.

I enjoyed watching MS Dhoni because he was nonchalant and made it look easy in tough conditions, but he was not the same keeper outside of home conditions. MS is the fastest stumper you will ever see, a gunfighter. The reason is because he is always moving in towards the stumps, he gets drawn to the stumps, but that makes it harder to get the fine edges.

Like batsmen or bowlers, you will find conservative and attacking keepers. It can be a personality thing, there are people with low-risk personalities who want to be safe, keep a clean sheet, but who aren't keen to risk a mistake to get the team forward. Keeping to the seamers is a good example. I remember keeping to Ben Hilfenhaus and James Faulkner a lot in state cricket when they were both in their pomp. I reckon I got Faulks a fair few wickets when the ball was reversing by keeping the batsman in his crease.

I remember in the last Test of the 2018 series against South Africa at Johannesburg, AB de Villiers was batting half a metre out of the crease to Chadd Sayers. Coming up to the stumps is not something you want to do, it's so much more difficult, chances are going to be harder to grab, but you can't let the batsman get away with it. I broke my thumb doing it, but it had to be done and it had the desired effect on AB who retreated to his crease. The history books will show that Chadd's first wicket was AB caught by me, they won't tell you how he was set up.

Flashy wicketkeepers aren't necessarily good keepers. The big diving, rolling catch gets everyone up and about and makes all the highlight reels but it is a dangerous practice and poor technique if the ball doesn't carry. If the ball is flying you get away with a bit of acrobatics, but if it drops on you like it does in England, you're gone. You have to have your feet on the ground and your eyes level to adjust to that, you can't adjust if you're flying through the air.

Plenty of fielding coaches come up with little tricks to help get you sharp as a wicketkeeper, but you need one that is transportable and one that you can do yourself. I take a golf ball with me everywhere and do a drill that I picked up from Ian Healy.

It's really simple, you bounce the ball off a wall and catch it, but it is specific too. Heals told me he would do it when something was bothering him: he would imagine the delivery and the shot and he'd replicate it over and over until he felt comfortable. If I'm feeling slightly off, I will go back to the hotel and head for the car park or get up early and go through the drill. I don't need anyone to come with me, I focus on what wasn't feeling right and I'll just work on that take, maybe rehearse it 50 times, until it feels better.

Most keepers I work with get bored with the golf ball in ten minutes. They want to dive and roll around, but I just keep throwing the ball at a wall and catching it for hours, going through scenarios that will hopefully play out in different circumstances. And you can do it anywhere. In Adelaide I've found myself in the laneway by the team hotel among the delivery trucks and drunks. At Bellerive, before the redevelopment, I had a spot out the back of the stands. I found a handy wall at our team hotel in Double Bay in Sydney, and in the Sandton complex in Johannesburg. It's a very transportable drill.

The dismissals I enjoy the most are the subtle ones that I think people don't appreciate – hopefully because I have made it look easy. The harder it is, the prouder I am of it, but sometimes only the bowler and I know how good a catch is, we know how many times that sort of edge beats the keeper because it is not expected. Nathan Lyon and I have enjoyed many of these wickets together. Occasionally Wadey will watch the replay and acknowledge the effort, and I can puff out my chest around another keeper, but nobody else in the team knows.

If Nathan is spinning it big and it gets the inside edge, that's an incredibly difficult catch. The other hard one is the delivery that misses the rough and goes straight. That's the one that takes years of practice. You have to hold your ground against all instinct. When you get one it's a great feeling, only I know how hard I work at that, going through drills where I'm saying to myself, 'Hits the rough, hits the rough, ooh it missed the rough . . .'

To some people all the preparation and practice might sound like an absolute grind – I imagine most of my teammates would think so – but I loved wicketkeeping and I wanted to be the best there was at the trade. I didn't mind all the extra hours training or the fact it was something of a secret society whose codes few really understand.

I'd made it to Sheffield Shield level, played in my state's first championship team, I'd even made the Australian one-day team, but the next step was the big one. I was prepared to put in tens of thousands of hours in case a vacancy came up .

My time was coming.

5

THE FIRST TEST

When you have something and you lose it or it's taken away from you, it casts what you had in a new light. Even before I blew everything up, I'd had reason to wonder what was going on in my head in the past. I guess the answer is that I had no perspective and no reason to question how things were going as long as they were going well. Who does? I was playing cricket, I was in a fast-flowing stream and everything was taking care of itself. There was no need to think or step back, that seemed like the worst thing I could do.

When 2010 came around I was 25 years old, I was sitting on Brad Haddin's shoulder ready to fill in when he was injured and in prime place to take over should his form slip or he retire. I'd found a spot in the one-day side and was going alright at that. By then I'd played 25 ODIs as the second keeper and was part of the ICC World Twenty20 squad in the Caribbean. My performances in the 50-over game earned me my first ever Cricket Australia contract.

You couldn't step outside and assess it all, I guess, for fear it would all fall apart the moment you let that happen. *Just don't think.*

I guess the other thing was that I hadn't so much made the next step because when I did play for Australia I was holding the place for Hadds until he was fit again. I was not making the next step so much as holding the wheel for Hadds until he recovered.

So, anyway, I made my Test debut that year and thinking about how little memory I have of that brought this reflection on. It was the biggest thing that ever happened to me but you couldn't let yourself get carried away or think about what it meant. Back then I tried not to analyse what was happening, I never went deep. If anything I took it a little bit for granted, I'd worked hard for it and it was an incredible privilege, but it was just another part of the journey that had been set for me. Things went well for me every time I took another step and now I'm not sure that was great. I just assumed that this was my destiny.

The 2009–10 summer passed and Hadds was still struggling with injury ahead of a two-Test series against Pakistan in England in July. There was a bit of talk in the press about who might take his place. Graham Manou had done it in the Ashes and some one-day games, a few others were in the mix, but in my head I was pretty confident that spot was mine. I was also screamingly nervous inside but you can't say that too loud.

They picked me and that was a dream come true.

Mum and Nan flew over. I didn't have a partner then. Shaun Tait and I used to talk about that on the one-day tour because he was single too, and the others would bring over their wives or girlfriends when they could. I think Shaun brought over his brother for the Test, and I brought my mum and nan. My club president from University, Paul McNamara, was in town and George Campbell, an overseas professional when I was young who did a lot of work with me in the early days, came to the game too.

All four of them came to the Royal Garden and were waiting in the foyer of the hotel when I got back from training one day. It was pretty surreal to see them all there and great to have the support. They wanted to go to lunch but I couldn't do it, I was too uptight, so I begged out and just went and sat in my room and tried to relax. I couldn't talk to anyone, I couldn't think about anything else but the game. I was crapping myself, absolutely crapping myself.

It wasn't the Ashes, but it was the Australian Test team captained by Ricky Ponting and it was Rick who presented me with my baggy green before play on an overcast London morning, 13 July 2010. Steve Smith got his first one, too.

Shane Watson, Simon Katich, Michael Hussey, Michael Clarke, Marcus North, Mitch Johnson, Ben Hilfenhaus and Doug Bollinger must have been in the circle as Punter said whatever he said to us. I don't remember anything at all. I've seen the famous photo of Steve and me with our new caps on. We look like we should still be at school. Two future captains. Two who would share fates that weren't so dissimilar over the next years although my game never reached the incredible heights Smithy's did. You have to marvel at the selectors who knew there was something in this kid who could field, bat and bowl, but hadn't really nailed down his brand. As you probably know, he was batting at No. 8 and bowling leggies in that series. Fancy Steve Smith batting below me.

Anyway, I was so nervous all my energy was consumed trying to keep it together. Pakistan won the toss and decided to try and exploit the overhead conditions by sending us in. That gave me a chance to be as nonchalant as possible in that sacred dressing room with its famous balcony.

It was a stop-start day. Light forced us off. Shane Watson didn't last long, he left one that hit his pads and was in the process of being given out lbw when the ball bounced into the stumps, but Simon Katich was grinding it out. Kat, it has to be said, was never easy on the eye as a batter but he'd found himself a method to match his level of determination that was a level above most other people. He top-scored with 50 in the innings.

Pakistan had quite the bowling line-up and everyone was in awe of Mohammad Amir, their teenage star. He'd taken a five-for at the MCG the year before and was shaping as one of the great bowling talents. It was only a month later that he got caught up in that sports betting sting by a tabloid newspaper that resulted in him doing three months in jail for match fixing. His captain Salman Butt and the senior quick Mohammad Amir also went down for that. It was one of the biggest stories in cricket at the time and had massive consequences for the three involved.

I'd figured I wouldn't have to bat for a while so I was able to get my heart rate down a bit, but when I saw Amir – it was the first time we'd seen much of him and he was quick and swinging it – I was thinking, 'Crap, he is pretty good.' Mohammed Asif at the other end was tall and swinging it too, Umar Gul was also quick and their spinners were good.

When the time came for me to bat, I felt like my feet had gone numb because I was so nervous. I don't remember leaving the dressing room, or walking through the Long Room, but when I got to the bottom of the stairs that lead to the grass there was a bit of a drop and I was worried that I couldn't feel the ground. I looked down as my feet landed on the Lord's grass and I have this mental snapshot of the Adidas stripes on the top of my batting boots as they made first contact with the turf. Ricky had given me these new shoes and I really liked them.

I had all these crazy thoughts during my brief period out there and was struggling to concentrate. I panicked at one point after I'd arrived at the crease that I hadn't marked centre but I was too embarrassed to ask the umpire so I asked Michael Hussey instead. Huss helped to calm me down, as he always did. I think I got off the mark through square leg or mid wicket but I really can't remember much about that day apart from my shoes landing on the grass.

I do, however, remember my first catch when Pakistan batted on day two. I got Imran Farhat off the bowling of fellow Tasmanian Ben Hilfenhaus. But the dismissal that will live with me was a leg side stumping of Salman Butt off the bowling of Marcus North. At that stage of the game, they were 2–186 and going alright. Punter brought Marcus on to bowl his first over and he got the first delivery to drift past the opener's pads and I did the rest. I've seen the replay and I reckon the one thing I did quicker than break the stumps was run into the arms of Ricky for a big hug. It was a good moment for two Tasmanians. Smithy took his first wickets in that innings too, which was pretty cool.

Bringing on Marcus North was an inspired move by the skipper. The part-timer finished with 6–55 and we won the game on the fourth day.

In the second innings I'd put on a partnership batting with Hilf and we had great fun. When he came to the middle, I asked him if he was going to take singles and he said there was no way he wanted to face Umar and I could have that end to myself. Then Hilf started throwing the bat at the ball and connecting and after a while he was having such a good time he was desperate to get on strike. I got 47-odd and he got to 56 not out. I was bowled off a low full toss, I played over the top of it. If I'd belted one more I'd have made a half-century on debut, but I got a bit ambitious aiming a drive at Umar and was bowled. Actually, the same bowler had caused me considerable embarrassment and discomfort when he'd got one to come back at me earlier and hit me where it hurts the most. I reckon I was sucking in deep breaths for half an hour. Or that's what it felt like. You don't get much sympathy in that situation and even when you do, you know the other bloke is trying not to laugh.

Hilf was someone who, in the state Under 19s, swung the ball but wasn't that fast. He moved from Ulverstone to Hobart on a rookie contract and needed a job and I think my dad organised work for him as a brickie's labourer with some friends of ours because Hilfy was playing with us at University. After a winter carrying bricks and pushing wheelbarrows, he just put on this muscle and he came back to the next pre-season and he was real quick. He'd filled out. He gained yards. He had the same action but he just got quicker and quicker. He's a good man, Hilf, used to love a beer.

That side at Lord's was the first team to have three genuine Tasmanians in it. Still probably the only one.

Plus Troy Cooley was there as bowling coach so we had a pretty good representation from the island and Mick Marshal was the analyst. David Boon and Jamie Cox were selectors at the time but I can't remember who was selector on that tour.

Huss sang the team song that night. He was unbelievable at that. Tradition has it that the singer runs through the highlights of the match. Huss would not miss anything, he'd go through the game listing five-fors, 50s, 100s, great catches or bits of fielding, personal bests – every little thing that happened. I don't remember if he called me out, I would have already been well into the beer. The sense of relief after all those nerves leading into the game was extraordinary. And we'd won.

I reckon I was drunk for a day and a half. I went way too hard. I rocked up the next day for the bus to Leeds and I was shattered. Smithy was the same. I think it was Punter who dragged us aside later and said it's okay to celebrate, that's fine, but don't make it a habit of going too hard or take it too far, particularly mid series.

Mum's scrapbook – of course she has one! – had this quote from Ricky:

His work behind the stumps was very sharp. It was a great stumping today, one sliding down the leg side behind a left-hander is always a hard one to take. That was a big moment in the game, really. Butt was playing beautifully and they're the sort of chances you hope your keeper or any of your fielders take. I thought he had an outstanding debut, as did Smith.

We went up to Leeds for the next match, won the toss, decided to bat and were bowled out for 88 despite T. Paine top-scoring with 17. My 33 in the second innings was only shaded by Punter's 66 but needless to say we were coming from a long way back. We never got back in that match and were easily beaten. Pakistan won the game with three wickets in hand.

My first Test series ended in a 1–1 draw. I'd kept well, held my own with the bat and despite the nerves had not felt out of my depth in Test match cricket.

Opportunities, obviously, kept presenting themselves and I was kept in the team for the series that followed against India because Hadds was not fit. I was really excited about getting the chance to keep in a Test match over there, it is probably the hardest place for a keeper because of the low bounce so it was going to be a good test of my skills and how they would stand up at this level.

I played my third Test at Mohali and a nice hundred by Shane Watson along with a half-century by Ricky put us in a reasonable position, but we lost Michael Hussey and Marcus North near stumps and I had to bat for the last bit of the day. The following morning Watto and I took our time, then Mitch Johnson joined me and started to take on Harbhajan Singh and Pragyan Ojha. He hit three sixes but the best I could manage at the other end was knocking Ojha over mid wicket for consecutive boundaries. I wasn't exactly flying, but I kept going and going and by tea I was 75 from a lot of balls. After 195 deliveries I was well set and on 92 – within sniffing distance of my first Test hundred.

I didn't get any closer. The 196th delivery I faced was a good ball from Zaheer Khan that caught my outside edge and an even better catch from VVS Laxman at second slip. You could say I was unlucky but I suppose I've left out the fact that MS Dhoni dropped me before I got off the mark. And again when I was on 86. I was definitely disappointed not to reach three figures, but the team was past 400 by that stage and there'd be plenty more chances to get that hundred. Well, at least I thought there'd be.

India won that game but they shouldn't have. When Ishant Sharma came out to bat, they were eight wickets down and needed 92 to win. They were nine down and still needed a few in the last over when Johnno had Pragyan Ojha trapped in front, but Billy Bowden said there was an edge on it. But that wasn't the end of it. The ball rolled to point and Ojha was out of his crease, not sure whether to run or not. Smithy tried to run him out but missed and gave away four overthrows. They got the two runs needed a couple of balls later and that was that.

There was a lot of unhappiness around that game because Cricket Australia had refused to step in and get Doug Bollinger or Michael Hussey a leave pass from their Indian Premier League sides in the Champions League so they only arrived a few days before the game. Doug broke down in the second innings which added to the bad feeling over the incident. I got a half-century in the next game at Bengaluru but we lost and there was a pretty bad vibe about the way the whole tour had gone. Australia had lost three consecutive Tests and the Ashes were on that summer.

I figured that I wasn't going to be part of the next squad and didn't allow myself to consider any other possibility. Having gone alright on the tour, there was, naturally, talk that I might be a threat to Hadds. There was no competition between us, we both respected each other and respected the pecking order. He was the incumbent and I would step back when he was ready. Hadds was interviewed in the newspapers at the time and I think his attitude reflected mine.

'All I've worried about is I'm available to play,' he told the journos. 'I've spent that long out of the game, no one has really crossed my thought process, it's just been about making sure I can get back and play cricket. Everyone has an opinion and that's never going to change and I'm not worried about anything else. I'm not one of those people who sit awake at night hoping someone nicks it or doesn't get runs. I spent all my career behind [Adam Gilchrist] so those sorts of things haven't crossed my thoughts. I'm not worried about who's going well or who's not.' He certainly had no need to worry about me.

I'd played four Tests, passed 50 a couple of times, almost got to a hundred. I was happy to wait my turn but the steady progress I had made to that point was not going to continue. In fact, things were about to go down the toilet. That was one of the last times I would bat with confidence or freedom. It was also one of the last times I'd bat that well. I would get back some semblance of who I was, but when I did next claw my way to a first-class century in 2019, somebody worked out it was 4738 days since my previous one. I would not walk onto the field with the Australian Test team for another seven years after that last Test in India.

A lot of that seven years was marked by the dull throbbing in my right index finger and doubt that nagged like water torture.

6

BREAKING POINT

For a long time I figured what happened on 21 November 2010, and the consequences of it, would be the worst thing that ever happened to me. That was a naive thought, there was worse to come, but back then that was what I had to deal with and it turned out I didn't deal with it all that well.

It started with the best intentions. That day I flew to Brisbane for a hit and giggle Twenty20 fundraising match for the Australian Cricketers' Association. I'd already played a Shield game for Tasmania to start the season and we'd finished a four-day match for Australia A against England the day before I flew up. It was odd to back up so quickly, but it was for a good cause, so I got up early that Saturday to leave Hobart, checked into the hotel at Southbank, had lunch and went back to bed for a while before getting up and getting ready for the match.

I'd been picked by my peers to play in the ACA All-Stars side against an Aussie Fans XI chosen by popular vote as part of what was an annual fundraising game for the association. I wasn't expecting to be in the Test side but it was fun to be in town. Brad Haddin was fit and the chief selector Rod Marsh said it was his spot. I was happy, Hadds had been injured for a couple of tours and would be rested in the future because he was playing all three formats, so if ever there was a period where it was a good time to be the back-up keeper that was it. I was getting games here and there, I'd played four Tests, more ODIs. I was making the most of the chance to be around that elite group whenever it came up and I knew if I could keep performing at Sheffield Shield level for a few more years I would be next in line. Being around players like Ponting, Clarke, Hussey, Katich, Watson and Brett Lee was making me a better player by association.

It was good to catch up with Hadds in Brisbane. He was always generous with me, we were similar characters, similar cricketers, we worked hard together on each other's games, did a bit of gym together and we enjoyed a night out too. We'd struck up a good relationship from the start. We had some separation in age, so it was a master and apprentice relationship, he wasn't threatened by me, he saw me as his successor and because we got on well he was more than happy to help me and we've been that way ever since.

It was actually a radical change in my game that sent me to Brisbane on that fateful night. Before the start of the previous season, Tim Coyle had come to me and said he wanted me to open in the first T20 game against New South Wales. I thought he was mad, I just wasn't a power hitter and to be honest when we did range hitting at training I tended to hide because it was embarrassing. I couldn't hit the ball very far at all. It took all my effort to get one over mid wicket.

In a panic I called an old neighbour and we went down to an oval at Lindisfarne and I got him to throw me some balls. I don't reckon I got one to the boundary for the first hour, but I kept working on it and after a while I started to find a groove. I changed my swing and that allowed me to clear mid wicket, then I adjusted my position and found a way to get it over cover point. I was away.

That game the Blues came down with all their stars and put on 194 batting first. I walked out with Rhett Lockyear and threw caution to the wind. I went down the wicket, hit Mitch Starc over mid off for four in his first over. When Moises Henriques came on, I went to town. First ball – a full toss – went over square leg for six, then a two through cover, a slog sweep for four, a pull shot out of the ground for six, another slog sweep for four and then a dot ball to appease the gods of cricket. Something had clicked in my game.

I reckon that being asked to open in T20 improved my batting in other formats, it added a bit of flair, a bit of confidence, and a few scoring shots that I didn't previously possess. My strike rate batting down the order in the previous season was 97.61 runs per 100 balls but in 2009–10 it went up to 207. Only Dave Warner had a better strike rate and I guess that's how we found ourselves walking out to open the batting in the All-Stars game.

They had Shaun Tait bowling from one end and Dirk Nannes from the other, both generated some serious heat, but Tait was the one known as the wild thing. Being the sort of character he is, Davey said we just have to pick an end and swing hard. He opted to take Dirk's bowling and I got Shaun. Thanks, Bull. I remember one of the first deliveries Dirk bowled to him was about 154 kph and he came down to me and said, 'Forget the plan.' It was every man for themselves and Dave got himself off strike with a single.

Dirk dropped one a bit short and wide to me and I cracked it over point for a four which on reflection was not the smartest thing to do. The next one was shorter and faster and aimed at my body. I tried to get on top of it but the bounce got me and it hit my index finger on the right hand. I knew immediately that I was in trouble. I started shaking my hand, which is usually a fair sign that it is something serious, as cricketers pride themselves on never showing it hurt. Cam White came up to ask if I was okay, I said I didn't think so, and he told me to take my glove off and have a look. I did and I immediately wished I hadn't.

Did I mention I was miked up at the time by Channel Nine?

Mark Taylor was commentating and asked me if I was alright. I said, 'Nah, mate, no good.' He asked me if I was going off. Of course I was – at the time the question was irritating, but in his defence he couldn't see what I could. I think he asked if it was broken and I reckon I was pretty short with him. I might have given a few more monosyllabic answers to questions on the way off the ground and basically that was the end of my commentary career with Channel Nine.

I then headed off to the hospital. The finger was broken at the top where the ball had hit and at the bottom where it had jarred into the bat handle. They splinted it up and I was back in the change rooms before the game was finished. I knew it would require a bit more attention, but they were going to fly me to Melbourne to get it sorted out. Someone packed my kit away for me.

I wasn't too worried at that stage, a broken finger is a broken finger. They put me on a plane the next morning but when I got off the plane it had swollen up big time. It was massive and too swollen to operate on. When they did operate on it, I had to stay in hospital for a few days because the swelling was over the top again.

I guess that was a warning sign of what was to come.

There was a bit of controversy after Tim Coyle did an interview that week saying the All-Stars game was a silly idea and not worth such risks, but to be honest it could have happened in the nets – well, it could have happened if Dirk Nannes was bowling flat out in the nets.

The doctors said my recovery period was going to be five or six weeks. I heard four. A couple of games. Looking back, my optimism was wildly off the mark. It wasn't four weeks, five weeks or even six weeks . . . more like seven years before I'd claw back to where I was.

I just wanted to get back to training as quickly as possible and then I could put my hand up for the World Cup which was set for India, Sri Lanka and Bangladesh in February. I promised myself I would be ready, that I would train and prepare like I was playing the next game.

I'd never really had a bad break before. I cracked my scapula playing footy when I was 15, someone drove a knee into my back. It was a state trial game and we were playing in Campbelltown 90 minutes from Hobart. I was in awful pain, but the St John's ambulance bloke said it took a lot of force to break a shoulderblade so it was almost certainly not broken. He said just go home and if it is still sore, go and get an X-ray. I felt every bump on that road home. It was killing me the next day so my parents took me to get an X-ray and it was almost broken in half.

The shoulder still gets sore every now and then when it gets cold, which is fairly regularly down here on the island, but not like the finger. That is unbelievable, shocking. On cold mornings I can't do anything, it aches, it's got terrible blood flow so it goes white and numb and I can't feel it, it looks disgusting. I can't write or train when it is too cold, it's hard to button up a shirt. This happens every morning in winter, I would have to move to a warmer state if I want to have a better start to the day.

It's been a horrible injury, but back then it was just a broken finger that'd be right in six weeks. Four weeks later, I was back at training. Ed Cowan had joined us in Tasmania and wrote a diary of the summer. On a Monday late in December, he wrote that while Australia was being murdered at the MCG in the Ashes: 'Tim Paine passed his fitness test on his, recovering incredibly quickly from his finger operation . . . His finger is still the size of a Hungarian sausage. I have been throwing him ball in the nets and watching him catch with tremendous pain.'

I was determined to be fit for the World Cup and so pushed through the pain at training sessions. I was being an idiot. I turned out for a couple of Big Bash games which meant Ed was out of the team. I opened in Perth against the Scorchers on 30 December – the injury happened

21 November – and hit 71 which anchored the innings, was my highest score in the BBL and earned me Man of the Match in a game we won easily.

I was back in the saddle and trying not to let on how much trouble I was in. It still hurt like hell; batting, keeping and at training. The thought of playing a World Cup didn't numb the pain, but it was enough reason to push through it.

In January I was named captain for the Prime Minister's XI game against England and got a half-century opening the batting, but we were beaten thanks to a great century from Ian Bell. Then I was picked to play for Australia in two T20s against England in the following weeks and named vice-captain, which was a further boost to my confidence and assurance that there was a future in the national team for me. I didn't get to bat in the first one, but had a bit of a swing at first drop below Dave Warner and Shane Watson at the MCG in mid-January. Shaun Tait, Brett Lee and Mitchell Johnson all played that game and I have to thank the person who decided quicks should be limited to four overs in this format because the fewer deliveries smacking into a sore hand the better.

I was lying to anybody who asked how my finger was going, hiding the swelling and the pain. People who saw the finger couldn't believe I was playing, but I dismissed all their concerns. I'd just say there was a bit of scar tissue so it's swollen.

The Australian selectors asked me play in the seventh ODI of the series against England in Perth at the back of the summer. Brad Haddin and I opened the batting, he got the gloves and I got to field, which was not fun. I winced every time I had to throw the ball, the finger throbbed something shocking and swelled up during the game, but I got away with it and kept going and iced it quietly in the change rooms.

It all paid off when I was picked in the squad for the 2011 World Cup. It was a great feeling to be part of the crew and even if my finger was in a bad state, I figured it had to get better sometime.

Our first game was to be against India in February, but I played a practice game in the lead-up while Brad rested and it was a miserable experience keeping to Mitchell Johnson. I pushed through because the chance of playing in the tournament was just too big to turn down, but it was agony. Had they not picked a second keeper for the World Cup, I might not have gone as hard, I would have had that time off. I managed to get through the game but Hadds knew how bad it was and afterwards when he asked me about it, I said to him that he couldn't have another rest because I didn't think I'd be able to get through another 50 overs behind the stumps.

It was good to have someone to confide in because mostly I was enduring this by myself. I kept masking it, icing it in my room, I didn't miss any training. I wouldn't admit there was a problem, putting on a big smile and dismissing any questions about my health. As you do. But the veil would drop when the hotel door closed and I would give in to the pain. Keeping secrets isn't easy, even those sorts. There was some relief in acknowledging the pain even if it was in private.

In the end we were knocked out by India in the quarter finals despite Ricky making a century, which was disappointing since we were playing for a fourth straight World Cup title. Even though my hand was still in trouble, the team's loss stung more. After the loss Ricky announced he was standing down as captain to give Michael Clarke a clear run at the next World Cup. It was a changing of the guard and I reckon it hurt Punter to do that but he always put the team first.

We played a series in Bangladesh after the World Cup and I was still hanging in there. Hadds played and opened in the first two ODIs and I got picked for the third game but ended up batting below Mitch Johnson who was sent in ahead of me to have a slog.

I was away when Tasmania beat New South Wales at Bellerive to win our second Sheffield Shield. Tom Triffitt took my job behind the stumps for Tasmania, as I was spending time in national teams, but mostly because I just couldn't get the finger right for a four-day game. It was a good win considering New South Wales made over 400 in the first innings thanks to a century each by

Phil Hughes and Simon Katich, but Ed Cowan had something to prove against his old side and responded with a century of his own.

Life kept rolling on and I kept waiting for my finger to get better but it wasn't getting a lot of rest or relaxation. I'd been picked up in January in the IPL by Pune Warriors for $270,000 – which is enough for a nice little place in Tassie. I went there thinking they wouldn't play me and they would let you run your own ship at training, but they picked me which was bloody inconvenient. I played two games but by now the finger was so swollen it looked like it would burst and the pain had finally worn me down. I had to admit I was done. I had to go home, I was no good. Geoff Marsh was coach and I'm sorry I let him down. I felt like shit about that.

If I had my time over I would have done different rehab and been honest with selectors and not gone to the World Cup, not gone to the IPL, but I was young and dumb and desperate and probably refusing to acknowledge how bad things were. I just kept pushing on and when the opportunities arose I felt like I had to take them. If I was an established player, I reckon I might have been smarter, but maybe not. When you are not established, you think you have to take every opportunity or someone else will; and when you are established, you think pretty much the same.

I got myself fit enough to hide the injury and be picked for an Australia A tour of Zimbabwe in July 2011. We had a good team: Dave Warner and Phil Hughes opened the batting, Usman Khawaja was at No. 3, Callum Ferguson and Mitch Marsh played, Pete Siddle, Trent Copeland and Ben Hilfenhaus were bowling. They made me captain and I returned the favour by scoring 98 in the first game. We won both matches but I didn't play another first-class game for 12 months.

The next summer, 2011–12, didn't go well. In fact, it didn't go at all. I didn't front for one single game at state or international level.

The trouble began when I was hit at the start of the year at training. Brendan Drew caught me with an innocuous delivery in the nets and broke the bone in my finger again. I was really worried by that. It wasn't a big blow and obviously the bone was really brittle but you can't play cricket and not get hit on the fingers. I had an operation and they took bone from my hip to help fix it. Then it broke again at training and they had to do the operation again.

There was a plate and eight pins holding my finger together by the time they'd finished all the operations. It still hurt but not as much as before, I could put on a jumper or clean my teeth without wincing. I was icing it and flying to Melbourne to use a hyperbaric chamber which was supposed to reduce the swelling, but it just wouldn't go down. At times I felt like someone was tasering me through the finger. If I bumped it the colour would drain from my face and I couldn't talk for a while.

The physical pain never receded so it was hard to forget even if I was batting okay, it was constantly sore, something I couldn't ignore. The finger was becoming the centre of my universe, I couldn't get away from it, people would talk to me about it because of the appearance of it, they'd have to comment and it would become part of the conversation. As I began to miss more and more games, everyone wanted to know what was going on.

I was already well practised at covering up because from the time I was a teenager until my mid 20s I used to bite my fingernails a lot, so I was always good at hiding them. I'd put my hand in my pocket but I couldn't fit it in my jeans pocket or it would hurt pushing it in because the scarring was on the outside. I developed other ways to keep my hand out of sight.

Then I noticed there was a clicking sound when I made a fist. I couldn't get up for a game all year and in February 2012 the Australian team came down to play an ODI in Hobart and so I went to see the medical staff. I opened and closed my fist and it was going click, click. They sent me for a scan and you could see the plate had cracked and the broken edge was pushing against the bone when I closed my hand. Missing the summer was hard but if it gave the finger time to repair, that was fine with me. One year out of your career isn't too bad.

Problem was, it wasn't getting any better. I was bouncing back and forth between Hobart and Melbourne where I was going to the hand clinic for more operations and rehab. Going to Victoria all the time wasn't so bad as I met a girl called Bonnie who'd moved over there from Hobart and asked her out. That was a pleasant distraction.

Tasmanian coach Tim Coyle was a good man and said, 'Why don't you go and stay in Melbourne for a month or two?' It was good to cut down on the travelling and I hooked up with a gym and spent a bit of time in and out of the hand clinic.

When I was in Tassie nothing changed, I was always around the boys at Bellerive, I was still enjoying it, just a bit frustrated that I couldn't play. There was always someone else who was injured to do work with. And I could stay connected to the group – I could go to gym, do some running, watch the team training, do top hand batting drills, there was even a period where I could do my golf ball drills.

That said, when the 2011–12 season went by without a single game of cricket and little improvement in the finger, I was probably starting to move past frustrated and on to worry. It was a real kick in the teeth when Peter Nevill and Matthew Wade were included in the squad for the West Indies when Hadds was unavailable.

You have to remember that you are dealing with a bloke who was so addicted to the game that Tim Coyle thought

I was obsessed and would sometimes send me home from training because he felt I should be doing something else with my life.

I'm a cricket tragic and will watch any and every game I can on TV, but the darkness was starting to loom and as the summer progressed I couldn't watch the Australians play. I guess I was just jealous, disappointed, frustrated . . . all those things. I started to go out a lot. Weekends were huge. I'd missed all that stuff when I was the right age to be doing it. I was on the tear because I didn't really have much to do and I suppose I was trying to forget the fact I wasn't playing cricket at such an important point in my career. But then one day I just snapped out of it and came back to that place where I, at least, lived like a cricketer even if I wasn't playing cricket.

By this stage people were catching on. People were asking what was going to happen, if I would make it back, it moved to a different kind of concern. Nobody was as positive as they'd been before and the game doesn't wait for anyone, it just keeps moving. If you are standing still, you get left further and further behind.

In July 2012 I found the fitness to join the Australia A side on a tour of England, but this time they made Ed Cowan captain. I liked Ed from the moment he arrived in Tasmania, he was a serious professional player who

made us a much better team. At training and on the field
he helped us improve because of the way he worked and
trained. He was dedicated in everything he did and he was
a nice fellow to boot. He moved down from New South
Wales because he wanted to play for Australia, not because
he wanted to play first-class cricket. We had quite an
ambitious group – George Bailey, Ben Hilfenhaus, Jason
Krejza, Xavier Doherty, James Faulkner, Alex Doolan –
these were guys who had played for Australia or were very
close, and Ed, like the rest of us, was really driven.

Ed was great on that Australia A tour and I was just
pumped to be part of it. I hadn't given myself a chance
of being selected so it was a pleasant surprise when I was.
I remember hanging out with Usman in Derbyshire,
there wasn't much on and most of the boys were playing
golf. I am hopeless at golf, it doesn't suit my personality
I reckon, I like to run around, that's my idea of sport. I
like playing in teams, I find walking around too boring
to take seriously. Cricketers take golf very seriously but
I don't enjoy it that way, I enjoy it with a few beers as a
social event, but the boys are mad about it.

The positive thing about all of this was that my keeping
was still in good order. I remember diving for a leg side
nick that got rid of Joe Root at Edgbaston, then somehow
hitting 59 off 78 balls and that felt okay. The selectors
didn't put any pressure on me and my confidence started
to return. I had to wear a guard on the finger and the

gloves were specially reinforced to protect the bone as the graft took.

That series was my first look at Joe Root, he was an opening batter at the time, he was rated highly and we'd heard about him. He was a little skinny fellow, still is, but smaller and skinnier back then. You could tell straight away how good he was. He hit the ball cleanly and moved well.

Ben Stokes and Mark Wood were also in the opposition at one stage or another. The first time I saw Stokes bat, he came out looking a bit untucked, gear all over the place. Nathan Coulter-Nile was bowling fast and he already had a few wickets. He bowled a full first ball and Stokes absolutely creamed it. I can remember Coults saying, 'Shot!' I'd heard a little bit about Stokes because he'd played at Durham and everyone thought he was going to be a gun, but he was just a bit of a loose cannon back then. The same with Mark Wood who came on first change; he was a skinny, small kid but he had that action he has now and he just whanged it down much quicker than you expected.

They had a decent attack too: Chris Woakes played in that game.

I kept well on that tour and was happy to go on it and in the last game I showed something with the bat and so I left with a bit of confidence. I read an interview I did at the time and I guess I must have had a shift in thinking, because I said that it was just a relief to be playing cricket and I hoped that one day I'd be back for the Ashes but the injury had given me a new perspective.

There was, however, another problem developing and it was to do with my batting. I had a special guard and gloves, but for most of this period I couldn't wrap my finger around the bat properly. The finger just won't do what it is supposed to anymore. When I drive my index finger sits off the wheel, it never touches the steering wheel. I had to change the way I brushed my teeth, change the way I wrote with a pen. It was like having someone else's finger. Obviously the impact on my cricket was the most serious side effect of the situation.

Everything in my batting had to adjust because of my finger and it threw my whole game out. I was a cover driving, off side player, I played the drive and cut, I'd modelled my technique on Jamie Cox, but because of my index finger I couldn't really hold the bat properly and so things started shifting. It's important not to be tight with your bottom hand, which means you hold the bat with your thumb and index finger, but I couldn't do that anymore. My index finger sits off the bat and I have to grip it with the other three fingers which makes me really bottom handed. My game became a mirror of itself, I went from scoring the bulk of my runs in the arc from gully to mid off, to scoring them all on the leg side.

Changing the way I held the bat changed the angle of the blade and where I hit the ball, so I had to adapt my game to it. But for 15 years, if the ball was pitched up I would cover drive, and I couldn't break the habit. Almost every time I attempted it, I nicked the ball. I had trained a certain way for so long and it was ingrained in me to go at it. It drove me mad how often I nicked balls that year. I tried to tell myself not to drive but my muscle memory was undermining me.

I'd come back for the 2012–13 season expecting to pick up from where I had left off. I'd had two interrupted summers and it was time to get on with it but I struggled with the bat. Tassie, however, were flying. Ricky Ponting played nine games with us and got three centuries and it all came together. We got into the Sheffield Shield final again and made the early running against Queensland. We were well placed after the first innings even though I got a duck. We were reduced to 6–56 in the second but James Faulkner and I had a bit of a swing. I hit 87, he got 89, that gave us a massive lead and we drew the game which was enough to win the Sheffield Shield.

It was our third Sheffield Shield trophy in six years, but this one was special because it was Ricky's. Tim Coyle was finishing up that season too, so it felt great to be part of that for both those guys. I reckon that group was playing really well because we had some extra motivation. Rick was pumped, he is as proud a Tasmanian as there is, and I wonder if those early years when there was no success must have been frustrating. I think he enjoyed being in this team because it was full of guys who had a bit of ambition and had worked hard and wanted to win and expected to win. Maybe it was his influence and legacy that got us to a place where we had so much confidence in Tasmanian cricket. It was great for him and Coyley, they'd both put so much in. And we adored both of them.

The other issue that was getting worse – and which I have struggled to admit – was that I was not only losing confidence in my stroke play, I was petrified of getting hit again. When I started to face guys who were a bit quicker, instead of concentrating on what they were going to bowl as they ran in, I was thinking, 'I hope he doesn't hit my finger again or I'm in all sorts of trouble.' I was in all sorts of trouble.

At first, it was that little bit of fear of being hit and from there it was a downward spiral, but of course I didn't tell anyone.

When I played in England after missing that season, I didn't get to bat in the first innings against Derbyshire and I remember I was watching the bowlers to work out which ones would break my finger and which one would bowl me. They had a left-armed quick called Mark Footitt who had been on the fringes of Test selection. I was surprised at how gentle he looked in the first dig, our guys were smacking him around, but when they sent me out to open in the seconds I swear he was bowling 20 kph faster and I was in a world of trouble. I was thinking, 'This is not what I want coming back into it.' Sure enough I went forward to a short ball that hit me flush in the helmet and flew on the full to mid on who caught it. I just wasn't watching the ball, I was so worried about getting hit in the hand that I didn't leave it or try and play a pull shot, I kind of just wore it.

When you're batting, if you are thinking about anything else but watching the ball and scoring, you are not going to make runs or last very long. I was not making runs. The drip feed of doubt was becoming a real problem. I was so focused on the fear of getting hit that I forgot what I do well when I'm batting well. If anyone asked, I did that cricketer thing of saying that I was going okay, that I was hitting them alright, that I just needed a little bit of luck. The truth was I was scared of getting hit and I couldn't think past that and so I couldn't score runs.

The fear started to get out of control and after a while I wouldn't sleep or eat before games because I was so worried about batting. I was difficult to live with.

During those years I was sometimes captaining state sides if George Bailey was away and I was doing a poor job. I was grumpy, stressed and taking my frustrations out on other people. The runs just wouldn't come and the anxiety grew.

It would start before I got to the crease, usually the day before. The opposition would name their team and I would look at their bowlers and see which ones would hit me, which ones would get me out. I would get up the next morning and was so uptight I couldn't eat which meant I had no energy. I was coming to games expecting to fail. I was just praying for a bit of luck, a dropped catch or a bad decision, and hoping that would be the point my old life would just come back to me. Things had to turn my way soon.

It even started to happen at grade cricket, all I could think about was getting out or getting hit so I was defeated before I got to the game. I had no idea how I would score runs. I started hiding, I'd find excuses not to be in the nets or if I had to I kept it as short as possible to make sure people didn't see how shit I was.

I hung on in the 2013–14 season, averaged 31.5 and got three half-centuries, but I was not the batsman I once was. I still couldn't grip the bat with the bottom hand. I was closed off and natural scoring options were weaknesses. Where once I was strong on driving on the front foot, now I was nicking off time and time again, I was becoming a bunny.

I became really hard to be around for my teammates and Bonnie. A year after we'd got together during my visits to the hand clinic in Melbourne she'd moved back to Hobart and in with me. I had a home in Sandy Bay at the time and was feeling quite grown up. What girl in her right mind could resist a handsome young cricketer with the world at his feet? Unfortunately the man she moved in with was not the man I became. I was miserable inside and miserable to be around.

It was a double-barrel thing, I was disappointed about where I was but I also felt like I'd let everyone down, my family, my club coaches, people that believed in me. In those days I couldn't talk on the phone to family after a game because I couldn't tell them that I'd failed again.

I still loved going to training, I still loved watching cricket, but I wasn't enjoying the game because I was convinced I was going to fail, and when I inevitably did fail I felt like I'd disappointed everyone. One thing about succeeding is you feel like you are providing joy to people who help you. There's an obvious flip side to this.

I don't think my best mates, family or partner had any idea what was going on in my head around this time. It got so bad I would cry on the couch when Bonnie was at work. I started becoming a recluse, I didn't want to social-ise with anybody because the fact my cricket had gone backward was the elephant in every room. Once, cricket was the first thing people spoke to me about. Now it was an awkward subject they danced around.

Eventually I visited Cricket Tasmania's personal development/welfare officer to see if I could do a TAFE course or something because I was starting to think that I'd need to find a job. Her name was Emma Harris and she was also our team psychologist. We started to talk about me moving on and this other stuff started coming out. I reckon I sat with her for 20 minutes and when I walked out of that room I felt instantly better; that was the first step and I took it by accident. It still took six months to get my game back but that was the starting point. Now I tell the younger players that you need people around who you can trust, talk to and share with. I realise now that it's braver to share than to deal with it yourself. Back then I was embarrassed, I thought I couldn't turn to people who'd helped me and who I thought expected me to deliver.

I got a little bit of focus back after some sessions with Emma and started to reflect on my life. I realised that being picked up at 16 wasn't ideal. It was probably too soon, I wasn't ready, I stopped focusing on important things outside of cricket. If I had my time again, I would do things a bit differently

7

SECOND CHANCE

I was feeling a bit better, but things went from bad to worse with my cricket.

In the summer of 2014–15 my keeping was fine but I averaged 17.7 with the bat in eight games. In the following summer I only got five games, kept fine, averaged 7 and was dropped from the Sheffield Shield side. It was no surprise when the 2016–17 Shield season rolled around that I was not included again, and I didn't get a game before Christmas. I was going backwards.

I spent a lot of time in those years playing club cricket for the University of Tasmania or in the second grade, which was essentially an Under 23 competition with a few dinosaurs thrown in. It was strange, I always felt better with the bat in the seconds and in that final season I had scores of 55, 49, 99, 5 and 120 in three games. I was alright in the Big Bash too.

At the end of the 2016 summer Bonnie and I got married at the Home Hill Winery. It was a fantastic day with family, friends and lots of my mates from cricket.

I had a two-year deal with the Hobart Hurricanes but my contract with the state side had run out. In the winter, Tassie signed Matty Wade and I was even further down the pecking order, but I'd already made the decision to leave Tasmania and my first-class cricket behind. It hadn't worked out the way I planned, I was 32 years old, I had no education or skills to speak of and it was pretty clear my best years were behind me. I was worn down by trying and failing, and if Bonnie and I were to have a financially secure future I needed to act.

The decision was also provoked by an offer to go to Melbourne and work for Kookaburra Sports. They wanted me to be a rep with them which would keep me around the game. Obviously I'd been thinking about my future and I'd been beating myself up about the fact I wasn't qualified for anything. I didn't go to a better school because I wanted to be with my mates, and I didn't have anything to recommend me to an employer except a crooked finger, a failing cricket career and the fact I'd played a few Tests way back in history.

In my worse moments I thought I'd screwed up my life, but the Kookaburra job offered a lifeline and you never know, maybe the Bushrangers might take a look at me if things went well. If they didn't, I had a job that kept me around the game and paid a modest wage – they were going to throw in a free phone!

What was then known as the Allan Border Medal was on in Sydney in late January and we went up to the Quay West on the day of the awards ceremony. I think Bonnie was up in our room at the Quay West when I went downstairs and met with the guy from Kookaburra to discuss my future. I told him I would take the job. I was going to be a marketing manager looking after players, but there was a career path there for me.

So I did the deal in the cafe that morning, put on the fancy suit and enjoyed my last ever Allan Border Medal. Davey Warner got the big gong for the second year running, ahead of Steve Smith and Mitchell Starc. Meg Lanning took out the Belinda Clark Medal.

The thing was, Tasmania didn't really want me enough. I had decided that if they gave me a two-year deal I would stay, but if it was one year I was going to take the Kookaburra job. I met with Andrew Dykes, who'd been our general manager for the past 13 years, and list manager Mike Farrell. I laid it out, making sure they knew I wasn't trying to bargain or threaten, I just wanted a two-year deal otherwise I needed to get on with the rest of my life.

They offered me a one-year deal. I wasn't upset but I'm not sure they thought I was being serious and it seemed to surprise them when I said thanks but no thanks.

Word had got around Melbourne and I was getting offers from a few clubs and it was like the next chapter of my life was starting already. It was kind of exciting.

Feeling a bit cheeky about it, I gave Ricky Ponting a call.

'Any places for sale near you?' I asked, knowing full well I couldn't afford to live anywhere near him. He'd forked out about $10 million for a house on the Golden Mile in Melbourne not far from Warney's place. He asked why and I told him and I could hear the gears in his mind grinding. He wasn't impressed. 'Fuck that,' he said. He wasn't happy at all about me leaving Tassie and said he would make some calls, but things were in play and Bonnie and I were already planning our life in Melbourne.

A couple of days later Nick Cummins, who had been the general manager of Sydney Thunder, gave me a call. He wanted to meet in Salamanca for coffee, he'd just been announced as the Cricket Tasmania's new CEO and wanted to have a chat. Punter had called him and told him about my plans. Nick was replacing David Johnston who'd been there for 19 years and while he hadn't started yet he was keen to make some changes – but I wasn't one of them. He said that he didn't care how bad I had been going, he wanted me around the group to guide them into a new era.

This was all a bit awkward.

I discussed it with Bonnie and we agreed that rather than uproot ourselves we'd stay in the town where we were born and I'd keep playing cricket. I rang Kookaburra and said, 'Aaah, sorry, I'm out.'

As luck would have it I was picked to play three Sheffield Shield matches at the back end of the summer and in the third of them I passed 3000 runs in that format, but I was still going at an average of 26.

Australia had shared the keeping duties between Pete Nevill and Matty Wade since Brad Haddin stopped playing in 2015. Watching opportunities go to other players was one of the hardest things. When the Test team came to Hobart to play South Africa in 2016–17 Pete had the job, but the game did not go well at all. Australia got done by an innings and 80 runs which is not exactly what you expect to happen at home. It clearly wasn't acceptable to the brass who saddled up and rode into town to read the riot act to the boys in the dressing rooms.

It was the fifth straight loss for the Test side and there were bodies that needed to be thrown under the bus. Pete had come in to replace Brad when he had to pull out of the Lord's Test in 2015 because his daughter Mia had been taken to hospital. When Hadds was ready to play again, Pete kept the job which caused some angst in the team. It didn't sit right with everybody as one of the core values of the coaching group at the time was family first, but a bloke who put his family first lost his spot. They made wholesale changes after the loss in Hobart and Wadey, who'd played a dozen or so Tests when Hadds was absent four years earlier, was brought back into the team.

It was funny how that drama basically played out in my hometown. It was like watching the girl you love break up with one guy and take up with another.

I think there was a vague sense that I'd be back in the mix at some time. Nathan Lyon had been asked at one stage and he said some good things about bowling with me behind the stumps in Australia A games. Hadds had also championed my cause. It was just a pity I was screwed in the head.

Things changed quickly at Bellerive with the new chief executive in the job. Our coach Dan Marsh was replaced with Adam Griffith. Matthew Wade came back. A few people thought I'd be upset that my friend from up the road would be given the gloves ahead of me, but England were coming to play the Ashes and it was pretty obvious Matty was going to be away playing for Australia for most of the summer so they'd need me to help out. I had no thoughts of playing for Australia at that stage.

Strange how things turn out.

When the summer rolled around we had our first game against Western Australia at the WACA and I went over with the team, but was made 12th man. Selectors couldn't find a place for me with Wadey obviously needing a bit of match practice before the summer so I was running drinks. Chasing 365 in the last innings we were bowled out for 63 so it was almost a good game to miss – if there is such a thing.

Greg Chappell came to town for the Under 19 Championships which were on in Hobart and he gave me a call and wanted to have a chat so we arranged to meet for coffee. Greg is a legend in Australian cricket and has this aura, but from the moment I met him I felt like we clicked. I think it was because I was a bit of a cheeky young bloke who respected his standing in the game, but wasn't so intimidated I couldn't have a casual conversation. He is a great storyteller and over the years I loved hearing his tales from days on the road. We'd spent a lot of time getting to know each other in Zimbabwe when I captained the Australia A side and done alright for myself back in 2013 and I think that really cemented the respect we had for each other.

We both barrack for Essendon too and so we chatted away about how bad that was going and at some point we got around to where I was at. He said the selectors wanted me to captain a Cricket Australia XI against England in Adelaide and Townsville. Because it was a young group, they wanted a senior player to keep them all in line. I didn't mind that at all, it gave me a chance to get a bit of a look at young Will Pucovski and a few of the other emerging cricketers.

When we got up to pay the bill and say our goodbyes, Greg said, 'Go over there, enjoy yourself, play well and you never know.' It was an intriguing way to end the conversation and the words went round in my head quite a bit after that. What did he mean? I got home to Bonnie and told her that he'd said something strange, but had to dismiss it because you don't want to get expectations up or anything. I reckon by the next day I'd forgotten all about it and was just looking forward to playing some cricket against the tourists.

I don't know if my confidence was sort of coming back, or not. I'd been talking to the psych and that was helping with my balance in life. Deep down I knew I was still a good player, but I wasn't sure if I could get going again. I just needed a lucky break. A dropped catch. A flukey 50. One good innings. I hoped I had something left, but to be honest I was thinking I was gone – still, there's always 'what if?'.

While I wasn't scoring runs in first-class cricket and in my darkest moments I never thought I would again, I was getting hundreds fairly consistently in club cricket and Second XI games. It was just that fear of failure that emerged every time I had to bat in first-class games. The anxiety would really eat away at me. I was hitting the ball well enough in the Big Bash at the start of the year. It was just a matter of getting that form from other grades out into the middle without that crippling anxiety robbing me of all confidence every time I stepped up to Shield level.

At the same time I was at the top of my game as a wicketkeeper and I knew it. In my mind I was still the best in the country and a few other people felt that too.

The work with a psych was helping and things had changed at home. Bonnie and I had our first child, Milla, in June 2017, and as anyone who has had a child will know, that shifts your perspective on everything. I'm not saying cricket took a back seat, but it certainly had some competition. All the boys who have children comment on how when you get back home you soon forget about the day. Being greeted by your kids instantly puts an end to any self-pity about a bad innings or a result, they don't care if you've made a golden duck or a double century. Which is not to say that the game doesn't still loom largest in almost every aspect of your life.

I only had a short session against the bowlers when I was in Adelaide for the Cricket Australia XI, but later I did have a bit of a one-on-one with Chris Rogers in the nets in Canberra because I am one of those people who likes to tinker and I'm never going to waste the chance to learn something from somebody who has obviously worked out a way to succeed at the top level. Chris wasn't the most gifted batter I ever played against, I say that with the most respect, but he was a gun because he'd worked it out. I hated playing against him because he just knew how to score and he'd put on a shitload of runs. There aren't a lot of players who have more than 25,000 first-class runs with 76 centuries at an average of almost 50. You have to have figured the game out to do that. He didn't get a long stint at Test cricket, but he played 24 games for Australia with an average of over 40. I got to like Chris over the week in the nets in Canberra. He's actually a funny guy, I'd never known that when we played each other, he'd always seemed so serious.

Looking back I didn't have the anxiety about my batting before I started with the Cricket Australia XI because in a way the innings didn't matter that much, I didn't think anything was on the line. Wadey was around for the next Shield game and I would be slotting in after that because he was most likely going to play the Tests.

England arrived with a bowling attack that included James Anderson and Chris Woakes and I knocked up a decent half-century in the first innings, holding things together in the middle order while the youngsters came and went, but they tore us apart in the second innings and we were soundly beaten. It had been three years since I'd made a first-class 50 so I was pretty happy.

Things got strange after that. I was supposed to go to Townsville the following day for another tour match with the Cricket Australia XI which meant I wasn't available for the Shield game at the MCG against Victoria even if they wanted to pick me, but when the game finished I got a phone call to tell me to come to Melbourne because they'd decided I should play there for Tassie. Something was going on, but I didn't know what. When we were leaving Adelaide I was chatting to Stuart Broad who'd played with us at the Hurricanes and he said, 'I'll see you in Townsville,' but I explained there'd been a change and he said, 'Ahhh, we thought there was something on.'

There was a lot of speculation about who would keep in the first Ashes Test. The contest was obviously between Pete Nevill and Matty Wade, they were first choice. Maybe Cricket Australia was just looking for some competitive tension. Some commentators were pointing to Alex Carey who'd just missed the cut from the GWS football team and gone back to cricket. The previous summer he'd broken the Sheffield Shield record for dismissals (59) and he'd scored over 500 runs. The only players who'd ever done the 500 and the 50 were former record-holder Chris Hartley (three times), Adam Gilchrist and Matthew Wade – and it was in Alex's first full season.

I spoke to George Bailey when I got to Melbourne and he said that all he knew was someone at headquarters wanted me to play the next Shield game even if I didn't keep wickets. We went to speak to Adam Griffith, the coach, and he asked what was going on – which was strange in itself. It didn't seem to sit right with Griff which is understandable because nobody wants selection dictated to them from outside the team. He said they were picking Wadey so someone had to be dropped and it turned out to be Jake Doran. They hadn't booked me a room so I had to share with our batting coach, Jeff Vaughan, which was fine by me as I liked having someone to talk to and we got on well.

George won the toss at the MCG, we batted and I was out for a duck. Oh well, that was that done.

I remember that in the rooms Alex Doolan asked me how I was. Usually I'd get cranky and kick a few cans, but I was strangely relaxed and said, 'It's just a game.' I hadn't expected to even play that season so being at the MCG was a bonus and I was having a bit of fun. I wasn't sure what was going on, nobody really was, but I was rolling with it.

In the first innings we got done for 172, with George contributing 106 runs, then we knocked them over for 144 with only Marcus Harris (86) and Dan Christian (35) reaching double figures. I fielded at slip next to Wadey who had the gloves and enjoyed it, got myself a couple of catches and we were batting again early on day two.

I was actually lucky to get a bat in the second innings. Our opener Alex Doolan took the opposition bowlers apart, George came in first drop and we were already 2–233 when I finally got out in the middle on the third day. Dools was 130 and on his way to a really big score. I wasn't feeling too bad going in, but I struggled to rotate the strike. I played only three scoring shots from the first 30-odd balls I faced, but at least they were all boundaries. Slowly I started to find a bit of rhythm. It probably helped that their bowlers were tiring and Dan Christian was kind enough to allow me a few more boundaries. I reached 50 and was 71 not out – Dools was 247 not out – when Bails declared at tea on day three.

That, friends, was my second half-century in a week but it was my first time past 50 in Sheffield Shield for four years – last time I'd got there was against South Australia in Hobart back in 2014.

We played out a boring draw and afterwards somebody said that one of the journalists from Cricket Australia's website wanted to interview me. I went over and he said something about it being a big moment to be called back into the Australian team: 'How do you feel, Tim?'

I said, 'Sorry, I don't know what you're talking about.'

The journalist told me it was all over Twitter. It may well have been but you'd reckon they'd have told me first if I was picked so I didn't get too excited.

I looked up that interview the other day. I said I was feeling good and that if there hadn't been changes at Cricket Tasmania I'd be working for Kookaburra, not playing at the MCG. I added that it was nice to be enjoying the game again.

The story pointed out that I'd played 26 one-day internationals between 2009 and 2011, made an ODI century in England and a 92 in India in one of my four Tests. Then there were the missing years. Apparently, if I did play at the Gabba in the next Test as the journos seemed to think I would, I'd equal Brad Hogg's Australian record of missing the most Tests – 78 – between my last and next match.

I wandered back to the dressing rooms and whispered to George what the journo had just said. I turned on my phone and there were no messages, no missed calls from the selectors. It sounded like a silly rumour. We had a beer with the Victorians, packed up our bags and jumped on the bus. I was sitting in the middle row of the bus with George, just chatting with the rest of the boys, when he typed one word on his screen and showed it to me:

CONFIRMED

My heart leapt and then just sank. Instant nerves took over. *Fuck me. What were they thinking? The Ashes. In Australia. What had I done? . . . God, be careful what you wish for.* I started panicking about the enormity of the challenge, my mind went straight to the negative stuff. I knew it would be a huge story and I knew I would be under massive pressure because nobody rated me, they all thought Wade or Nevill should have the job. It was going to look like the selectors were so desperate they had to go back to a bloke from Tassie who couldn't even hold his spot in state cricket. I wasn't even keeping.

Still, nobody had confirmed it to me.

We got to the hotel and the boys decided we'd drop off our gear then go to a bar and have a beer. As I walked into my room, my phone rang. It was chief selector, Trevor Hohns. My heart skipped a beat, again. Trevor said something like, 'We're ringing to let you know we're picking you in the first Test against England. We just want to pick the best wicketkeeper and we think it is you, plus you've been batting well.' I was in shock even after all the rumours.

And then I got a text from Wadey asking if I'd been picked. I rang him back and told him. He said he thought so, as the selectors had told him he was out but wouldn't say who was in. Peter Nevill, who'd been playing in Brisbane, was on the plane flying home, which he wouldn't have been doing if he was picked because the Test team was due to gather there.

It was fine between Wadey and me. I got the feeling that he'd had enough of the pressure of keeping and batting, after a few Test series that didn't go well for him. I'd always thought it was unfair that, for some reason, his keeping was marked much harder than other's. If he made a mistake, it was replayed 20 times. I don't want to speak for him, but I do know that sometimes all the scrutiny and criticism can wear you down.

After that I called Mum and Bonnie. Still focusing on the negatives, I called my mate James Henderson, a fellow Tasmanian who managed Ricky Ponting, and said, 'I need some help because I'm going to get crucified here.' James had a sports management company called DSEG in Melbourne and he arranged to meet me in the morning to talk it through.

When I got to the pub to join the Tassie boys, everyone was having a beer. Wadey looked relaxed, Vaughny my roommate was absolutely stoked for me.

It was strange and awesome to be in that moment with Jeff Vaughan. During the pre-season I'd sat down with him and he'd asked me, 'What's the problem, how in god's name aren't you scoring runs?' As our batting coach, he saw things. I'd confided in him that it was all mental, I was lacking confidence. He said, 'I look at you and you are a terrific player, but now I get it.' That summer he'd give me throwdowns and he would say, 'Righto, Boxing Day, Stuart Broad bowling, the field is up,' or 'Now I'm Jimmy Anderson, I'm coming around the wicket, it's the last hour, you have to hang on.' It was all a bit of fun, but maybe it proves the power of positive thinking – his not mine.

I lay wide awake staring at the ceiling that night, listening to Vaughny sleep and wondering how the hell this had happened.

The next day reality hit and the squad was announced: David Warner, Cameron Bancroft, Usman Khawaja, Steve Smith (c), Peter Handscomb, Shaun Marsh, Tim Paine,

Mitchell Starc, Pat Cummins, Nathan Lyon, Josh Hazlewood, Jackson Bird.

The reviews were in by the time I got up and they were pretty much as I'd expected. Veteran cricket writer Robert 'Crash' Craddock wrote: 'Tim Paine's elevation to Test wicketkeeper in place of his old backyard rival Matthew Wade shows how totally confused Australia is over this crucial position. Never has Australia had less faith in its Test custodians since the heartbreak years of the mid-1980s when five keepers were tried in four years after Rod Marsh left and before Ian Healy arrived.'

Stuart MacGill was clearly not happy with me getting the nod ahead of Peter Nevill and let the world know via social media. Naturally, the papers picked up on his comments.

Everyone on social media was asking, 'How the hell have they gone back to this bloke?' It wasn't seen as an inspired choice, I hadn't banged the door down, it looked like desperation by the selectors. A bloke in his 12th summer, a bloke who wasn't first choice keeper for his state, one who hadn't scored a run since WG Grace was a boy . . .

Before the Test began I ducked back to Tasmania to pick up some stuff. There was media at the airport when I got back. All my gear from Cricket Australia was sent to Bellerive and so I had to swing by and get that. I found the baggy green which hadn't seen the light of day for a hell of a long time and started to get my stuff together at home. Bonnie, god bless her, couldn't understand why I seemed so anxious. I told her I'd wanted this all my life and now I didn't know if I could do it. They'd picked me for my wicketkeeping, but all that did was heighten the scrutiny on my wicketkeeping and I thought everyone was going to be picking the shit out of it.

Then, as I was getting ready to leave, I decided to change the way I was thinking. I just thought, 'Bugger it, I'll just go up there and make the most of this. I'll try my best but I'll have some fun because I didn't do that first time around.' Nobody was expecting much of me and how rare in life is it to get a second chance?

8

STEPPING UP

Seven long and occasionally dark years after making that fateful trip to Brisbane on the eve of the 2010–11 Ashes, I'm on the plane again with a second chance at a career in Test cricket that nobody, least of all me, saw coming.

The bloke who couldn't get a start in the Sheffield Shield. The bloke who is still not sure how to hold a bat. But I'm the still the bloke who backs his keeping ability against anyone, anywhere. And, this time, I have nothing to lose. They've locked in the team for the first two games, so even if I fail and get dropped I will have played in two Ashes Tests. I've gone from caring too much to almost care free.

There were plenty of well-wishers in Hobart as I boarded the plane with my baggy green – slightly musty from all those years in the cupboard. We made our way up the eastern seaboard, flying past Melbourne where I probably would have been starting work as a rep for Kookaburra but for a series of circumstances.

If I hadn't called Ricky . . .

If Cricket Tasmania hadn't replaced the CEO that month . . .

If Greg Chappell hadn't kept faith in me when even I had lost it . . .

This was bonus time and I was going to make the most of it, which is the attitude I brought to Brisbane this time. When I arrived we did a round of interviews and I remember Crash going hard at me. I defused the situation quickly by saying that I was as shocked as he was, but I was there now and I was going to do my best. I could see everyone in the media room sit back as if to say, 'Yeah, fair enough.' If I'd gotten my back up, it would have been different. But I was honest with them because what else could I say or do? I'd been on the record for some time saying that I was not batting well but I was still a good keeper. 'I've been picked for my keeping,' I said. 'I'm here to do a job.'

I was barely the new boy, I'd played with most of the Test team at some point somewhere over the years. Steve Smith and I debuted together. David Warner, Usman Khawaja,

Nathan Lyon, Shaun Marsh and I had played together and against each other for a decade or more. Jackson Bird was a Tasmanian so we spoke the same language. There may have been a lot of noise in the media about Matthew Wade or Peter Nevill missing out, but these blokes knew I could keep and most were as excited as I was.

For Smithy it was his first Ashes as captain and he is the sort of bloke who is happy to have experience around him. Darren Lehmann was an experienced coach and an easy bloke to get along with. Boof was laidback and just as he had a way of triggering stupid things in batsmen on the field when he was a player – I will never get over how he taunted me to try to hit that sweep shot years ago in the Shield – he could trigger self-belief in his players with similar economy.

I remember Boof saying to us that the next six to eight weeks would be the best time of our lives. The Ashes are a carnival and you have to just strap yourself in for the ride. In every town the public are on a cricket high, the media presence doubles or triples, the attention is relentless and you can either be intimidated by it or embrace it. This time, I was lapping it up.

Bonnie had flown up with Milla to join me and she was blown away by the atmosphere. Everywhere we went for dinner, coffee or a walk, people on the street around Southbank were stopping and talking to us. The English fans were there a week before, decked out in all their gear. She said to me, 'I finally get it.' She now understood why I was so freaked out when I got selected. Since we'd been together I'd pretty much been in the lost years of my career, so she'd only seen me play a few state games, and she didn't really get how big Test cricket or the Ashes was. Before she'd flown up she'd had to google how long a Test match lasted so she could work out what to pack for the trip.

At the first net session I did the warm-ups then engaged in my keeping drills and thought about having to go and bat. I had been fretting about having to face the quicks in the nets. Starc, Hazlewood and Cummins are no fun, then there was Bird and Lyon. I was going to spend as little time as I could in there and hopefully I'd at least be able to avoid the seamers. I still had this thing in my head where I was scared of getting hit on the hand by anything back of a length and I knew that if they pitched it up, one of three things would happen: I'd get hit on the pads, I'd nick it or I'd get bowled. But somehow, putting on the Australian tracksuit in the morning changed my mindset. I'm a tragic for a bit of kit. When I did my glove work I held on to some screamers and I could sense that the others were impressed. I think Davey, Smithy, Shaun Marsh and maybe Cam Bancroft were in the cordon and I could feel their approval.

When I got to the nets the seamers were pitching them up early and none of the three things I listed above happened. In fact, I hit the ball out of the middle from the start, I connected with almost everything. I went really well. I then went into the side nets for throwdowns with our batting coach Graeme Hick and Boof which also went well.

Walking back to the dressing rooms when the session was finished, Boof said, 'I can't understand how you haven't been scoring runs . . . I've watched you, you're an excellent batter, it has got me fucked.' I laughed nervously and said that I was just going to go out there and play some shots and see how it went. He said, 'Mate, just play the way you want to play, have fun – you could score ten Test hundreds.' I don't know that he believed it, but I reckon it was the best piece of coaching I have ever had because I walked into the rooms thinking, 'Darren Lehmann thinks I'm a good batter.' I didn't feel like a good batter but I was hoping he knew better than me.

Still, when that first day rocked around I was sick with anxiety. It was horrible, I felt terrible. The closer we got to the ground, the worse I felt. Everything seemed so big. The anthem. The crowds. The excitement. My nerves were out of control and I just couldn't enjoy any of it. Then it got worse once the match began.

Nathan was bowling and I dropped their No. 3 James Vince. The ball drifted and bounced and it wasn't the edge that got me, it was the bounce. I hadn't kept at the Gabba for ages and it hit me high on the palms. Vince was playing well, I saw he was going to nick it, but it just got a bit big on me and I dropped it. I'd been picked for my keeping and it was a shameful start.

I wanted to dig a hole and bury myself, I just wanted to go home, but when it was shown on the replay Smithy came over and gave me a pat on the shoulder like he understood what had happened and I felt a bit better. Normally when I drop a catch as a wicketkeeper I don't want the ball coming near me for the next ten minutes. I don't know why this was different, but I squatted down for the next delivery, thinking, 'Just give me the same catch.' My mindset had completely changed. I wanted another chance to show I could do it. I did end up catching out my opposite number Jonny Bairstow before England finished with 302 runs.

In our innings I was on 13 when James Anderson bowled a ripper to me and Jonny Bairstow returned the favour with a very good catch behind the stumps. Steve Smith top scored with an unbeaten 141 to get us to 328.

There wasn't much between the two sides after the first innings, but Josh Hazlewood and Nathan Lyon ripped through their top order in the second. Nathan got one to turn big on Moeen Ali and I had his bails off in an instant. The umpire sent it upstairs and it was as close as you get, but we had him by a millimetre. It was an important wicket and it ended his innings on 40 when he could have gone on with it and posted a big tally. It also sent a message to anyone who'd questioned why I was there.

We won the match without losing a wicket in the second innings and that was that. Smithy got Man of the Match for his 141 not out that set the game up. I'd played in my first Ashes Test, we'd got a victory and the beer tasted pretty good that night in the rooms. The song sounded even better. These days Nathan was singing it after Huss had handed the honour to him. We didn't get silly and I kept a lid on it because I wanted to enjoy every bit of this second chance at life.

While the chat with Boof had really boosted my confidence before the game, I'd also been talking a lot with Brad Haddin who was working as an assistant coach and he kept emphasising that it was my job to 'bat like a wicket-keeper', that if we were 5–300 I should play my shots and if we were 5–60 I should do the same. I was there to keep the game moving. I said, 'That's all very well in theory, Hadds, but a bit harder to actually put into action.' Still, he was right and it further emphasised the idea that nobody was expecting too much from me.

The second Test was in Adelaide – it is a Test everyone loves. There's no better cricket town. The team stays in a hotel close to the ground, in fact everything in Adelaide is close to the ground, so you can walk across the footbridge and past the gum trees to training. You can just feel the excitement. It's a place that loves its cricket and it's great to play in a ground that has a bit of history and atmosphere.

We batted first. When I joined Shaun Marsh at the wicket we were 5–209 and struggling a bit, but I found the middle early with a couple of fours off Jimmy Anderson and took the pressure off SOS and the next thing you know I had 50 from 91 balls. That felt great, but then Craig Overton bounced me with two fielders out. Every coach will tell you to duck under that one, but instinct took over and I took him on. I absolutely nailed the shot and it went straight at head height to Moeen Ali who was at deep square leg. I'd taken the bait and I was out for 59. I was fuming in the rooms because I knew we were on the verge of taking them down. SOS and I had put on 85 and got us almost to 300. I was batting beautifully up to that point and was ready to launch.

I had my head down in the dressing rooms but I saw a pair of shoes approaching and I knew they were Boof's. I thought, 'Here we go,' because any coach had the right to tear into a batsman for doing that and I'd experienced it plenty of times in Tasmania. Tim Coyle was not afraid of letting you know if you had screwed up. I looked up as Boof got close and said, 'Sorry mate.' But Boof hadn't come into the rooms to roast me, or even to talk to me, he was on his way to do something else. He just paused and said, 'Don't be sorry, next time put it 20 rows back,' and he kept walking.

In the second innings we were chasing runs for another declaration and I top-edged a hook which Craig Overton caught. It wasn't a good shot and again I was steaming afterwards, thinking I'd buggered that up. This time Boof walked by, patted me on the shoulder and congratulated me for my intent. He was impressed I hadn't batted for myself.

The coaching thing is funny, and some coaches just don't understand what a negative effect they can have. I remember in a game for Tasmania against Victoria where they were bouncing me and I was getting on top of the pull shot and running them down for singles. When I came off for a break, one coach told me to stop taking that risk, while another said, 'You've scored 15 runs from it, you're in control, keep going.' What's a bloke to do?

After the Test we were having a beer and Graeme Hick came up and said, 'We're going to Perth, you've just got out hooking and pulling, they'll target that.' He told me to make sure I had my plans in place if I was going to play it, because they'd have this field and that field waiting for me. I said, 'Fair enough, I have to watch that,' and then I started to get nervous, thinking, 'I hope I don't play one on instinct and get out again or people will be up me.' Later I mentioned to Boof that I was going to have to watch that shot in Perth because they'd be targeting me with the short ball. 'Bullshit,' he said, 'the WACA is the best place in the world to play the pull shot, get after them.'

That changed my thinking and I walked out to bat in the third Test hoping they would bowl short to me. That's what I love about Darren Lehmann, he made me believe in myself when I didn't. As I said, I don't know if he did believe in me, I've never asked him, but it worked. I felt safe to make a mistake.

When we had them eight down and were cruising towards victory, it was the first time since the series started that I allowed myself to really relax and enjoy it. I looked around at the team and the ground, the place was packed, and I just thought, 'I can't believe this, I'm having so much fun and we're about to go 2–0 up in the Ashes.' One month ago I was nowhere and now I was here.

We won the Test in Adelaide and the minimum guarantee I had of two Tests had stretched out a bit. Getting that 50 stopped people death-riding my batting and I'd done a good job behind the stumps.

There was to be a lot of criticism not too long after this series about the way Australia played its cricket, but as far as I know there were no incidents that needed the match referee to be involved. The Ashes are the most intense contest you can be involved in. Players on both sides go so hard, it means so much, there is nothing like it, the competitiveness is incredible. I remember the first half hour in Brisbane and it was just so full on. The tension was explosive, the focus of everybody on the ground was next level.

Davey Warner wouldn't let up on their batsmen, he needled them, poked them, he called them out for what they were. He was always in control, he wasn't abusive, but he was at them. He'd say, 'You're an average player, look at your numbers,' and he knew what he was talking about, there's no point saying that to a bloke averaging 60. He was always looking for a psychological edge and trying to unsettle the other side. He did his homework too. He would talk to Joe Root a lot about his conversion rate, Root couldn't escape it, Davey knew every stat, how many times he'd got out between 50 and 100, and he'd say to him, 'You've got to convert this time or the press will crucify you,' which was true. 'Flintoff will be over you in his column, Vaughny will criticise you on the television, they're just waiting for you to get another start and not convert.' These were the blokes who'd already had a go at Root.

Davey had stopped talking for a few years after being slammed by Cricket Australia chief executive James Sutherland, but there was a push for him to bring it back and get in people's faces so he obliged in this series. He's a team player and he's happy to do what is needed most of the time. He went at Jonny Bairstow after he heard that Jonny was on it in Perth and had greeted Cam Bancroft with a strange sort of head butt late at night in a nightclub.

It wasn't a big incident, Bangers thought nothing of it at the time, but Davey played it up, saying, 'We know what you did,' and Jonny got really defensive and started to worry about it. At one point he ran down to the boundary to chat to management, so he was clearly distracted. England's management took that incident so seriously they imposed a curfew on the team which must have upset the players because it was stupid.

As far as we were concerned, the aim was to upset the batter. With Moeen Ali we knew he was hopeless against Nathan Lyon so whenever he walked out, the cry would go up: 'Get Nathan on.' We'd pretend we didn't know Dawid Malan's name, I'd call him Dale and someone would correct me. It was schoolboy stuff, but I don't think we went over the top, I don't think we were abusive or disrespectful to the game, or personal. It was just constant niggling, we talked about them a lot rather than to them. There weren't too many balls being bowled without something being said, but other teams are just as bad when they get the chance.

Our bowlers were ruthless at their tail with the short stuff, that was at a time when all three were properly fast. Some people questioned that, but we were just focused on doing what we had to do to win and part of that was bowling short to the tail. It had worked for Mitch Johnson in the previous home series. It made them really uncomfortable. It zapped their confidence, you almost felt like it fed into their bowling. Some of those bowlers came over with nightmares of Johnno and while this attack wasn't as quick, there were three of them – Mitchell Starc, Pat Cummins and Josh Hazlewood – and they were all fast and never let up. Boof was very keen on maintaining the bouncer barrage at the tail and it proved very effective. One way you know you are getting an edge in the series is when bowlers start getting annoyed at their top order for letting them down, they want to have a decent break between innings and they don't want to have to do any serious work with the bat. We made sure it was serious every time they had to bat and that just kept them on edge.

In Perth we played at the WACA which was a ground on its last legs, but one that held so many memories for those of us who love Test cricket. It was the home of Rod Marsh and Dennis Lillee. There was the stand Mark Waugh hit that incredible six on to. The little patch near the light towers where Adam Gilchrist hit those sixes against Monty Panesar in 2006–07 on the way to that incredible hundred. I'd played there in plenty of state games but to be part of an Ashes Test at the WACA was to be part of history.

They got off to a decent start. Dawid Malan scored 140 and made sure I remembered his name, Jonny Bairstow shrugged off the controversy early in the tour and scored 119 and they reached 403. It seemed like a lot, but

Steve Smith was at the height of his powers and peeled off 239 then Mitch Marsh, who'd come in for Pete Handscomb, hit 181. I was 49 not out when Smithy declared with us on 9–662. We'd pushed on a little after lunch on the fourth day, but it was time to get them in and when Nathan holed out Smithy called it. I'd have liked another half-century, but I was happy to settle for the chance at another Test win.

We had them and we knew it. We were playing well, our bowlers were all over them, there was a great feel in the team. A number of guys were on top of their game: Smithy was batting on another level, Davey was flying, Shaun was scoring centuries, Mitch Marsh had gone big, Starc was bowling fast, Cummins too and Josh was relentless.

The next day, the Monday, we had them nine down and were on the verge of securing the Ashes when I had to take a little break. I had tears in my eyes, I had to take my sunnies off to wipe them so I could see. Cummins was steaming in, we were flying. That iconic ground. David Warner over there. Steve Smith standing next to me. I was thinking, 'This is living.' I have goosebumps even now thinking about it.

I flew back home to join Bonnie and Milla after that and things were put back into context. Bonnie's dad, Thomas Maggs, had invited us for dinner at his place and she left before me while I sorted myself out, but soon after she rang and sounded really upset. He'd had a stroke, called for an ambulance and then called her and was on his way to hospital. It didn't sound too serious. I said I'd meet Bonnie there. Tom was awake when I got there, but they took him away to do some tests. Soon after the doctor came in and said he's had a catastrophic bleed and he's not going to make it. We slept on the floor and a fold-out bed in the hospital for a few nights. Bonnie wouldn't leave, she was really close to her father. I'd go home sometimes and pick up Milla from Mum who was minding her for us.

Tom was a legend in the Antarctic community. He'd been a radio operator at Mawson back in the 1970s and an officer in charge at Casey as well as leading a few voyages. He knew people all over the world and had lived life to the fullest. He died on Christmas Eve with Bonnie and her sister Georgie holding his hand. They were playing his favourite band, Pink Floyd, for him when he stopped breathing.

Bonnie rang me and she was so upset. It was awful because this was another of those times when I wasn't there for her. I'd left that morning to join the team in Melbourne.

After the call I didn't feel like going to the traditional team Christmas lunch with the others so I went out with Nathan Lyon and his mum and dad.

I remember feeling really sad when they played the anthems before the match at the MCG the next day.

That place is amazing with the stands packed on the first morning of a Boxing Day Test — it's an incredible occasion — but my thoughts were elsewhere. We won the toss and batted so I had time to regroup a bit.

Mum, Dad, my younger sister, my nan and some of Uncle Rob's family were at the ground. She's a marvel, Nan, she's over 90 now but she still loves her cricket. I walked all the way around the back of the stands to a box someone had given them and I'll never forget the hug she gave me when she saw me. She was delighted to be there and I was delighted that the lady who'd been at so many of my games, and fed me countless sandwiches in the front seat of her car at grounds in Hobart, was there to watch me on the big stage. This was a bit of payback to my family.

We did okay in the first innings, Davey batted his pants off for another hundred in no time at all, but we were bowled out for 327 and probably should have got a lot more. The wicket was stone cold dead. Alastair Cook came out to bat and stayed there for the next ten hours. I spent more than 600 minutes staring at his arse and I can tell you he batted unbelievably. The wicket was flat, but it was hard to score on and he just buckled down. He batted the same way for the entire time, he had his plans and he stuck to them, and he ended up with a record

244 not out. I can't remember him ever going the slog or drifting away from his plans. That was some feat of concentration. Jackson Bird picked a bad match to come into the side and ended up with 0–108 from 30 overs. Nathan bowled 42 overs but at least he picked up three wickets for his efforts.

Smithy made a hundred in the second innings. It was his third of the series and he was batting unbelievably. He was standing there almost French-cricket style so he could steer the ball where he wanted. I was so emotionally drained during the game that at one point I went downstairs to one of the rooms and fell asleep watching the game on television.

The Test ended in a draw. The ICC gave the pitch a poor rating and so they should have. Wickets have to be competitive for batters and bowlers. The wicket was so poor I kept up to the stumps when Mitch Marsh was bowling in an attempt to force a mistake.

In Sydney, we beat them by an innings and 123 runs. The wheels had fallen off for them, Joe Root got sick, but he's a tough competitor and he pushed on scoring two half-centuries despite spending one night in hospital with dehydration. It was stinking hot and must have been awful for him. The temperature in the middle on at least one day was over 50°C. It was inhumane but you don't feel it so much when you are winning. You suffer when you are on the losing side. Usman and both Marsh brothers got centuries when we batted while I boosted the average with a nice little 38 not out, but by then we were 7–649 and there was no point going on.

The heat never let up during the match and the last wicket was a relief more than anything – I took the catch off Anderson, he missed it, it came off his shoulder, but nobody had the energy to argue.

It was a great party later. We drank with the English for a while which is one of the things I really enjoy, I love talking to other cricketers and when you've played five Tests against them there's a lot to catch up on. They went back to the hotel and we stayed there very late before someone called us onto the ground in front of the SCG members' stand.

We went out there in pitch dark not knowing what was going on, then somebody fired up the big screen and played a long highlight reel of the Ashes with the sound pumped through the speakers.

It was an extraordinary feeling, watching it in the dark, all the highs and lows. When it was finished Nathan led us in the team song.

I went home to Hobart the next day and slept on the couch for four days. I'd get up to eat and then just lie down again. If you are mentally or physically tired, you can get through, but I was both and I needed to sleep. You don't sleep well during Test matches anyway, or I don't. I remember when we finished the series, I thought,

'That's it, I've played an Ashes I can die happy,' but there was more in store for me.

When I first got into the team all I wanted to do was play well enough in the first two Tests to get to the WACA for a Test. Then, when we got there, I thought, 'If I go alright now I could go to South Africa,' and that would be brilliant because they were flying and it would be a red hot series.

Now I was the Australian Test wicketkeeper with an Ashes series win to his name.

9

SANDPAPERGATE

Where do I start with all of this?
What did we know?
Could we have stopped it?
How did things get to such a place?
Was David Warner a scapegoat? Was Cameron Bancroft
the innocent party?

I remember the excitement ahead of the South African
tour. Life was going along beautifully. I've just played five
Ashes Tests I never expected to play and now they want
me to do my bit for three Test matches in South Africa.
We were up and about, we had taken the best of what
England could muster and won the Ashes 4–0 and now it
was time to take on the Proteas.

The circus rolls on. The fun continues.

It's fair to say these series had developed a heat of their own. The cricket was always good, but on and off the field things often got strained. Australia had won the last series in South Africa and there'd been a bit of carry on. Then they came over here in 2016–17, beat us in our own backyard and that had cost a few blokes their places in the team. In that series Faf du Plessis got charged with ball-tampering for using a peppermint and they had a real tantrum over the penalty. They were roughing up journos in the airport and outside their team hotel. They flew in their chief executive Haroon Lorgat who took on the ICC's chief executive Dave Richardson over the issue and went as far as to indicate that Richardson was part of a 'ball shining brigade' when he played for South Africa – a charge he has strongly refuted, but an indication of how low Cricket South Africa were willing to go.

Faf was one of those South African players who could rile people up. In 2014 he accused Australians of carrying on like wild dogs during a previous series so some of our boys howled like wild dogs when he got out in the next innings. In 2016–17, Faf rolled through an airport with a peppermint on his tongue which he poked out for the cameras to see – he was making a mockery of the charges.

To be fair to him, everybody used mints, but when others got caught they accepted the penalty. The South Africans seemed to think they didn't have to and would behave the same way when Kagiso Rabada got suspended in 2018 (more of that soon).

Things often boiled over against the Proteas. I remember the clash between Dale Steyn and Michael Clarke in 2014. Pup lost it at the time and called him a cheat but was man enough to realise that and apologise publicly later, but it just showed you how heated things got between the two teams. Clarke was not the sort of player to say things like that. Steyn declared on the next tour that he wouldn't forgive him for what was said until he got a personal apology.

Australian teams were always up for the fight, maybe even started their fair share, but if you listen to the South Africans they're always the innocent victims and that's never, ever been the case.

Still, we lost sight of how our behaviour looked and that was all we could control.

They were waiting for us with baseball bats in 2018. It felt like we were under siege from the start of the series, but if you put that aside the first couple of Tests were fantastic, intensive, competitive cricket.

Some of us went over early and played a four-day game and got in 20 days on the ground before the series started, but Dave Warner and a few of the others headed to New Zealand for a T20 series. Davey captained and they held their nerve in some tight chases for an impressive win. He enjoyed that, he is a good captain with lots of ideas and a good approach when he is put in charge. One of the dumbest things to come out of the controversy that followed was a Cricket Australia lifetime leadership ban on him. It is unfair and unwise. Now he captains in the IPL or wherever and Australia misses out on his astute leadership. Hopefully that will change and they'll revoke the ban, I know there's been talk of it.

Thankfully, as I learned when I was captain, he has remained a great contributor and support to subsequent skippers. David is a team man first, some people underestimate him, but anyone who has played with him knows it.

There was always talk of a rivalry between him and Steve Smith but I never saw or heard anything that made me think that. He's competitive, but we all are.

We started with a hit-out in Benoni and then moved to the seaside town of Durban for the first Test. South Africa has great beaches and from the early days we had a bit of a coffee and beach club in the mornings. Mitch Marsh came up with the slogan that 'Every day starts better on the beach' so I joined him down there for the sunrise over the Indian Ocean and soon there were a few others including Davey and Cam Bancroft. Frank Dimasi, our security guy, a hardened old Melbourne homicide copper who barracks for Collingwood and is everyone's mate, used to come down too.

Marshy was right, it was a good way to start the day. Durban is a hectic place and Test cricket is a hectic occupation but the beach was empty in the morning and it cleared your head.

Then there were the games. We batted first in Durban and a lot of people contributed. Mitch was knocked over by Vernon Philander on 96, but he had continued the great form he'd shown when given a chance in the Ashes. Dave and Steve both got half-centuries. When it came to the Proteas' turn, Mitch Starc got the ball reversing beautifully. He tore through them, taking 5–34, and we took a big lead. We didn't go as well in our second innings, but Cam got a half-century and we had a lead of over 400 which was too much for them. We went one–nil up and were feeling good about ourselves.

It was willing on the field from the start. Davey was being similar to how he was against England, he was heckling relentlessly, he would never stop. He wasn't yelling abuse, he was just baiting them constantly from backward point or second slip. They were the same, they had a lot of players in their side who liked to mouth off.

In their second innings Aiden Markram had hesitated on a quick single and sent AB de Villiers back, Davey swooped on it, threw to AB's end and Nathan completed the run-out as AB dived for his ground. He then dropped the ball at the crease. Davey was celebrating like a demon, yelling out to nobody in particular that it was a terrible mistake running out AB de Villiers. It was aimed at Markram but I'm not even sure he was looking at him, he was just letting it be known.

It didn't go down well. The pics of Davey yelling made him look angry and vicious when he was exuberant, elated.

Meanwhile, Nathan looked like he'd dropped the ball onto AB while he was on the ground and the camera angle made it appear a lot worse than it was. Anyone who knows Nathan Lyon knows he is not like that, he wouldn't disrespect an opponent by dropping the ball on him, that sort of behaviour is not in his wheelhouse. Nathan rang AB to clear things up after the game and that kind of shows you what sort of man he is. We love Gaz, he doesn't have a lot to say, but when he does it's often very funny. He's a deep thinker about the game and definitely the greatest off spinner we've had. He's stuck at a very difficult craft in the face of criticism and indifferent selection panels over the years. He just kept turning up and now at the time of writing this he has 400 wickets and I won't be surprised if he reaches 500 or more. There's no reason he shouldn't keep going until he is 40 or older.

I mentioned that Davey was chirpy and he was particularly keen to talk to Quinton de Kock when he was batting. He was into him every ball about being overweight, unprofessional, having a big off-season on the food, playing a shit shot, then he was at him about lunch, what he would eat, suggesting he probably couldn't wait to get to the buffet . . . It was essentially harmless but he was relentless.

Davey was at him on the way off for lunch on day four. I was nearby and heard the whole conversation. David was upset because he thought he'd heard de Kock make comments about his wife, Candice, but then the South African team came up with a story that David had started it by making a comment about de Kock's sister. I was there, I was the one holding them apart and I know how it unfolded. In my view, David had every right to be upset.

Naturally the footage got leaked to their media and we looked like the bad guys again. Both players got fined but we felt we were stitched up on that one.

They bowled better than us and squared the series in Port Elizabeth, which is now known as Gqeberha, but again there was trouble. Kagiso Rabada had the ball reversing early and took 11 wickets for the match, but he fell into old bad habits.

Rabada is a brilliant bowler when things go his way but he gets carried away with the aggression after taking wickets. Just over a year before, he'd been sanctioned by the ICC for running into Niroshan Dickwella and then he'd copped a suspension for abusing Ben Stokes. In February he'd been in trouble again for the same thing with Shikhar Dhawan. He just didn't want to learn.

In Port Elizabeth he ran into Steve Smith after dismissing him and then backed it up by getting in Dave Warner's face and giving him a spray after he got him out. It is one thing to give a player a spray, it's quite another to intrude into their personal space or make contact. It's something you should never see in cricket. You don't have to be Einstein to work out what's going to happen one day if bowlers are allowed to make contact with dismissed batsmen or even to get into their face.

These incidents happened despite the match referees meeting with both captains and coaches before the Test and asking everyone to cool it a bit. Everyone needed to take a deep breath, but it was hard not to get caught up in it all which was our mistake.

Rabada was suspended for the rest of the series which was appropriate, but again Cricket South Africa weren't willing to take their punishment and they hired some big deal lawyer to run an appeal after we landed in Cape Town for the third Test. It was all a big legal show and the hearing went on for a day.

Somehow he got off. It was galling for us and particularly for Steve who'd put up with the bloke running into him. I think Steve let it get to him and, in a way, we all did.

Some of what was going on around the ground was disgraceful. Two Cricket South Africa executives had photos of themselves taken with a group of fans wearing Sonny Bill Williams masks, which was a reference to a thing between the footballer and Candice Warner before she was married to David. After he got fined for the altercation with de Kock, Davey put out a statement saying he was ashamed of his behaviour but that he'd been putting up with abuse about his wife and Sonny Bill from the crowd without reacting. He had only lost it when he thought he heard a South African player say it to his face. I think most people would understand that.

Rather than stamping out the behaviour, Cricket South Africa officials decided to join the circus and pose for that photo.

It felt like we were being provoked, but it was hard to put your finger on. Stump mikes were turned right up when we were in the field but not when they were fielding, the camera was following us but not them, their team manager was stirring shit up, they leaked that security video from the first Test to try and make Davey look bad, they rorted the system to get Rabada off . . .

In Cape Town I think a dozen people from the crowd were ejected for vile comments about our families. One grub followed Dave up the race, yelling from a metre or two away after he'd just got out. I don't know how Bull kept his cool in those situations and on reflection I feel the team let him down by not offering him more support. He was turning up every day as if nothing was bothering him, but that's Dave. I can see now he was masking a lot of pain and we should have known it. I can only imagine what it was like to be going through that with your wife and three little girls.

We had a long break before the Cape Town Test started on 22 March and there is no better place in the world to be when you don't have too much to do. Table Mountain seems to sit in the middle of the town, the oceans (two of them meet nearby) are broad, the wineries just outside of town are a great way to spend a day and the place just has that holiday feel. Good bars, cafes, restaurants. Fresh air. Time to kill. We all enjoyed the break even if it was in that period that we heard Rabada had somehow got off the charge and would play.

South Africa made 311 batting first which was mostly down to an undefeated 141 from opener Dean Elgar and 64 from AB de Villiers. Unfortunately we got bundled out for 255 and only got there thanks to 77 from Cam Bancroft at the top of the order and a freewheeling 47 from Nathan Lyon. I was 34 not out when the innings ended early on day three which was a Saturday.

They started to pull away as the day progressed and by tea they were 3–151. The ball wasn't reversing for us and batting was easy.

What happened next will be the subject of speculation for the rest of time. There are so many people with so many theories, so much whispering and speculating.

I suspect nobody will ever be satisfied they know the full story of how we got to this place. I'm not sure I even understand myself.

A lot of commentators have said since that everybody has to know what's going on in a dressing room, but that's rubbish. Cricketers keep a lot to themselves, even in the happiest teams. Coaches and support staff do the same. There's coaches and players, batters and bowlers, cliques and mates. Coffee clubs, bowling cartels, walking groups, bonds formed in junior or state cricket, bonds formed on the road with the national team. Conversations in corners, thoughts kept private, things shared and things not shared.

The other thing that people should know is that the Cape Town change room is divided by the shower and toilet block and players have to split up either side for the duration of the Test. The coaches are in another room. In Cape Town you are literally a team divided. Something can happen in one room and the people in the other two would have no idea.

Everyone out there was shocked when they looked up on the big screen and saw Cameron Bancroft with a piece of sandpaper in his hand. I was stunned. We all were. I can let you in on the fact that over my years in the game I'd heard talk about guys taping small pieces of sandpaper onto their fingers, but this was next level. It was a Test match and it was on the big screen and it looked terrible.

My heart sank, I was thinking, 'What the fuck?' A sense of dread came over us all. They kept showing images on the screen and the umpires called Bancroft over.

You've all seen the footage.

Smithy ran over to the umpires and then came back to the slips. He was clearly very agitated and distracted. I can remember him saying at some point that as captain he was going to be in trouble, he was pretty dejected about it. The crowd by this stage had worked themselves into a frenzy and the atmosphere was unsettling to say the least. I think at one point Steve ran off the field. I don't know if he was feeling unwell or wanted to talk to Darren Lehmann, but I think he was unwell.

Cam mustn't have done a very good job with the sand-paper because when the umpires examined the ball they didn't even change it. Still, it's an offence and one that could see him banned for two matches. Unfortunately, he made it worse for himself by misleading the umpires about what was in his pockets (by now I think he'd stuffed the sandpaper down his pants). Of his own volition he went and apologised to the umpires that night for being dishonest with them on the field.

As I said, ball tampering might be a huge crime in some people's eyes but as far as the ICC was concerned it was only a two-match penalty at most.

Steve and Cameron were charged by the ICC, but Cameron was not suspended. He actually hadn't done anything to the ball. Smithy got a one match suspension. Dave Richardson, the CEO of the ICC, put out a statement when the sanctions were revealed. It spoke more about the ugly nature of the series than sandpaper:

The decision made by the leadership group of the Australian team to act in this way is clearly contrary to the spirit of the game, risks causing significant damage to the integrity of the match, the players and the sport itself and is therefore 'serious' in nature. As captain, Steve Smith must take full responsibility for the actions of his players and it is appropriate that he be suspended.

The game needs to have a hard look at itself. In recent weeks we have seen incidents of ugly sledging, send-offs, dissent against umpires' decisions, a walk-off, ball tampering and some ordinary off-field behaviour.

The ICC needs to do more to prevent poor behavior and better police the spirit of the game, defining more clearly what is expected of players and enforcing the regulations in a consistent fashion. In addition and most importantly Member countries need to show more accountability for their teams' conduct. Winning is important but not at the expense of the spirit of the game which is intrinsic and precious to the sport of cricket. We have to raise the bar across all areas.

Of course it didn't end there. The media were treating this as the biggest story in the world. The top brass of Australian cricket had all jumped on planes and headed to the Cullinan Hotel where we were staying. This was not going to go away with a one match ban.

This situation felt different, but the game had always treated ball tampering as a misdemeanour. Officials tended to turn a blind eye or issue a slap on the wrist. But the reaction from the Australian public was extraordinary. On reflection it sent a broader message about their expectations of us as players, and the disconnect that had developed between us and those expectations. We'd got caught up in our own world and lost focus.

Every team tampers with the ball to some degree, especially when they're looking for reverse swing. It's no secret. It's well known at every level of the game.

They throw it into the square, they 'manage' it like scientists in a lab, nobody with sweaty hands can touch it, only certain fielders apply the saliva, some spinners aren't allowed near it because they have clammy hands. Fielders have to return the ball a certain way. If it bounces on the wrong side, heaven help them. When I'm keeper I have to know if we are looking for reverse or conventional swing. If it's reverse, the team knows to throw it in on the bounce, ideally into the bowlers' footmarks. If you get that right, you can get it going reverse quite often, but once it's going I have to make sure it doesn't bounce again because a mark on the shiny side will end that party in a minute. If we are looking for conventional swing we are more protective of the ball.

Throwing it into the rough is against the rules and if you are too obvious the umpires will have a go at you, but it's hard to police and in most people's minds it's not a big deal. Umpires never seem too keen on stamping it out, in fact they rarely want to make a big deal of any of this stuff. In state and international cricket a lot of things go down that the officials turn a blind eye to. A lot of the umpires have played cricket at a senior level and know it is an unspoken part of it. Match referees sometimes tell teams to give it a rest but it rarely gets more serious than a verbal warning.

So much of it goes on and nobody admits to it. People do what they can and everybody moans about the other side doing it, but there are no cleanskins in cricket and there weren't in that game.

Three years before the incident with the mints in Australia, Faf du Plessis had been caught using the zip on his trousers and got fined for that. A year later Vernon Philander got caught doing the same thing. So South Africa had been caught at it three times in five years.

On another tour there were allegations about a wicket-keeper gluing something abrasive to his gloves so he could scratch the ball at will.

Former England captain Michael Atherton was accused of using dirt he kept in his pocket, though he denied tampering. Mick Lewis infamously kicked the ball into the gutter and scraped it on the concrete when he was bowling coach of the Victorians. A year earlier the Redbacks skipper and former South African player, Johan Botha, got done during a match. Sachin Tendulkar was suspended once but eventually cleared on appeal.

Don't even start me on players using their thumbnail. I saw it happen in the fourth Test of that series. Think about that. After everything that had happened in Cape Town, after all the headlines and bans and carry on. I was standing at the bowlers' end in the next Test when a shot came up on the screen of a South African player at mid off having a huge crack at the ball. The television director, who had played an active role in catching out Cam, immediately pulled the shot off the screen. We went to the umpires about it, which might seem a bit poor, but we'd been slaughtered and were convinced they'd been up to it since the first Test. But the footage got lost. As it would.

I had to laugh the other day, I was watching a Test when one of the hosts asked an old quick from another country how they used to get it to reverse so much and it was a really awkward moment. The bowler answered that you held your wrist here and dried this side of the ball, but the real answer was that 99 times out of 100 someone had scratched the shit out of the ball. There's always someone who has a thumbnail as hard as a cat's head.

Can you imagine what they were taking onto the field in the days before there were so many cameras? There was no need to hide it then. That's why you don't see the ball reverse now like it did in that era. They could have been using anything and from what I've heard they were.

In county cricket everyone knew about the Murray Mints. In his book Monty Panesar admitted that it was his role to look after the ball and admitted to using sunscreen, mints and even the zipper on his trousers. Marcus Trescothick wrote in his book about how it was his job to do that work on the ball in Ashes Tests for Simon Jones and Andrew Flintoff.

Everyone has done it over the years and at all levels, whether it's sunscreen, mints, bottle tops, thumbnails, sandpaper. Because players meet each other in county cricket, the Indian and Caribbean premier leagues, Big Bash or even at club level, these practices get handed around and are commonplace.

There's talk the New South Wales side got schooled in the craft by a visiting international bowler in the seventies.

Nobody, however, would admit it if asked. It is cricket's dirty secret. I think that is part of why the issue became so big. Everyone did it and everyone denied it.

Other cricket players were stunned by the way our three were treated by Cricket Australia. I think some of them were happy to see them get caught, because you like it when someone else gets caught, but they were horrified by the lengths of the bans. I'll say it again, the penalty for that offence under the code of conduct is two games maximum.

There were bad choices made that day and it is an event which has tarnished all our reputations, but there certainly wasn't any team meeting, saying, 'This is what we're going to do.' The team just knew that if we were going to get it to reverse we had to be on our toes about throwing it in on the bounce and stopping that once it started to go.

Every team had a ball manager because somebody had to identify a side from early in the game to shine for conventional swing and then work on it through the game for when it went the other way. Nobody else was allowed to do any work on it for fear of undoing what had been achieved. Davey was our ball manager and he'd often say, 'Don't worry boys, I'll get it going,' and he would and everybody was rapt when he got the ball to reverse.

It was his job.

Reverse swing is a huge thing in cricket at this time and every team goes out of their way to try and achieve it, and always have. The South Africans were very, very good at getting it going and they'd had it reversing ridiculously early in some innings. If the opposition didn't do the same they were at a clear disadvantage.

I know teams will sometimes lift the quarter seam.

Someone with a well-manicured thumbnail can cut the seam and flick up that little bit of the leather which makes it swerve out of the bowler's hand. You can see when a team does that, suddenly the ball starts deviating in the air, leaving a batsman playing at something that isn't there.

The South Africans were on to Davey moaning about the bandages on his hands from the start of the series but his hands were in a bad way, they were full of hot spots from slips catching, so he had padding everywhere and anyway you can't do anything to a ball using bandages. The broadcasters and the home team were so obsessed about his bandages that the cameras were on them from very early in the series. I remember he wrote Candice and his girls' names on the taping just to wind everyone up. Plenty of the players have their hands wrapped up like that. A lot of the guys wear training gloves to protect their hands because the ball does a lot of damage when you are trying to catch it or stop it when it's travelling at high speed.

None of this excuses what happened – it was shameful – but goes some way to explaining the confusion most players felt at this point.

Ball-tampering was not a big deal for cricketers, but this incident took on a life of its own.

★

I think we all knew that when we saw the shots of Bangers on the big screen, even if we didn't want to admit it, that it was going to be huge. The ground was giving way under our feet and for some time it felt like we'd never hit the bottom.

Dressing rooms can be pretty intense places, they can be full of joy or despair, but I have never been in one that felt the way those rooms felt in Cape Town after that day. It was quiet, people were coming and going in and out of huddles in side rooms. There was a sense that this was bigger than we knew. Our minds were racing. *It's not a big deal, is it? She'll be right, mate.* Most of us predicted a small penalty at best, but it felt like our world had been knocked a little off its axis and this could go anywhere.

Our team manager Gavin Dovey, Darren Lehmann and a few others were with Smithy and Cam trying to figure out what to do next. The rest of us were trying unsuccessfully to carry on as if nothing had happened.

Journalists were waiting on the other side of the ground for someone to show up at the media conference and answer questions about what was going on. Like everybody else they were in the dark about what exactly had taken place on the field. People saw what they saw but nobody really knew. Eventually Smithy resolved that he was going to meet it head on. It was a good instinct and one born of the right intentions. He wanted to accept responsibility and stand by Cam at the presser, but they didn't tell the whole truth, they claimed it wasn't sandpaper and came up with some story about it being tape and grit. It was madness, who cared what it was? I can't help but think that if we'd told the truth the fall-out might not have been so bad afterwards.

I know that there were people in the camp saying they shouldn't have done the media conference, they could have waited until the match referee made their report and handled it then, but they decided to get ahead of the curve.

I watched the media conference from the change rooms and it was horrible. Smithy said he wasn't proud of what he'd done, that he was embarrassed. We all were. He said, 'My integrity, the team's integrity, the leadership group's integrity, has come into question and rightfully so.'

Towards the end, a journo asked Smithy if he could continue as captain – for me, at that point, it seemed ridiculous. It was a two-match ban at most. Since then I've wondered about Mike Atherton and what happened with him. He was captain, he got caught using sand or dirt on the ball and was done for it, but he has continued on to be one of the most respected people in the game. I think he is a fantastic commentator and he was gutsy batsman in his time. Steve is an all-time great and he deserves the same respect. Everybody makes mistakes.

Atherton wrote about it in his book, *Opening Up*, and there were a few parallels, starting with the fact the umpire didn't bother changing the ball – the same thing that happened in our game. He was caught by the cameras and wasn't honest when called in by the match referee, which was a bit like us. He was hounded by the media but nothing like what Dave, Steve and Cam would get – he got off with just a fine.

It was a gloomy trip back to Cape Town and our hotel that night.

I didn't sleep and I reckon there wasn't an Australian in that Cape Town hotel that wasn't lying awake, wondering what the hell had just happened and how it would be received. I felt anxious and sick in the stomach, but I never looked at my phone. Maybe I didn't want to know about the reaction, maybe I just wanted to give it a bit of space. When morning finally came, I rolled over and looked at my phone and felt the blood drain from my face. I reckon the screen was generating heat.

It was worse than I could have imagined.

Words like 'shame' and 'cheat' were being bandied about. Printed in capitals. Everywhere you looked was the word 'cheat'. It's such an ugly term.

The reaction was so intense. It was headline news everywhere. It was as if everything else in life had stopped to focus on what had happened over here. Everybody was laying in their boots. Ex-players, current players, politicians and the PM, commentators, radio jocks, mums and dads, it was the biggest pile-on ever. It felt like all of Australia was against us.

THE PRICE PAID

It would stay like that for weeks. It was clear to all of us that this had not gone down well at home. I can't imagine how the outrage could have been greater and I have to be honest that it was confusing for us at first, but maybe that's because we knew that ball-tampering was part of the game and the public didn't. Or didn't want it to be. Maybe it was our fault for making it cricket's dark secret for all those years.

It became apparent that this wasn't just about using sandpaper on the ball, it was about the way we played cricket, the way the public perceived us. It wasn't so much a wake-up call as being woken with a bucket of cold water and being dragged onto the street by an angry mob.

It took me a while to see the big picture, there was so much noise, so many thoughts, but I eventually got it.

Frankly, there was no way of getting away from it.

And things were moving so fast.

The next morning we sat shellshocked over breakfast. Almost numb. I went to the ground early to have a hit because I would have to bat that day. The nets are a long way from the change rooms and when the team arrived they called on the radio for me to finish up and come back because there was a meeting.

When we got together, Steve said he was standing down as captain then Dave got up and said he'd be standing down from his role as vice-captain. They looked shattered. We all felt much the same. That's when Trevor Hohns got up and said I'd be captain for the rest of the game. That was the first I'd heard of it.

The boys weren't in a great place. Everybody was emotional, but Trevor said we had to do the best to pick ourselves up and play out the rest of the game.

So, there I was, just eight Tests into my return and 12 into my career and I was interim captain with the job of leading the Australian Test team onto the field.

As we ran out we were abused by the crowd who were calling us 'fucking cheats' and worse. Nobody's heart or head was in it that day, we had a crack, but as I said it was like the earth had been kicked out from under our feet. Poor old Nathan Lyon took his 300th wicket (Rabada stumped by me) but there wasn't a lot of celebration.

I had to do the media conference at the end of the game because I was the acting Test captain.

You can't imagine worse circumstances to do a presser. The reaction had multiplied during the day and Prime Minister Malcolm Turnbull had even come out and had a go at us. The PM said it was a 'disgrace'. He used the 'cheating' word and called it a 'shocking affront to Australia'. The chief executive of Cricket Australia, James Sutherland, called it a 'sad day for Australian cricket' and said they would be taking it further.

News had come through during the day that Smithy had copped a one-match ban and lost his match fee, while Cam got three demerit points which meant that technically he could play the next Test. That was the ICC's response to the incident.

So there was a bit to deal with in the media conference and I was not looking forward to it at all. You need a clear head to handle these situations and that was the last thing any of us had.

Recently I looked up what I said to see how I went.

They asked me how I felt to be made acting captain and I said it was 'not the circumstances that anyone would like to be sitting here' and that it had been a 'really bizarre, strange, horrible 24 hours'. I focused on the cricket a bit, saying there was no excuse for how bad we'd been in the last hour of the game and that it had rubbed salt in the wounds. Then they asked me about Steve and Cameron.

'They're not great . . . they're struggling, but probably the reality and the enormity of what's happened is starting to sink in,' I said. 'I don't think we all would have expected this to be as big as it has been and particularly the fall-out that we have seen from back home, I think the reality and enormity of it has sunk in.'

I said I couldn't comment on what the prime minister had to say about us. The last thing we needed at that point of proceedings was for me to get caught up in a slanging match with him. Somebody asked me if tonight was the lowest I'd ever felt on a cricket field, but I told them it wasn't, that had been 24 hours earlier when we walked off the field after Cameron had been caught.

After that we slunk back to the hotel and hung around another day because the Test had finished early, but nobody was in the mood to enjoy the sights of Cape Town. Pat Howard and head of integrity, Iain Roy, arrived that day and I reckon James Sutherland came the next day. There was a lot of stuff going on and none of it was good. We were a long way from those carefree mornings on the beach in Durban all of three weeks before.

We flew to Johannesburg in a storm of emotions. We were shocked. Browbeaten. In our minds we weren't cheats, we weren't what these people were saying we were. We thought everyone else had lost perspective, but maybe it was us who'd lost perspective. We'd certainly lost respect and we were being beaten up by everyone who had a grudge against us. It was hard not to be defensive and it was hard not to feel sorry for our three teammates at the centre of the storm, they were shattered.

There was no leaving this one behind.

We were staying in Sandton as usual, an upmarket shopping district in Jo'burg where the hotels are connected to the shopping malls and shops by a series of tunnels above the streets and below them. You never have to walk outside. You can dine in restaurants around an open square named after Nelson Mandela, but it's the only time you ever need to leave the hotel. It sounds a little over the top but Jo'burg is like that, the locals don't walk around the streets and they have security like you wouldn't believe. There's a lot of serious crime about.

We weren't going anywhere even if we wanted to. A media pack set itself up on the street outside the hotel. American cable networks sent people to cover the story. The English lapped it up, their media loves it when Australia is in trouble. It was big news everywhere. The *New York Times* ran a story in their news pages about it and you can imagine how many of their readers know or care about cricket.

Cricket Australia did its best to add to our sense of being under siege. Some of us were called into a room and interrogated.

Bonnie and Milla and my mum had come over for the Cape Town part of the trip as had most of the players' partners. It was good to have some distraction, but it wasn't exactly fun for anyone.

Davey had his family there the whole time, but Steve and Cam were alone. Things were tense and horrible. I think Davey felt abandoned and that nobody was looking out for him. He'd copped so much heat for his behaviour on the field and then there was what he was going through with the crowd. For a while there he cut himself off from all of us and removed himself from the team WhatsApp group and I can understand that. The personal abuse was taking its toll before this, but things had gone from bad to worse.

On reflection all three of them should have had more support. Maybe we could have done more as a group or organisation, not enough people put themselves in their shoes.

It was a really weird time. We were all walking around in a daze and at one point I got a call from Pat Howard to come up to see him and James Sutherland in an office they'd set up near the hotel's business centre. I waited outside and when they called me in James said that the board had met and I was now the 46th Test captain.

I suppose they must have asked me at one stage if I wanted to do the job, but I don't remember and all of that was kind of secondary compared to everything else.

James said he was going to tell the media that Steve, David and Cameron were all being sent home and that the board would decide on sanctions after it had examined the interim report. He told the media the issue here was bigger than the technicalities of ball–tampering and that the 'integrity and reputation of Australian cricket' was at stake.

Bonnie was somewhere with Milla and I went up to our room and I remember looking out at the sunset, it was a vivid orange-pink sky – you get enormous sunsets in Africa – and the door opened and Mum came in. She stood there for a while, she could see I was a bit shaken, and then she said, 'What's going on?' I told her that I'd just been appointed Test captain and she asked if it was temporary. I said, 'Nope, full time,' and I don't normally swear in front of Mum but I did.

I genuinely didn't know whether to cry or what, I was in shock.

There were rumours flying around that Darren Lehmann was going to resign – he said he was determined to stay on and support us, but he was taking it hard. Like a lot of us, he wasn't sleeping and couldn't get any peace. I went to see him that night in his room and he told me he would be around for me.

James Sutherland had told the media that no other players or support staff were involved, including Darren, and they appeared publicly to have his back.

I spent time making my way along the corridor, talking to some of the boys. Some time with Cameron and some with Steve. As I said Davey had his family there, in fact he had a few other people there, including a mate and his brother-in-law.

At some point all the players were called into a room and Pat told us that Steve and Dave had each been given a 12-month ban and Cameron nine months. Steve got a one-year ban from leadership roles but Dave got a lifetime ban. There was a sense the administration were out to get him. He was often a thorn in their side and had been quite outspoken during a contract dispute which had gotten ugly the year before.

The next morning they packed their bags. We were trying to have our breakfast and there were people coming and going. There was a huge media pack outside and some of the Australian journos had set up in the corner of the hotel foyer which was also the breakfast area. Smithy even went over and spoke to them before he left. I remember giving him a hug goodbye. We were both pretty emotional.

I was due to front up at my first pre-match captain's media conference before training day at the Wanderers Stadium and caught the bus early to the ground with a few of the coaches. It's funny but I can't recall if Darren Lehmann was on the bus, but I do remember when we got there that I was about to head across to talk to the journos and someone told me to wait because Boof was going first.

I saw him outside the room having a cigarette and I asked what was going on and he said he was going to stand down.

Darren is a good man, he is a real softy. I loved playing under him, he'd filled me with confidence I didn't know I had when I joined the team a few months earlier, and he'd brought out the best in me. He loved the boys and he was broken. There was talk he'd already quit or should be sacked and his family was copping it, and I think he just wanted to take the heat off them, or off us.

I went into the room and sat in the corner as he did the presser. He was a mess. Red-eyed from crying. He'd been adamant he was going to stay with us. He had a change of heart, apparently, but I couldn't help but feel that he'd been pushed.

Dave and Steve returned home to those awful scenes in the airports. Seeing Davey and his family harassed like that was wrong. Watching Smithy's tearful media conference was heartbreaking.

Meanwhile, the team was in disarray. Joe Burns and Matt Renshaw flew over in case we needed extra players. Mitch Starc broke down and Chadd Sayers got the chance to play.

After the presser we went out and trained. Somebody had plugged an Australian playlist into the stadium sound system. Often we train with music playing from a large jukebox/speaker thing but this was pumping out like we were at a rock concert and every song seemed to have another meaning.

One of the journos later showed me a message he'd received from a former English player who now worked in the media. It said: 'Making them walk the plank like that in public was disgusting for an offence few players give a hoot about . . . talk about an overreaction by the many, made me feel queasy.'

I still feel like Steve, Dave and Cam copped the brunt of it, and Boof too, but I have wondered if there was a point where we could have said something or done something differently. Everyone was a part of it to some degree — would it have worked out better for those three players if we had owned it as a team? I think it would have.

We played my first Test as Australian captain in a daze. The umpire Ian Gould wrote in his book that he'd never officiated in a quieter match. He said we were like zombies. We lost, but for the first time in my life I can truly say that the game seemed secondary.

The scale of my task as captain became apparent after all the noise died down. I had been placed in charge of a team whose best players were suspended and whose public standing was in the gutter. We talked a lot in the next months about values, but I didn't need any reviews or consultants to tell me we had a major problem, and I didn't need a report to see that things had to change.

It was going to be a long, slow process and there were going to be hiccups, but I loved Australian cricket and it was a task I was willing to put my heart into. Fortunately, I would not be alone in the rebuilding process, which every single person involved bought into without question.

We were going to struggle without Steve and Dave, but we had to keep our heads down and our eyes on the task at hand. Essentially, we were on probation and we were going to have to prove ourselves again to gain back the public's trust.

I was determined to help restore Australian cricket's reputation.

10

A NEW GUARD

Australia, with a new coach, a new captain and a squad that was missing six of its best players, took the first tentative step across the scorched earth and towards a new future in England in June 2018. Steve Smith and Dave Warner were a few months into 12-month suspensions, Pat Cummins, Josh Hazlewood, Mitchell Starc and Mitch Marsh were all unavailable. Cam Bancroft was studying how to be a yoga teacher.

It was at the camp ahead of our flight to England that allegations were made by the Cricket Tasmania employee, and I was investigated and cleared. I don't think anyone else knew what was going on, for now at least.

Justin Langer wanted me to be captain of the ODI team because I think he was keen to have consistent captaincy across the three formats. I was happy to do the job, but by the time the away series was over I was just as happy not to do it. I think one-day cricket had passed me by.

We got soundly beaten. It wasn't unsurprising but it wasn't much fun. We were playing the best team in the world and they were on fire.

We could have won the first game at The Oval when we had them 6–163 chasing 215, but David Willey smacked it around at the end. We had Billy Stanlake, Michael Neser, Kane Richardson and Andrew Tye bowling. It wasn't exactly an experienced attack and it didn't help that I put down a tough skied ball when Josh Buttler was batting. He didn't make a lot more runs but it would have kept up our momentum.

We could have won the second game too. They scored 342 and thanks to an unbelievable hundred from Shaun Marsh we were well in the chase, but we stuffed it up at the end.

They were way too good at Trent Bridge. Alex Hales got 147, Jonny Bairstow 139 and Jason Roy 82. It was a massacre. There's no way we could chase down 481. We put on 310 thanks to hundreds from Marsh and Aaron Finch at Durham but they got into our inexperienced attack and ran that down pretty easily. Then they got the runs in Manchester with nine balls remaining.

All things considered I reckon we weren't as bad as the result of the series suggested. It was a research and development exercise in some ways. Obviously things would change when the big boys were available.

One of the things JL and I identified about my captaincy during the one-day tour of the UK was that I'd got too wrapped up in things. I was overtraining and trying too hard to lead from the front. I never go well when I try too hard and going over the top with the training side of things left me physically and mentally tired.

I'd actually gone on a study tour of the United States with JL, Cricket Australia's chief executive James Sutherland, the high performance manager Pat Howard and coaching consultant Darren Holder. On that trip we discussed a lot of things about leadership and the direction we wanted to take Australian cricket. One of the conclusions we came to around me was that I was a better captain and player when I was relaxed and not trying to be anything other than myself. JL was assigned the role of tapping me on my shoulder if I was trying or training too hard.

In October 2018 we headed to the UAE for two Test matches against Pakistan. It was the first Test tour with me as captain and JL as coach and the first Test Australia would play since returning from South Africa. We were up for it but we knew we were up against it.

Australian cricket was coming from a long way back in the public's eye and we were missing four of the best players in the world with Pat Cummins, Josh Hazlewood, Steve Smith and Dave Warner unavailable. Our batting in particular was exposed, but it gave us a chance to blood some new players. Aaron Finch was picked because other guys had not taken their chances and he'd scored a heap of hundreds in one-day cricket. JL was big on the fact that in Test cricket you needed to have blokes scoring hundreds if you are going to win, and we thought Finchy was more likely to score them than blokes who weren't getting them in Shield cricket. The other thinking was that the UAE, where the ball doesn't do a lot, would suit him.

Matthew Renshaw would have played the first Test, but he got concussed in the warm-up game fielding at short leg. We brought in Marnus Labuschagne to replace Renners. I always liked the way Marnus played, he'd done well against us in Sheffield Shield games and caught my eye with the little things he did. He was always up for the game, he ran hard between the wickets, he was good in the field, he had energy, he was a team man and he didn't shut up which was a result of his endless enthusiasm, but it made him very, very hard to like when you were playing against him. He was an annoying opponent, he was cheeky, always chatting, but he was the kind of player you wanted in your team. He and guys like Dave Warner bring something to a side. They are relentless and it lifts everyone around them. Sometimes you just need a bit of noise and enthusiasm.

Marnus hadn't done a lot at Shield level yet but there was something about him. Graeme Hick had been the coach on a previous Australia A series and Marnus had impressed him. Greg Chappell was always a big supporter and he was the loudest voice, I think, in pushing us to give him a chance at Test level. We were on the same page on that. Greg copped flak from various people over the years but he got that right, in fact he got a lot of things right. It was his role to spot talent and he was very good at it. He'd seen something in Steve Smith at a young age, also in Glenn Maxwell. He'd pushed for David Warner as a future Test player when I think even New South Wales didn't recognise him as the talent he was. Phillip Hughes was another he got right very early. People would say these guys didn't have the technique or whatever, but Greg saw through that stuff. Marnus had a poor average in Shield cricket at that time, but GC knew there was more there.

Because Renners was concussed Marnus had moved up to bat at No. 6 in the practice game. He was 39 not out when we declared. We gave him a bowl in the second innings and liked what we saw. He was a better bowler than we'd thought. JL warmed to him, he always liked blokes who trained hard and were up for the game. So we brought him in to play the Test.

Travis Head was another who got his chance. He'd been very impressive in the warm-up game and had got a hundred on the Australia A tour of India before that. They'd made him captain of South Australia when he was very young and he'd already got some exposure playing white ball cricket for Australia. Travis was one of those people who we thought not only had the ability to play Test cricket but, because of the way he plays it, he had the ability to win matches. He can change the course of the game very quickly. I love the way he plays and while people were a bit cynical at first, I think they came around after a while. He's got to have a clear role, but when he has the licence to back himself he can do things others can't.

Heady and Rishabh Pant are a bit similar, they can change the momentum of a Test match rapidly. You have to accept that every now and then they will play an ordinary shot, but every now and then they can be devastating. We'd seen that in Heady's games for South Australia and we were starting to see it in Test match cricket too. He can hit a ball so hard and has a great eye so that even when he is not in position, he middles the ball. These days he is confident enough to back himself and I think that's because he's been backed too.

The first Test match was among the glistening skyscrapers and devastating heat of Dubai. It's a strange place.

You drive out of the city on these massive roads and find yourself in the Sports City which is another bit of reclaimed desert. Look one way and all you can see are these towers dominating the skyline, look another and you half expect to see camels rolling over the dunes. They've plonked this joint right in the middle of the sand. Everything is man-made. It's so hot that nobody really goes out and about much. All the restaurants are in massive shopping malls which are like cities within cities, and if you do find yourself eating on a balcony or in an outdoor setting there's a bank of air-conditioners keeping you alive. There's a beach but the water is like a warm bath. It's a long way from Hobart.

We lost the toss, Pakistan batted and they scored the best part of 500 while we slowly cooked under the desert sun. We were going alright in reply, Finchy and Usman put on 140, but then we lost the next ten wickets for 60 runs and were completely out of the game. It was cruel how little time we got to spend in the dressing room.

The batting, with the exception of our openers, had been disappointing, but one thing I was impressed with was the way our bowlers stuck to the task in both innings. I remember walking off when Pakistan got that big score in the first innings, thinking that our bowlers had really had a crack on a flat wicket against a good batting line-up when it was stinking, stinking hot.

Pakistan had got the best of the conditions batting first and our batsmen, who were all inexperienced, struggled against their spin when it did start to turn on the third day. They had a bit of a swing to set us a total in their second innings. We needed 462 to win, which was not impossible but highly improbable, especially after we lost Finch and both Marsh brothers with the score on 87 on the fourth evening.

We were five down in the second session of the last day when I walked out to join Usman who'd already brought up a hundred. I was determined to dig in and defend, he was happy to hang around. Usi was incredible in those innings and showed signs of what was to come when he would make another return to Test cricket a few years later. He was under so much scrutiny about the way he played spin bowling and they had very good spinners, but he took them on. He was reverse sweeping Yasir Shah from what seemed like the first over he faced. It was really brave, if that shot didn't come off people would have been all over him, but when it did it allowed him to break the shackles of their bowlers.

It was one of the better innings I've ever seen.

Usman was out for 141 and I lost Mitch Starc and Peter Siddle as partners in quick succession afterwards. Nathan Lyon was pretty nervous when he came out, he prefers having a hit to having to hold them out, but he hung around for 50 minutes and we pulled off a draw which

I was pretty happy with. I was 61 not out and it was nice, in my first real Test as captain, to walk off having been part of the rescue mission. Nobody really expected us to save that game but I had been confident from the start of the innings.

I remember that in the last overs of the game there were a few runs on offer when they brought the field up to stop the single and I started taking them. I copped a bit of good-natured flak from our assistant coach David Saker about that. I told him I hadn't scored enough Test runs to leave any out there.

When we did get that game over the line, I gestured to the balcony for everyone to keep a lid on it. It was a draw not a win, we had done okay but we needed to do better.

We drove across to Abu Dhabi for the second Test. Lost the toss again, batted poorly and found ourselves pretty comprehensively beaten. It was disappointing, especially as we'd got them out for 282 when they batted in the first innings. Mohammad Abbas, their medium pacer, tore through us in our first innings and we were knocked over for 145, and then he did the same as we got rolled for 164 in the second.

That wasn't great, but we bowled well again, especially Nathan Lyon. We'd had them 5–57 on the first day but Sarfaraz Ahmed changed the momentum of the game. I remember Marnus getting run out in bizarre fashion at the non-striker's end in the first innings which kind of summed up our day. Usman didn't even get out for the second innings because he'd hurt his knee.

I wasn't all that happy at the end of the series and had a bit to say in the media about the way we were collapsing. It had been a bit of a pattern in recent years. I added that it would be a pretty exciting time to be a batsman in Sheffield Shield cricket because there were spots up for grabs for anyone who was scoring hundreds.

There was a T20 and some ODIs after the Tests but Aaron Finch had, rightly, replaced me as captain and Alex Carey was given a chance behind the stumps. It was the right call.

Bonnie and I had our second child Charlie just before I left so it was good to get back home. I'd had to run off on the tour pretty much straight after he was born. And we were moving house. Problem was I had back-to-back Sheffield Shield games which I needed to play before the home Tests, so cricket kind of took precedence again.

People were questioning whether I was the right man to lead Australia. Shane Warne wasn't convinced. I think Geoff Lawson had a go too. It didn't worry me. It was a big job, I was willing to give it my best shot and if I wasn't up to it, that was okay. I focused on what I could do, not what I couldn't.

Because I came in from outside the team and was slightly older, the other players trusted me a bit more because I had no alliances, no baggage. In that first six months I built strong relationships with my teammates and got to know them well. I just knew if I was myself that was all I could be. It didn't bother me what Warney said because I didn't know him and he didn't know me. Same with Lawson. There was a time when I would have gone ballistic about that stuff, but I'd moved past that. If it was someone who knew me and who I shared respect with, it might be different. If I wasn't getting things right, JL would discuss it with me and there were also a few other people around who could guide me. Somewhere along the way I developed a thick skin and if people thought I was no good as a keeper or a captain, that was fine.

Don't get me wrong, though, I am fiercely competitive. I wanted to captain the best team in the world, I wanted to get us to the Test championship, I wanted to be the best player I could be.

That summer Virat Kohli and the Indians came over and I reckon that Virat could smell a big opportunity. Warner and Smith were good for more than 200 runs a game (they basically averaged 100 runs an innings between them) but they were still banned. Our batting line-up was a long way from settled and we were on notice about the way we played cricket. The public had made that very clear in the reaction to the South African scandal and it had been emphasised in an inquiry into the culture of Australian cricket.

Virat loves a fight, loves to lord it over the opposition, he plays on the edge, and he saw the opportunity to try and dominate us when we were essentially feeling our way. It was a very difficult period to be an Australian player, it was hard, you couldn't say a thing on the field or you'd get nailed for it. It wasn't enjoyable. We didn't want to abuse people and carry on, but you wanted to be able to compete and part of cricket is competing mentally with the opposition, trying to distract each other and make them doubt themselves. It was important if the opposition came at us that we were able to stand up to them, but it felt a little bit like we were fighting with one hand behind our back.

Our major problem, however, was that India came here with three world-class quicks. They'd always had great batters but the bowlers had let them down in previous trips to Australia. The first Test was played in Adelaide, which was odd as Australia had always played the first match of the summer in Brisbane and had a great record there. Apparently India had demanded they play either Brisbane or Adelaide, but not both.

Marnus Labuschagne and Mitch Marsh were dropped from the side, Marcus Harris came in to make his debut as an opener with Aaron Finch, and Pete Handscomb batted in the middle order. There'd been some talk about not playing Finchy at home, but we stuck with him after he went well in the UAE, even though we knew that the conditions and bowlers were going to test his technique. He was bowled by Ishant Sharma for a duck in the first innings and didn't ask for a review when given out caught off the pad in the second. If he had, he'd have been okay and things might have turned out differently. Instead he found himself under pressure from the start.

We had Josh Hazlewood and Pat Cummins back and we rolled India, who batted first, for 250. We actually had them 5–86 but Cheteshwar Pujara dug in and contributed half their score. The highlight of that innings was Usman's screamer in the gully to remove Virat for 3 off Pat's bowling. We didn't do enough in our innings and were out for 235. Honours were even but they put on 301 when they batted again. We nearly got those runs. We were in trouble at 9–251 but Josh walked out to join Nathan Lyon in the middle and they put on 30-odd by lunch on day five. Unfortunately, we didn't get any closer.

India had won the first Test of the series.

From there we went to Perth and that's when things really heated up. Virat was in our face the whole time and he just pushed it too far. I got tired of his rubbish on the third day when he had a bit to say over an appeal against me while I was batting. He was taunting me, saying that if I stuffed it up we'd be two–nil. I said something like,

'You still have to bat yet big head,' and of course a few people thought I'd called him a dickhead. Walking off at stumps that night, there was a bit of back and forth.

I think there was some nervousness around how that would be perceived by the public, but it seemed to me that they like to see sportspeople going at each other within reason. It shows it matters. To see the argument continue on the way off the ground was a bit odd but it was a sign that there was something on the line here. Virat started referring to me as the 'stand-in captain' but that didn't worry me at all, I thought it was pretty funny.

At one point on the fourth day I hit a single and he ran from mid off to get in my way then stood at the crease blocking me. I could have held my line and run through him but I didn't. Still, I wasn't going to let him behave like this, even if the umpires and match officials were. He shouldn't have got that close, it should never get physical, but I enjoyed the test of wills. I stood up to him and the umpires stepped in when I told him he was getting a bit silly.

I had to stop Virat carrying on. I had to draw a line and say we wouldn't put up with his nonsense. I would have done it earlier but we were so nervous about that stuff.

Virat was the sort of player I enjoyed taking on, he was so easy to fire up. You could walk past him and say some-thing about him, not to him, and he would react. They are the players you have the most fun with. You didn't have to make eye contact with Virat and he would bite. He was one of the best batters in the world and he wasn't going to let a bloke like me say anything and he never let a comment go unanswered. He loved a clash and it was a bit of fun. I can't stand it when people say, 'Don't get stuck into him, it gets him going,' that's the biggest load of crap in cricket. Are they going to focus more because you said something? He was averaging 60 anyway.

We weren't a great team that summer. Put in Warner, Smith, Khawaja and Labuschagne and we would have been very different, but two of them weren't available and the other two weren't in the team just yet. Test cricket is hard when you don't score enough runs but in that Perth game we'd at least got past 300 when we batted first and that was incentive for our bowlers. Nathan Lyon took five in the first innings and three in the second and deserved the Man of the Match award that came his way.

We'd squared the series and in a way straightened ourselves up as a cricket side. I felt like we were a little less apologetic, a bit more assertive. People seemed to like the fact I'd stood up to Virat.

Unfortunately, we lost the toss in Melbourne and India batted our attack into the ground on another disappointing MCG deck. Pujara was out there forever, making another century, Kohli hung around for a long while and our bowlers had sent down 170 overs when they declared on 7–433. The wicket looked flat when we bowled, but

Jasprit Bumrah turned it on to take 6–33 and roll us for a pathetic 151 when India got a chance. At least Pat Cummins went one better and took 6–27 in an equally impressive bowling display when they batted a second time, but even though we held them to 8–106 declared we were now behind by 399 and we just didn't have that many runs in our inexperienced batting line-up.

We headed up to Sydney hoping to level the series in the new year. Finchy didn't make it into the side. He'd done his best, but as good as he is opening in the white ball formats – one of the greats – he just couldn't translate that to Test match cricket. We moved Usman up to open for the last game which meant we needed someone to bat at No. 3. Marnus was brought into the side and naturally he was happy to do it. That's what you've got to love about Marnus, he's up for anything if it means being part of the game. He always wants to bowl, he is always looking for a run-out or a catch, and if there's a spot in the batting order to fill he'll take it. Pete Handscomb, who had been replaced by Mitch Marsh in Melbourne, was brought back in too.

India batted us into the ground. Cheteshwar Pujara scored 193 and my little mate Rishabh Pant knocked up a ridiculous 159 not out to allow them to declare on 7–622.

We knocked up 300 batting second but it was nowhere near enough, we weren't ever getting back into that game, and when rain wiped out the last day it fizzled into a draw.

India had clinched its first series victory in Australia. It wasn't a great feeling to be on the end of that loss. Their experienced players like Pujara, Virat and Bumrah had stood up in the big moments and Rishabh's knock showed the depth of talent they had. India notched up five centuries in the series but we had nobody who reached 80. It annoyed me that we'd let a few moments slide in Adelaide, it is always hard to come back after losing the first Test, but Travis Head had shown something and Marnus was clearly a player who could more than hold his own at this level. With Steve and Dave to come back in, I thought we had the makings of a good Test side.

And we were due to get them back for the next assignment which was a winter trip to England for the Ashes. I was quietly confident, but before that we had two Tests against Sri Lanka to round out the summer.

JL said in the media that he was having sleepless nights worrying about being beaten by Sri Lanka at the Gabba. I wasn't worried at all, we had the attack to beat them and our batting was taking shape despite the absences. Joe Burns came in to open with Marcus Harris, Usman dropped down to No. 3 and Marnus to No. 4, Travis Head was below him and then we had Kurtis Patterson who had forced his way in at the last minute. He wasn't in the squad, but demanded selection after making a century in the Shield on a spicy deck at Perth before Christmas and a pair of them for the Cricket Australia XI in the tour match against the visitors. Their bowlers couldn't get him out in either innings. There was a bit of to and fro among the coaches about bringing him into the squad, but I was strongly of the opinion that we do what it takes to have the best XI for the Test.

JL had been saying that runs were currency and there was an emphasis on finding batters who could hang around and score centuries. Kurtis had just done that while nobody in the team had achieved it in the Tests against India. A lot of people were expecting Will Pucovski to play but he was never in the mix to my knowledge. Josh Hazlewood was still unavailable and James Pattinson got himself suspended for using a homophobic slur in the Shield game on the eve of the Test. He only found out when we got to Brisbane before the match and was pretty emotional when he broke the news to us. His pace would have been handy, but we had Jhye Richardson ready to go.

It's good for the whole group to have a cap presentation ceremony before play, it puts things into context, reminds players of where their journey started and it's exciting to see nervous new players achieve their dream. Puts a smile on your face. On the first morning of the Test, Jhye and Kurtis were both given their first baggy greens.

Jhye was straight to work after Sri Lanka won the toss and chose to bat. Towards the back end of his spell, he was rewarded with his first wicket when Joe Burns caught Dinesh Chandimal low at second slip. He finished with 3–26 and we rolled Sri Lanka for 144. Our seamers were just too much for them to handle on a Gabba strip that always does a bit early in the game. They just weren't used to conditions like that. They would have been in a lot more trouble if Niroshan Dickwella hadn't backed himself to score a quick-fire 64.

Marnus and Travis both scored 80s when we batted, but again nobody went on to score a hundred so the century drought continued. We posted 323 runs and Sri Lanka struggled again in their second innings. Pat Cummins was just way too good for them. To be honest he was proving to be too good for most batsmen. If there's a better bowler in the world, I haven't seen them. He is fast, skilful, aggressive and a bloody nightmare to face. He took 6–23 and we didn't have to bat again.

The cricket caravan moved to Canberra for a Test match at Manuka Oval. As a Tasmanian I have to question why it was being played there and not next to Nan's house in Hobart. Seriously. Tasmanian cricket had to beg for crumbs from the table at the best of times because Melbourne, Sydney, Adelaide, Perth and Brisbane were in front of us. Now Canberra comes along and we have to compete with them for the sixth match – when there is one.

That said, it was kind of fun to play the inaugural men's Test on the ground. It was even better because the runs flowed. Joe Burns scored 180, Travis Head 161 and Kurtis Patterson 114 after we won the toss and chose to bat. Their attack just didn't have the firepower to challenge our batsmen. I declared when I was 45 not out – it would have been nice to go on, but we'd reached tea on day two and were 5–534. A bit of red ink is always nice for the averages.

Their openers, Dimuth Karunaratne and Lahiru Thirimanne, found the wicket a bit easier to handle and had a bit of a crack, but Mitch Starc found his range and took 5–54. He'd been struggling a bit for rhythm in the summer. This time he just turned up and bowled flat out and it was too much for the opposition. Dhananjaya de Silva was out hit wicket after Starcy hit him in the helmet and knocked him backward when he tried to pull a short one. Their batters were not having much fun. Jhye Richardson hit Kusal Perera in the helmet and he had to be helped from the ground with concussion. Karunaratne had really worried us when he'd been hit in the neck by Pat Cummins on the Saturday. He did not look well after that incident and was taken away in an ambulance, but after a night in hospital he came good and was able to come in and replace Perera when he retired hurt. It takes a bit of courage to come back into the fray like that, so good on him.

We were 300-odd in front after the first innings but batted again to make sure we got a result. This time

I waited until Usman got his century before bringing us in with the score at 3–196. Head was 59 not out when we declared.

Starcy picked up another five wickets in their second innings, Pat took 3–15 from eight overs and that was that.

It was nice to get a few wins and to get a bit of reward after losing to South Africa, Pakistan and India in our three previous series. Our Test team was training hard, JL was flogging us, he was putting his stamp on the place, setting really high standards. Fielding sessions were like running sessions. Our lungs were hanging out half the time. He was sending messages to the younger blokes about what international cricket is all about.

The other great motivator was that we looked up and knew that David Warner, Steve Smith and Cameron Bancroft would be available for our next assignment, which was the Ashes. Marnus was looking good, so was Kurtis Patterson and Joe Burns. Usman was a constant, Travis had found his range and Jhye had proved himself. Although he hadn't played, Michael Neser had come into the group and showed how good a cricketer he was. He was a revelation, actually. He is a gun bowler, a handy lower order batter, he fields his arse off and is just great to have around the group. He impressed everyone in that period and that's why he stayed involved. We were finding out about these players, and they were stepping up and showing character, which was just what Australian cricket needed.

11

REDEMPTION

I doubt Australia will ever get a preparation for an Ashes series like it did in 2019. We sent a preliminary 14-man A team over for a big series against whoever would play them, while others played in the 2019 World Cup and some like Marnus Labuschagne honed their skills in the county circuit. All eyes were on Steve Smith and David Warner who were making their comeback to cricket. The World Cup was a good way for them to test the waters and get used to the reception they would receive.

It felt like every elite Australian player was in the UK and we all came together in late July at Southampton to play a practice game which would determine who would be in the Ashes squad. There's a photo somewhere of all

25 players who fought it out for a place in the side on the landing at the Hampshire ground and it looks great.

A lot of players had a good lead-in. Matty Wade got centuries against Northamptonshire and Derbyshire, Travis Head got one in the unofficial Test and Marnus had laid down a marker with a string of them for Derby. Wadey actually wasn't even going to come on the tour as his second child was due, but his wife Julia had told him he'd regret it if he didn't give Test cricket one more crack so he changed his mind.

There was competition for spots and there was a real buzz in the air. I remember rocking up to the hotel and Marnus was running around the foyer like an excited puppy, greeting everybody as they arrived from various locations. It's kind of an odd set-up there because the hotel is out of town and part of the ground, so you could actually watch play from your room if you were so inclined. There's a golf course and a nearby gym but there's not a lot else to do but hang out with the boys and train.

We trained on the outground but used the Ageas Bowl for the three-day game.

We divided into two groups: the Brad Haddin XII and the Graeme Hick XII. The ground staff struck the first blow for England by preparing an unbelievably poor pitch for us to tune up on. Balls were flying off a length which would be okay if others weren't shooting through low. You weren't sure if it would hit your shin or your ankle.

It was a nightmare trying to bat. There was every chance we'd lose a bunch of batsmen to broken fingers. Or ankles. Nobody could get a run to save themselves in the first innings.

Marnus top-scored with 41 for the Haddins and Mitch Marsh with 29 for the Hicks. It was rubbish and if it had been a real game it would have been abandoned; it was also unusually hot which made it hard going for everyone. One bloke who made the most of it, however, was Cam Bancroft who somehow hung on for 93 not out on the last day. Nobody had got within a mile of that and it was a reminder of why he'd been in the side before his ban. It was a tight contest between him and Joe Burns for a seat on the bus, but that innings got Cam over the line. Michael Neser and Jackson Bird were in competition for the last bowling spot and Ness had actually made holiday plans which he had to cancel after he was named in the 17-man Ashes squad.

It was a strange morning when the selectors called everyone in one by one for a meeting in a room near the breakfast room to tell them if they were staying for the Ashes or being let go. A procession of players made their way to see Trevor Hohns and then emerged with their fate decided. Some packed up to leave for wherever, while the rest of us got our gear together.

That night I took the squad and a couple of the others who were still there out for dinner to mark the commencement of the campaign proper. The captain gets an allowance to do this and it's a good way to get a series started. Everyone thought it was hilarious that I had to pay – remember, I'm known as a tight-arse. Davey Warner looked up from the wine list to confirm I was footing the bill and, when I said yes, he promptly ordered Dom Perignon. It's a tradition to stitch up the captain.

The next morning we jumped on the team bus for the drive up to Birmingham for the first Test and there was a nice sort of tension in the air. It had taken a bit for a few of us to get to this point and now the real fun was due to start. There was a lot to do when we hit town, with photo shoots, (lots and lots of) interviews, functions and even the odd bit of training. The Ashes are a huge event and there's so much goes on around the cricket. A horde of Australian media head over and every day there's a roster for blokes to do interviews with this radio station or that newspaper. I'm not complaining about this, quite the opposite, it's a great thing that so many people put so much value on the series.

I had the bigger room – 'captain's suite' – at the team hotel and it was near the landing where there was a lot of coming and going. I made the decision to leave my door open most of the time so people could come in and out. My suite became the card room, sometimes there were eight or nine people hanging around there. None of the partners were in town, nobody was going out on the beers and dinner was usually over early, so it was a bit like a school camp. It was a good bonding period.

Another of the rituals for a Test captain is the pre-match media conference on the day before the game. This (listen to me with all my experience) usually involves getting asked about who is in the XI, what I think of the pitch, whether we'll bat first and all that stuff. The English journos had gone easy on me the year before during our one-day tour because I think they felt sorry for me, but the stakes were higher this time.

I remember making my way up the stairs from the dressing rooms to the media conference and I was pretty relaxed, but the moment I opened the door it was clear this was different to anything I'd done before. For starters, it was the size of it. There were so many people crammed into a section of an odd-shaped space which is also the media dining room. There was a different mood, a different feel, it was tense, as if the journos were nervous about the big series and you could almost see a split in the media in the way they'd arranged themselves with the Australians on one side and English on the other.

There were a couple of questions from the Australian journos about the cricket and the XI to kick things off. I reckon the very first question I got from the English was from a quietly spoken older guy, who said:

'We've seen Alex Carey do well in the World Cup and obviously you took over this job in difficult circumstances a year ago but it is harder to justify your place when we've seen Carey do well – [Matthew] Wade's probably going to play as a batsman, do you feel under pressure to justify your place?'

I didn't see that coming, but I didn't get my back up because there was an eternal truth about my spot in the team and my role as captain.

'No, not at all,' I said. 'I'm 34 years old, mate. I don't really care about my place in the side anymore. I'm here to do a job. I've been put in this team to captain and keep wicket to the best of my ability. That's all I can do. At 34 years of age if you're looking further ahead than the next Test match you're kidding yourself. I realise how lucky I am – the position I've come from and the position I'm now in. I'm not going to waste time looking over my shoulder. I'm enjoying the job that I'm doing.'

I always try to answer as honestly as I can, otherwise journos will keep asking the same question. I remember being interviewed about the Indians coming back in 2020–21 and them calling me the accidental captain. Someone asked if I was annoyed by that label and I said, 'No, why would it, it's true, I actually am an accidental captain, you can't deny this wasn't meant to happen but it did and I'm here to do a job now. I am an accidental captain, it is a fact.' Same as when everyone was shocked about my selection for the Ashes two years earlier, and I said that I was as shocked as the guy asking the question.

The English journo started asking me questions about playing in England and particularly at Edgbaston and the crowd. I must admit I was kind of confused about the point of this. Then one asked me if there was a more intimidating ground and I said, 'I could name you 15,' which caused a bit of a murmur to go around the room and a lot of stories to be written. But I literally had no idea about the reputation of Edgbaston or the crowd that inhabited its Hollies Stand. I wasn't being a smart-arse or trying to deflect it, I just didn't know. After the presser, our Welsh-born media officer Brian Murgatroyd raised his eyebrows about my answers and I said to him, 'You don't play the ground, mate.' Murgers didn't say much but I got the distinct impression that he thought I was about to discover the opposite.

It was odd to have the local media come at me like this, it was almost as if they were part of the England team in a way. I had gone into the presser feeling relaxed and open but I had to change my approach on the spot. I thought they were testing me to see if I was up to leading the team and if they could get me to snap or say something silly or be angry. As a sports lover I watch lots of pressers and they often heat up. When a coach or player reacts angrily, I always think, 'Oh no, why did you do that? You've just given them a headline or a story.' I hope I never fall for it.

Still, it's hard to go into those high-pressure ones and not get swept up in the mood. You have to stay relaxed, it's a waste of my energy to get caught up in things off the ground or have an argument with a journalist that will be used against me. I just try to go with it, sometimes even agree with them and that often shuts it off. If you keep pushing back they keep at it, but I reckon even that day they backed off because they could see I wasn't going to rise to it.

About five seconds into the Test I realised what the English journos were on about. That Edgbaston crowd is insane! I wouldn't say it was intimidating, it was awesome, they were all dressed up, they were almost deranged with passion, they didn't shut up from the first ball to the last, and they were very, very funny. They kept us entertained the whole time we were on the field. Me and the boys in the slips were always pointing out something that was going on over there. I've played a lot of cricket in grounds where nobody is taking any notice at all so I will take any attention I can get.

English crowds are a circus but in a good way. They love dressing up no matter how old they are. And, even when they're being nasty, there's something comical about it. They were obviously not going to miss the chance to have a go at us about sandpapergate, especially with the suspended players back in the team. They'd be waiting for us when we got to the ground on the bus and they'd boo us all the way into the change rooms and then they were out there on the footpath again in the evening to pick up where they'd left off. They followed the bus for as far as they could in the traffic from the ground, there were blokes in hardware store uniforms, heaps of them were holding pieces of sandpaper. One guy walked beside the bus halfway back from the ground to the hotel just working on a ball with a bit of paper as we crawled along in the traffic. I said to the boys that it was a once-in-a-lifetime experience to be abused like this, so make the most of it. The boys loved it. It was impossible not to laugh. Smithy and Dave lapped it up.

The crowd booed Smithy when he walked out to bat, they booed his fours, they booed his 50 and then they booed his hundred. And they had to boo it again when he batted in the next innings. I know he was ready to show everyone just how good he was on return, but the crowd's abuse made him doubly determined. They had poked the bear and the response was something else. They booed Davey just as much but they had a lot more time to get into Smithy over the course of the series. Not that Dave was avoiding it. He volunteered to field in front of the Hollies stand where all the abuse was coming from and when they sang a song about him crying on the telly he joined in. When they asked him about sandpaper he pulled out his pockets to show they were empty, for a laugh.

We'd made a clear plan that in England we had to adapt our bowling and bowlers to their conditions, particularly our seamers. Peter Siddle, who had vast experience in county cricket, was given the nod ahead of Josh Hazlewood, while James Pattinson came in for Mitch Starc.

All up there were six changes from the XI that played our last Test in Abu Dhabi. Travis Head got a start in front of Mitch Marsh, while Steve Smith, Dave Warner and Cameron Bancroft were all back from their bans. Pat Cummins was back after injury and so any way you look at it this was a vastly more experienced outfit than the last one I led. I suppose the question most asked was how Smith, Warner and Bancroft would go given all they'd been through. Davey and Steve, in particular, were the focus of most attention, Cam seemed to slip under the radar.

I won the toss and chose to bat in conditions that were challenging. Joe Root said it wasn't a bad toss to lose and when we were 3–35 with Warner, Bancroft and Usman gone, it seemed he was right. It went from bad to worse as the day progressed, but Smithy stayed out there and looked to be batting in a different game to the rest of us. Late in the day we were 8–122 and really in trouble. Warney was commentating at that stage and said if we were out for 140 it was game over, but Peter Siddle came out and hung on desperately as Steve continued to play on his own planet. They put on 88 for the ninth wicket. They were critical runs. When Sidds left, Nathan Lyon came out and the real fun began. Smithy hit Moeen over cow corner to get to 99 with a six and then Stokes through covers to bring up the hundred. You could see how emotional he was and we were just as excited on the balcony. He played some incredible shots as the clock ticked past 6 pm and the English bowlers tired – Jimmy Anderson bowled four overs early and no more, so they were a bowler short. Smithy was the last man out on 144 and we'd made it to 284. The last two wickets had put on 162 runs and every one of them was worth its weight in gold.

Steve Smith's innings was the best I have ever seen given his circumstances and the situation we were in. The bloke had been out of cricket for a year. He was coming back from an elbow injury, he had lost the captaincy and lost 12 months in the game when he was at the top of his career, but he had gained a hunger to make up for lost time. His focus and desire were next-level. His execution eccentric but effective. Nothing could shake or distract him.

Rory Burns countered with a century for them and they took an 80-run lead after the first innings. Smithy backed up in his second innings with 142 that was almost as good as his effort in the first. The icing on the cake was a hard-hitting 110 from Matty Wade which put us 398 runs in front when we declared. Not that long ago I'd replaced Wadey in the side and now he was back as a batsman. He had made a last-minute decision to come and had evolved into a world-class player. He is tough as nails and brave in his shot selection and it really paid off for us in this Test.

England had to bat late on day four and I opened the bowling with Peter Siddle and Nathan Lyon. The reason I chose Sidds was because England's medium pacers had been the most effective against us. Nathan got the ball because I wanted him to get a few overs under his belt and hopefully a wicket so he would sleep well and not feel too much weight of expectation on the last day. He didn't get a wicket that night but the next day he got their opener Jason Roy, their captain Joe Root, as well as Joe Denly, Ben Stokes, Moeen Ali and Stuart Broad, to finish with 6–49.

We'd won the first match by 251 runs and were 1–0 up in the Ashes.

There was a distinct change of atmosphere on that fifth day. For the previous four days there'd been so much noise from the crowd that you couldn't hear what the slips were saying, but on the fifth day you could have a conversation with mid off. Fortress Edgbaston no more.

There was a lot of talk around the bowling selections, but we knew from past experience that bowling the way we did in Australia wasn't going to work. We had two good bowlers on the sidelines, but we knew we needed to have flexibility and have the courage to use bowlers for the conditions – it wasn't about picking our best bowlers, it was about picking our best bowlers for the conditions. No Australian side had won a series in England since 2001. We liked Siddle in those conditions because he'd been playing county cricket for years and knew how to go about it. Pattinson bowled the house down in Southampton, he was quick, moved it around and got it in good areas. It was a line-ball decision to go with him over Josh Hazlewood for the first Test, but we felt Patto was coming off more cricket and just seemed ready to go.

Josh was a bit disappointed to miss out and you'd expect that. But he was primed for the second Test, we got him in and he stayed in. Hoff is a supreme bowling talent, I think sometimes Australians don't know just how good he is.

Mitch Starc had been told he would not always be in the team and he'd prepared himself. We knew how good he was and he bowled fast, but in England we needed him to bowl a little bit slower and get it in the right area because in England you are not blowing teams out with pace. We went over with a plan to be patient and wait for them to make mistakes, it's not something we normally do in Australia but over there you have to. That's one of the reasons we picked Pete Siddle and Michael Neser in the squad. A lot of big players put their feet up when they get dropped, but Starcy worked his backside off the whole series, getting drinks, doing everything he could for his teammates. He was awesome off the field and that set an impeccable example for everyone else.

One of the really good things about playing the Ashes in England is that the team travels on a bus. Everywhere else you catch planes and it's just not the same. With planes everyone shuffles through airports with pods in their ears and they use the short bus rides from hotels to grounds and airports to catch up on calls or texts or whatever. The same thing happens on a bus in England for 15 minutes then people start looking for something to do, whether it is playing cards or having a chat. Having everyone in that close proximity develops a sense of camaraderie, there's always something happening, it's always good fun and at the same time if you want to be alone there's enough room so you can sit downstairs or in a corner.

The bus is also our space, like a dressing room on wheels. You change hotel rooms every game, but the bus is the constant. It's a secure environment, nobody else can hear us or see us, and it means not having to go in and out of airports and do the transfers. For Smith and Warner especially, planes could be a hassle as there were always people looking for autographs and photos.

You set up your area on the bus and it is yours for the whole tour. You can leave stuff there, which doesn't sound like a big deal but it makes life so much easier when you are travelling around. I tend to lose things regularly so it is handy not to have to cart my stuff in and out of dressing rooms, hotel rooms and the like.

We'd had the same bus for the Australia A tour, so I was on it for months, and I had marked out my territory before the Test squad was even named. There were eight or ten tables, and you could have a table to yourself if you wanted to. The two at the back were prime real estate because they were close to the kitchen where the coffee machine was.

I was up the back left-hand side, facing the back of the bus on the last table. Smithy mostly sat next to me and Hoff sat opposite us with Travis Head. That was our four. We were always playing cards and as the stakes rose we tended to get a few standing around in the aisle so it might be six or seven.

The table across from us had Usman, Marnus, Ness and a revolving seat where Davey or Starcy would rotate and they would play UNO. Davey usually liked to sit down in the little bit at the front with Franky our security man and Popeye our bus driver.

JL sat in the middle of the bus which made him accessible but not too close. The rest of the coaches spread out.

There were televisions and on the Australia A tour we'd be watching the World Cup as we drove from game to game. We'd watch the premier league, but if there was nothing of interest on telly we'd play cards and have some music on. Mostly we played cards.

The card game of choice during the A series was 31, but the day we left Southampton to start the Ashes tour, Smithy doubled it to 62 and then the game took a bit longer. There was always money involved. It was usually about ten quid a round, but sometimes when we were on a 2–3 hour trip we were getting a few rounds in; obviously when we moved to 62 it reduced how many rounds and how much money was involved.

Heady was so bad at it that Hoff and Smithy figured out they needed to sit next to him because he'd always be throwing out good cards. He got slightly better as the tour went on, but was never any good. He was no good at concentrating, he'd always be on his phone and texting and he'd make poor decisions.

Josh Hazlewood, on the other hand, is like a professional card player. He would just smash us, he would have made a fortune on that trip, he's probably still waiting for me to pay. Hoff is great in that environment, he is not what people expect him to be, he is a very funny guy and very quick. He's a ripping bloke.

Fortunately I didn't see Smithy's guitar on the bus; he didn't take it on because he was way too competitive and always wanted to play cards. We got totally hooked on it, we could sneak in two or three hands on the way to the ground from the hotel. There was no small talk when we were in the zone, it was sit down, deal and play. It was a good distraction on the way in and it'd create a bit of banter and lift the mood.

We went to Worcestershire, which is a nice little town, for a tour match after the first Test and the plan was for me to rest from that game, but because we had a number of players involved in the World Cup we let them go to London early so I ended up being the 11th player of sorts. I played but I didn't bat or wicketkeep. It was a pretty chilled time and we needed it. You burn a lot of emotional energy in and around an event like the first Test of an Ashes. Naturally we were buoyed by the win but it didn't hurt to cool our heels for a while. I think it was especially important for Steve and Dave to take some time off.

And then it was back on the bus for the three-hour drive to London where we checked in at the Royal Garden Hotel ahead of the second Test at Lord's. It was on again. Nine years after playing my first Test at the home of cricket, I was back. This time, however, it was the Ashes and things had gone up a notch.

There were Australians everywhere. The executives from Cricket Australia never miss a London Test and all sorts of characters come to town. Former players are thick on the ground. The former prime minister John Howard is a regular sight in the foyer in the morning as he heads out for a walk in his Cricket Australia tracksuit. There's an incredible buzz. It rained the first day, which was a bummer, we didn't even get to have the toss, but we weren't too worried because four days is usually time enough to finish a Test match in England.

James Anderson was out of the series, it was a blow to England, but they had Jofra Archer waiting on the sidelines ready to go. There'd been a lot of talk about Jofra. He was going to be England's saviour. Wadey and I had played with him for the Hobart Hurricanes and we knew how good he was and how quick he could be. In the team meeting we spoke about making him bowl lots of overs in lots of spells, thinking his pace would drop and he would grow less interested because we didn't think he was fit enough. Jofra had never played a five-day game before so we thought if we could just keep bringing him back into the attack he would wear down. We were wrong, he really surprised us with his ability to back up for spell after spell. We just thought he could bowl fast, but Sidds and the boys from county cricket warned that he could move it around and he did. He surprised all of us with his ability and his appetite for the contest. He was still running

in and bowling with real aggression come the fifth Test –
ask Wadey, who was on the receiving end of it, and he'll
tell you.

James Pattinson made way for Josh Hazlewood in the
team for the second Test but all the excitement about
playing at Lord's was washed away when we woke that
morning to low skies and persistent rain. It was frustrating but we hung around playing cards and entertaining
ourselves and came back the next day for the toss. I won
again but the pitch was spicier and the clouds lower than
Edgbaston so I gave England first shot at batting. We
bowled them out for 258 and had to bat a tricky session
late in the day, which Davey did not survive.

Our top order found it hard going again. Day three
was interrupted by rain and when we did bat it was
bloody hard work. At the close of play we were 4–80.
Cam, Usman and Travis all before lunch and we didn't
get back on after the break. Wadey was 0 not out overnight and he was gone soon after play started on day four,
but that man Steve Smith was going about his business,
batting in his own universe yet again. He made it look
easier than it was, but you'd join him on the pitch and
it was as hairy as all get out. He was cruising along and
everyone else was just trying to hold on for dear life.
I joined him after the first hour and knew that if I could
just stay there for a little while we'd be better off. I was
hanging on desperately when Smithy got to 50, but soon

after Jofra got me with one I nicked onto my pad for an easy catch. I scored 23 and had been out there an hour and a half.

Jofra was all he was pumped up to be and a bit more at Lord's. He was really hard to handle with that stock ball that came down the slope and in to the right-hander and he was giving us hell. They had catchers around the bat and some back behind square, and while I'd normally have pulled those sorts of deliveries the bounce was uneven and the pitch was two paced. You couldn't risk the cross bat shot and you couldn't risk getting under the ball for fear of being hit. I got stuck in between a few times before I got out.

England took the new ball in Jofra's next spell after I was out, it was getting dark at the ground and that made things even more difficult. He started bowling even faster and into the body, Smithy had nowhere to go. He was getting battered. It was an amazing contest, I reckon everyone watching had goosebumps. Soon after he got hit on the arm and it looked serious, but he carried on.

Eventually Smithy got one that he couldn't get out of the way and it hit him in the neck at over 145 kph. He dropped like he'd been king hit and just lay facedown on the pitch. For those of us on the balcony, that was a horrible feeling, horrible. Instantly our thoughts went back to what happened to Phil Hughes – there was something about the way he fell. When we saw the replay it was even more chilling because the ball appeared to hit him in the same spot.

After a while Smithy moved and we all breathed again. The doctor ran out to assess him and we all tried to calm down a bit. England's medical staff rushed out too which shows you just how serious the situation looked. It was decided, wisely, that he come off. He'd been hit in the arm a few overs earlier and there was a bit of concern that he may have done some damage in that incident too. They didn't bring him into the change rooms, they took him to a room out the back.

We were 6–203 at the time. Sidds went in to bat and he said later he knew he was in for real trouble when he was greeted in the Long Room by the sorry sight of the best batsman in the world who had just had his helmet smacked in and probably a broken arm as well. Nathan Lyon was next in and he was absolutely shitting himself, which lightened the mood for the rest of us. He was sweating and had gone a very pale colour. He possibly looked worse than Steve.

Hadds and I went into the room when they brought Smithy up and he was more worried about his arm than his head. He had a bit of a stiff neck where he was hit, but his arm was really sore. He recovered enough to go out and bat again after Sidds was out. He'd been booed off by sections of the crowd and there were boos when he walked back on, but the Australian fans gave him the sort of reception the effort deserved.

It was an odd reprise. He played a strange little cameo where he belted a few then left one that trapped him in front and was out for 92 to the bowling of Mark Wood. Still, as he would point out, Jofra didn't get him. We had gotten within eight runs of their total which was a good effort and by stumps that night had them 4–96 thanks in part to Pat Cummins picking up the wickets of Jason Roy and Joe Root with consecutive deliveries.

Steve Waugh was with us in England as a mentor for the group and I got into a habit of heading out every morning with him, Sidds, Mitch Marsh and cameraman Andre Mauger at 7 am to find a good coffee and have a bit of a walk. Sidds knew all the good coffee spots. Mitch had started the walking club before the first Test which was something he'd done in South Africa as well. There's no better team man than Mitch Marsh. He's always up for fun, always entertaining someone somehow. He knows how to take the stress out of serious situations. I loved the walks. It was about getting up in the morning and getting out of your room. Your nerves can be really frazzled in a series like that so for me it was good to be around the boys and doing something with people who are going through the same thing.

There's something about Steve Waugh that helped keep me relaxed too. He is very grounding, he is not an excitable bloke, but he doesn't like England and he likes to win. I could bounce ideas off him and he was always so laidback and clear about what the situation was. I'd talk out my day with him very casually, ask him what he thought we should do if certain circumstances arose and he'd lay it out in simple terms. Some days we didn't talk about cricket at all but other days I pumped him for information.

When we got back to the foyer of the hotel after our morning coffee walk, I saw Smithy at reception and he didn't look well. I asked if he was alright and he said, 'Nah, I'm no good.' He'd just done some tests upstairs with a doctor and he had delayed concussion.

This was the first Test series that ever allowed a concussion substitute and to be honest I don't think we'd really thought too much about it, but thank god they did. It was obvious that Marnus was the one to come in as replacement but he'd already left for the ground to get a bit of work in. I realised I had a bit of a problem on my hands because I know how hard he trains and nobody had told him that Smithy was in trouble, so if he was left to his own devices he'd have thrashed himself that morning. I got into a car with one of the staff and by the time I got there Marnus was already batting in the nets. I dashed over and said, 'I think you're going to play, mate.'

I'll never forget his face when I told him, it just lit up with the biggest smile, no sign of nerves, he wasn't intimidated by the opportunity, he was up for it, more than up for it. Every day is like Christmas for Marnus, so you can imagine how huge this was to be back in the team.

Ben Stokes made a hundred on the fifth day and they set us 266 to win or – depending on how you look at it – 48 overs to survive in difficult conditions. Our top order struggled again, but this time we didn't have Smithy to save us. Turns out we had the next best thing.

The second ball Jofra bowled to Marnus was a 147 kph bouncer that smashed straight into his grille, and knocked him down. Before anyone could process what had happened, he'd sprung up and was staring back at Jofra as if to say, 'Is that all you've got?' I knew how good Marnus was and I knew he was ready, so I was confident he could hold his own, but when I saw that I realised his hunger was next level. Everyone says they want it, but some freeze and some fly when the moment comes. He flew. Marnus took off that day and probably hasn't touched down again since.

Our substitute Smith batted beautifully and got us out of trouble, but then he swept one into short leg's foot when he was on 59 and they gave him out when Joe Root dived forward to catch it. It was a shocking decision, the ball was on the ground, it wasn't a catch, but Marnus was given out with the game about five minutes shy of being called off. Jofra was back on and generating some heat in the dark. As a watcher of cricket, it drives me mad when they go

They start them young in Tassie and this is me in December 1986 at the age of two struggling with the size of the bat and pads (above). I got the cricket gear for my birthday from Dad who is seen helping me try them on (left).

Mum wanted a photo of my sister Meagan in her new school uniform and I wanted to show off my replica 'baggy green' so I squeezed into the shot. I'm just four years old, but how's the attitude?

This young rooster looks pretty proud of himself. I've just collected three gold medals in the 1992 Lauderdale Primary Mini Olympics. I'd finished first in the Mini Marathon and the 100 metres, and our team had triumphed in the indoor cricket competition.

When you start young you hit milestones early and here are the boys at the Lauderdale Junior Football Club chairing me off in my 100th match in July 1999 – I was fourteen. I loved my football and I still talk a good game.

There's nothing better than a team photo and this is a classic from one of the underage Tasmanian state teams from the Under 19s championships in Newcastle. That's seventeen-year-old me in the first row, second from left, doing my best to look like the blokes on the walls of every club in the land.

In October 2007 I played one of the best innings of my life at the WACA. Somehow I scored a double century in the game against Western Australia. The world was at my feet back then, but innings like this were to prove few and far between.

Notice something in this picture from the 2006–07 Sheffield Shield final at Bellerive Oval? I haven't got the gloves on, but I'm pretty happy in this moment. Damien Wright has just taken the last Blues wicket and Tasmania's won our first Sheffield Shield trophy. That's Michael Di Venuto with the ball in his hand after Wrighty trapped Doug Bollinger in front to seal our victory.

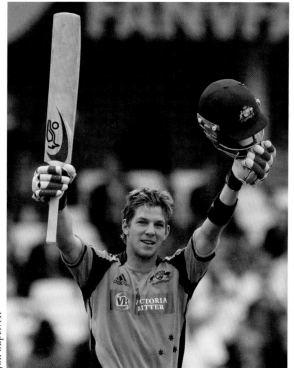

I get to raise the bat after bringing up my first century for Australia in a one-day international against England at Trent Bridge in 2007. It was just my seventh game but I had Mr Cricket, Michael Hussey, to guide me out in the middle.

Men like Ricky Ponting don't believe in the fist bump. Here he is giving me a solid handshake after I reached my half-century in the first ODI against India at the Reliance Stadium, Vadodara, in October 2009.

The huge moment when Ricky Ponting hands me my first baggy green cap ahead of the Test between Pakistan and Australia at Lord's in July 2010. I'm surrounded by legends: that's Steve Smith on my right, Simon Katich to my left, then fellow Tasmanian Troy Cooley, assistant coach Justin Langer and the great Shane Watson.

Steve Smith and me in front of the Lord's grandstand in our brand new baggy greens. I cannot believe how young we look in this picture and I cannot believe I was ahead of Smithy in the batting order.

An X-ray of my right index finger after surgery. This 2010 injury would plague my batting for years and keep me out of the national team until 2017. It still aches on a Tassie winter morning.

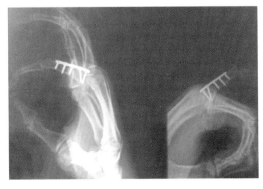

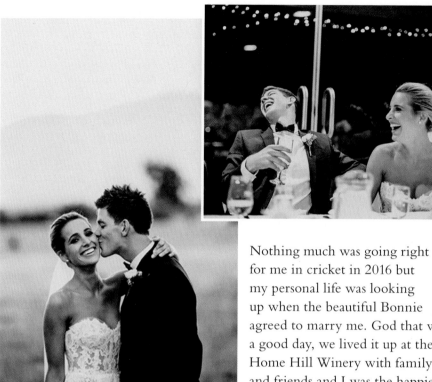

Nothing much was going right for me in cricket in 2016 but my personal life was looking up when the beautiful Bonnie agreed to marry me. God that was a good day, we lived it up at the Home Hill Winery with family and friends and I was the happiest man on the island.

Jono Searle/AAP Image

It's 2017 and I am playing my first Ashes series, a second chance at international cricket after nearly giving it all up. Usman Khawaja, a partially obscured Steve Smith, Dave Warner, Cameron Bancroft in the helmet and me coming around the back are pretty happy with Dave's catch to remove Jake Ball off the bowling of Mitchell Starc on the second day of the first Ashes Test at the Gabba.

Sarah Reed/Newspix

Joe Root was batting on day four of the second Ashes Test against England and I've pulled in a difficult catch high to my left off the bowling of Mitchell Starc. I'm convinced it is out, but the review shows it hit the top of his pad.

On Boxing Day in 2017 I snuck out of the dressing rooms and round to see my nan who was 90 years old. She had been there for all our junior football and cricket, parked in her car, armed with sandwiches and that special love grandmothers have. It meant a lot to have her there on that day.

Nikki Davis Jones/Newspix

After becoming Australian captain the level of interest from the media in me went up a level. Here's Bonnie, Milla and I posing in the garden for a magazine article in May 2018. This was a strange time as Australian cricket was still reeling from the sandpaper controversy and we weren't sure how the world would greet us the next time we played.

Penny Stephens/AAP Image

After the recriminations came the reviews and much of the winter of 2018 was spent working out a way forward for Australian cricket. On the day Cricket Australia published its Cultural Review, Josh Hazlewood and I presented a player review that we'd all worked on behind the scenes with the help of the Australian Cricketers' Association.

Sarah Reed Photography/Newspix

My first assignment as permanent Test captain was a battle for the Border–Gavaskar Trophy. Here's Virat Kohli and I sharing a picture opportunity ahead of the first Test in Adelaide in December 2018. The Indian captain is one of the most intense cricketers I've ever played against.

David Gray/AAP Image

We've won the series against the Sri Lankans at Manuka in February 2019 and the boys are pretty happy to put a trophy on the shelves and a long summer behind us. Kurtis Patterson (middle) had scored 114 not out in just his second and to this point last Test innings.

Our coach Justin Langer (right) loved getting legends from other sports around the team and it was pretty cool to catch up with Socceroos coach Graham Arnold (middle) at a nets session at Lord's in August 2019.

Marnus Labuschagne and I are convinced Jofra Archer had nicked the ball in this Test match at The Oval in 2019 but the umpire wasn't so sure and gave it not out. We reviewed and he was on his way soon after this moment.

We've just won the fourth Test at Old Trafford, Manchester and know we are now the first Australian team in 18 years to bring the Ashes home from England. You can tell from my elation that I'm pretty happy with the team's effort and they look pretty chuffed too.

Rui Vieira/AP

Kirsty Wigglesworth/AP

I get to hold the (replica) little urn aloft as the boys unleash the champagne after the fifth Ashes Test at The Oval in London, September 2019. We didn't win that Test, but if you've lost the battle yet won the war you get over it pretty quick.

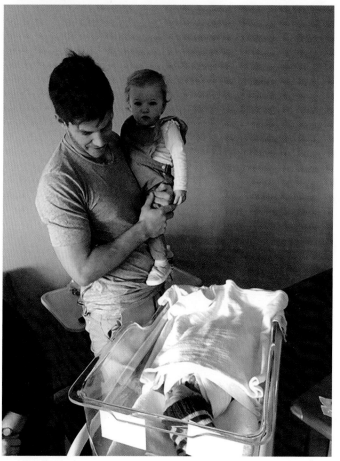

Cricketers spend a lot of time on the road and when the kids arrive that means a lot of one-on-one time in hotel rooms. Top left I'm feeding Milla while catching up on a bit of television, and that's me reading to her (right) in another hotel room in another town. And here's me introducing Milla to Charlie after his birth in September 2018.

I love this pic of Bonnie and Milla in the SCG change rooms in January 2018. It is an extraordinary place full of cricket memories and probably the one we all like best even though others are more modern and functional.

Bonnie holds the recently born Charlie and I've got Milla on the MCG that summer before the Boxing Day Test against India in December 2018.

I grew up with a cricket bat in my hand in Lauderdale and Charlie was pretty quick to pick one up too. This is him and me in the MCG change rooms in December 2019.

Dan Himbrechts/AAP Images

Being a cricketer means getting the best seats in the house and I was pumped to be out there when Marnus brought up his first Test double century against New Zealand at the SCG in January 2020.

Dave Hunt/AAP Image

I've just dropped India's Mayank Agarwal on day two of the first Test against India in Adelaide on 18 December 2020 and you can tell by the look on my face that it's not a good feeling. Worse was to come later in the series.

Cricket's full of rituals and I love getting out in the middle to inspect the wicket before the crowd arrives. Here's me and JL giving the pitch a once over before the fourth Test against India at the Gabba in January 2021, just over a year before he resigned as coach.

I tried to hold it together as I read a prepared statement about standing down from the captaincy to the media in November 2021, but when I got to the bit about family I started losing it.

Above: Four generations of my family in one pic. That's my 94-year-old nan with Charlie on her lap, I'm holding Milla and that's my lovely mum Sally on my left.

Left: Family holidays away from the game were rare and precious, this is the four of us in Noosa in early 2022 as we tried to find an escape from everything that had happened that summer and work out our way forward.

A throwback photo to me and Bonnie having a great time on the beach at Camps Bay, Cape Town in 2018, right around the time I became the 'accidental captain'. I count myself lucky to have shared the highs and lows of my life and my career with the woman I love, gorgeous on the outside and inside.

off and the light is okay, but there is a point where low light is dangerous. You only have to see what happened to Smith or Hughes to understand the consequences are quite serious if you can't pick up the ball properly. It still seems to me that the rule isn't applied consistently. If you are in the slips or even keeping, there is nothing worse than when the light reaches that point where you can't judge it – you can see the ball but you pick it up late and have to hold your nerve.

Wadey and I got out cheaply after Marnus and they had us six down with ten overs to play, but Pat Cummins and Travis Head were still there when the umpires finally pulled the pin and the game was saved. We had at least protected our 1–0 lead in the series.

We all assumed Smithy would be fine for the third Test at Leeds, but there was only a three-day break between games and he couldn't shake it off. He actually seemed to get worse as the time went on so we ruled him out pretty early. It was pretty disappointing to lose the best batsman in your side, probably the best batsman in the world, but Marnus was playing as well as anyone at that point. The way he batted at Lord's confirmed what we'd seen the whole time we'd been away. We weren't expecting him to do exactly as well as he did, but there was a sense we weren't set that far back. A bit of air was out of the tyres but not too much. The other thing was Davey Warner hadn't really got going yet so we were expecting him to make a bit more of a contribution with the bat. We had a problem with both openers misfiring and made the decision to drop Cam Bancroft.

Actually, do we have to talk about Headingley? It's not my favourite topic. Don't get me wrong, it was incredible to be part of that game, we were part of history, it's just that being on the wrong side of the ledger was a bit irritating.

England won the toss and bowled and it was horribly overcast and dark, the lights were on all day and the ball was doing heaps. Davey came good and contributed 61, he and Marnus got us to 2–130, but when they both fell we nosedived and were all out for 179 at the end of the day.

It wasn't much but Josh Hazlewood had a point to prove and his 5–39, along with Pat Cummins's 3–23 and James Pattinson's 2–9, saw them rolled for 67. Everything went right that second day. Joe Denly was their only batsman to reach double figures.

Marnus posted his third successive half-century in the next innings (run out for 80!) and they had to chase 329 to win. We had them on toast, but I just thought that we'd left the door slightly ajar by not getting a 350 lead. There was a moment there where we could have been more ruthless. Having said that, Ben Stokes had bowled his heart out and restricted us to what was a good lead but not a crushing one. The wicket was not difficult, but the movement was in the air and that last day the sun was out.

Stokes was incredible with the bat but he made an impression with the ball when all seemed lost. He bowled and bowled and bowled again in our second innings. When they brought Jofra on to give him a break, the quick got cramp halfway through the first over and so Stokes got the ball back and kept going. It was an unbelievable effort. Wadey and I were waiting to go in and we were sitting there, saying, 'This has to be his last over,' and that was at about seven overs in. He basically bowled 24 overs straight. He got the wickets of Head and Wade which stopped us closing out the game.

Then Ben came out and batted and batted and batted. And batted a bit more. He'd played a terrible stroke first innings, but knuckled down early in his second. He hardly scored a run for a long time, but when he got going his momentum was unstoppable.

Ben Stokes is different – he's a Kiwi, for a start. On the field he's a genuine competitor. Stuart Broad and James Anderson have that attitude too, they just keep coming, they don't stop or give up even when you are on top of the game, they don't give you an easy run, they don't stop competing. We could be miles ahead in a Test match, and have been a few times in Australia, but Anderson and Broad would just keep coming like Stokes did that day. Whenever they've got the ball in hand, it is total effort and they have huge skills so when you put that package together, it's fearsome. Stokes is the same but he does it with bat and ball.

Still, when we removed Chris Woakes and Stuart Broad, we had them 9–286 and all we had to do was knock over Jack Leach. We had 17 balls at Leach, but couldn't get him out. I was putting the field back to give Stokes the single, but I made some mistakes and they put on 74 together to win the game.

I got a lot of criticism for my tactics that day but there's not a heap I would change. There were probably a few times where I should have brought the field up a ball earlier but Ben was hitting everything for four and I didn't want to make it any easier for him. If I brought them up, he hit them for four; if I left them back, he hit them for four. Yes, I would make a couple of different decisions but that was only a few balls. That field and that philosophy have been used hundreds of times, but that day it didn't work. Stokes had a day out.

We should have had that last wicket when Pat Cummins threw to Nathan Lyon and Leach was short of his crease after a mix-up, but Gaz didn't take the ball cleanly. It was a perfect throw from Cummo and I saw it going into Gaz's hands. They were both at the wrong end and on the replay you can see me running down the pitch with my arms in the air in celebration as the ball is returned. Gaz is usually as clean as clean in the field. He has beautiful hands.

And the throw couldn't have been any better. It was just one of those moments, what can you say?

The next ball Nathan trapped Stokes dead in front, but the umpire gave him not out. We had no reviews left. I still really struggle with the umpire's match awareness in that situation. It was out, but even if you didn't think so you had to at least concede it was extremely close. With a Test match on the line, the umpire has to have the awareness that we have no reviews left and they do. Joel should have given him out even if he had a bit of doubt because England were in position to call for a review and if he was wrong then it would be overturned and no harm done. You want the right decision for the good of the game. It was hitting middle stump halfway up. The error was frustrating, it cost us the Test match, but I've dropped catches, I've played bad shots, we all make mistakes under pressure. The thing is, as a player, I don't have the luxury of falling back on technology to compensate for my mistake, an umpire does.

An over earlier a catch had just eluded Marcus Harris, so we'd created three opportunities to win the match but hadn't got there. They won the game four balls after the lbw was turned down. It still makes me sad now, it still makes me want to kick a rubbish bin. If we had won we would have broken their spirits completely, but they came to Manchester still in the series.

Nathan fell to the ground when Stokes hit the winning runs and I walked over to him and pulled him up. I'd gone straight into captain mode and was thinking about how to deal with this. We were all devastated but we couldn't let that consume us. It was one game, we couldn't let it destroy us no matter how rotten it was to be on the wrong side of it.

JL had kicked the bin over in the coaches' box, but he was really good with us. He went around the boys, saying, 'Bad luck, you tried your guts out.'

I came out of the shower and could see that the boys weren't in a good place and I knew I had to talk to them. I remember I said that even though we'd lost the match, I honestly thought at that point we were a better team than them, we had them covered, even in their conditions. I reminded them that for four days we controlled that Test. It took a once-in-a-lifetime effort from one bloke to drag them over the line. Yes, we made a few errors but on the whole we'd played 13 days of Test cricket and we'd been in control of most of them. It was disappointing but we had to understand that this was a big series, it wasn't one Test, and we needed to keep playing.

That said, I struggled to sleep that night. I felt physically sick, I've never felt anything like it. It was such a big series, such a big moment. I was frustrated and playing it over and over in my head a million times. The catch. The review. The run-out. The fields. I felt like crap the next morning and even worse when JL announced that we were going to review the match. It was the last thing any of us wanted to do and some in the room struggled to even look at the replays.

However, when we left that room, it was like I'd been unburdened of some guilt or something. I got it off my chest that I'd made a mistake about the fields. I think everybody felt the same relief. We all headed across for breakfast and the mood had changed considerably.

The boys got around Nathan who was pretty quiet. He takes things hard. He is not a vocal person on the field, but you can read his body language. He was a real barometer for us even though he didn't say much. If Gaz was up and about, we were up and about – we could give him the ball and he would change a game for us, or he would take a great catch, pull off a good bit of fielding. But if we saw him a bit down, it had the opposite effect. I remember talking to him later and saying I didn't think he realised how important he was to the group's confidence. I wanted to make sure that when we got back to training he was ready to fire.

We headed up to Derby to chill out and play a tour game before coming back for the fourth Test at Manchester. On the practice day Cam Bancroft, who'd used his time off while suspended to become a yoga instructor, took us for a class to kick things off and we played a game of touch footy which was a good way to blow off some steam.

Brad Haddin, who was an assistant coach and a close ally through this period, had to leave us in the middle of the night after getting a call to say his daughter Mia had been admitted to hospital. That helped put things into perspective too. Losing a Test was nothing like what he was going through with a sick child.

After a break in Derby we felt refreshed and headed to Manchester for the fourth Test. Home of Manchester United and Manchester City. I was loving the tour and loving England. I could very easily live there. I love the small villages and the big cities. And the weather's not that different to Hobart. I love that the English are fanatical about their sport; their football, their cricket, their darts, they just love it all and I am like that. You have big teams around the corner in every town in England. In London you've got Chelsea, Tottenham, Lord's and The Oval. The best sporting brands, the best sportsmen in the world, right on your doorstep, I find that fascinating. In Notts you've got two football teams and the cricket.

In a strange way I really enjoyed the people who showed up to abuse us too – I respect their passion and their ability to go hard all day from first ball to last. I even loved it when the Barmy Army was giving it to us on the field. I'd be batting or wicketkeeping and thinking, 'I can't believe I am here experiencing this.' For years I'd watched them going nuts on television and now I was living it. When the Barmy Army is chanting your name it's surreal, it's almost like you've entered your television or you're living out your dream, which I guess I was.

In Sydney, at the end of the previous Ashes, our team went over to the stands and clapped the Barmy Army. They'd been there for five Tests without anything to cheer about, but they'd sung their songs and abused us all day every day, and as a player you love that atmosphere and in the end they showed us some respect and we gave it back. During the COVID-19 lockdowns, we played with no crowds and it was horrendous, soulless, you just want a bit of spirit out there.

The biggest surprise when we got to Manchester was the wicket. I had thought on the way there that England would juice up the pitch to bring their bowlers back into the series, but we got there and it was flat as flat. We left Peter Siddle out and brought Mitchell Starc in for James Pattinson. We wanted that extra speed and the left-armer's footmarks would give Nathan Lyon something to aim at when it broke up. That paid off towards the end of the game when he picked up Joe Denly and Jofra Archer.

The Test was packed and it was loud. We won the toss which got us off on the right foot as it looked like a good wicket to bat on. The big inclusion for us was Steve Smith. For the first time we'd have him and Marnus in the side together. We lost Dave Warner and Marcus Harris early, then those two came together and we were away. Marnus was out for 67 but Steve had another point to prove. I'm not sure I've seen a batter in better form than he was that series and it is worth noting that we hadn't won either game that he'd been absent from.

Smithy made up for lost time and scored a double century and we got to declare on 8–497. How well was he going? In four innings he had scores of 144, 142, 92 and 211. He followed up with an 82 in the second innings and we won the game easily. Jofra still hadn't got him out. They persisted on bowling short, but he was fine with that as it took his stumps out of the equation. They could do it all day as far as he was concerned.

It was a sweet victory, it was a complete game of cricket, we played very well and it was a win off a shattering loss, people forget that. It was impressive without the context, but it was even better given what had happened in the week before in a game we should have won. A lot of teams would have broken after Headingley but we bounced back and played brilliantly. I knew we were a better team than them.

And, of course, we'd retained the Ashes. We'd done good.

We celebrated that night, but we kept a lid on it. I didn't drink much because there was still work to do and the others were too professional to get carried away.

At The Oval in the fifth Test we made mistakes and a lot of people will say that one of them was to put England in when I won the toss. JL was saying that morning that we should definitely bat, but I wasn't sure, I really didn't know. I always ask the team what they think we should do, I'm making a decision for the batsmen and bowlers, not for me. The overwhelming feedback was to bowl. If your best batsmen say they reckon we should bowl, you listen because if they don't want to bat then it's best not to ask them to and you can be sure the other side's openers feel exactly the same way.

The conditions were overcast and the wicket was doing plenty, but we didn't bowl at our best and we were awful in the field. It didn't help that Pete Siddle strained a muscle three balls into his first over of the game. It doesn't matter what you do first in a game if you don't do it well. People get stuck on the toss as the reason we lost, that's what the hindsight specialists say, but what if we'd won the toss and batted as poorly as we caught and bowled? What if we were bowled out for 25? You just don't know but what I do know is that we bowled poorly and caught poorly. That's what people should focus on.

Did I mention we lost the game? It was a little deflating to end like that, but as I said, we'd done something a lot of very good Australian teams had failed to do and we got over our disappointment pretty quickly. We were exhausted but we were all happy with what we'd achieved. The Ashes were coming home with us. We were the first team since Steve Waugh's in 2001 to do that.

★

People talk about the 2005 series as one of the great contests and it was, but I reckon 2019 was up there. Sure, it didn't have Warne, Ponting, McGrath, Flintoff or Pietersen, but it had some very, very good cricketers and the quality of the cricket was equal to that series. The 2019 series had Jofra, Broad, Anderson, Stokes, Root, Smith, Lyon, Cummins and Hazlewood. They were all-time greats and Marnus Labuschagne was on his way to being one.

JL was cranky the day after the Test. We were told to be in the team room at 11 am and we all turned up in our casual clothes because we'd been on tour for months and we just wanted to go and have a beer as a group before heading our separate ways. We thought it was going to be a quick debrief about flights and checking out of the hotel but nah, the first thing that happened was we were kept waiting for 45 minutes while the staff finished their meeting and we were pretty cranky about that and then they came in and told us what we didn't do well in that game. There is a time and place for that, but it wasn't then. It should have been a focus on the positives, about the strides we'd made, that no one thought we were any good and yet we did what other teams hadn't achieved, but they wanted to focus on the negatives.

We finally went to the pub and it was great to sit together and have a beer, but I didn't get on it because I had to go and have an X-ray on my right ring finger which I'd broken in Manchester. It was only a small fracture and it wasn't displaced but I had to get it checked out because the next day I was going to France with Bonnie and the kids. It takes a while to wind down from a tour like that, but we holed up in little village called Eygalières. Apparently Hugh Grant had a house next to us but we didn't see him when we were there. I bet he was ducking me because he didn't want to talk about the Ashes.

12

GROUNDED

The summer of 2019–20 was the first time we got to play at home after getting the band back together. Dave Warner and Steve Smith were with us and ready to play their first Test matches in Australia since their bans, we had a full strength bowling line-up and Pakistan were due for two Tests in our backyard before New Zealand came across the ditch.

It was going to be a very different prospect for Pakistan to the one they'd faced when we took them on in the UAE a little over 12 months ago. We were a new-look team and we were in good form.

We'd got some experience into our younger batsmen. Smithy was flying, but Warner was coming off a nightmare in England. Stuart Broad had his number and he'd posted scores of 2, 8, 3, 5, 61, 0, 0, 0, 5, 11. Most people would let that get to them, but Bull is made of tougher stuff than that and the way he handled himself is a mark of the sort of person he is. Players who let their poor form affect their mood can be a real liability on a tour. David Warner is not one of those. He does whatever he is asked to do and in that situation he kept turning up as if there was nothing wrong. You would never know that he was being tormented by Broad, never know that he was getting knocked over for fun. He kept that smile on his face, he kept his energy up on the field, on the bus and around the group. He caught brilliantly at Headingley. He is an amazing character and the ultimate team man.

There were, naturally, questions about his place in the side before the summer started. People wondered if he had lost it in the year off. I knew he hadn't. I'd seen him in the nets, he'd lost nothing. I'd also seen what he'd faced in England, he'd been on the end of some brilliant bowling from Broad that was uniquely challenging to him as a left-hander. In England the bounce isn't great and he had to play at the ball on or about off stump, in Australia he could let that go. Broady had him cornered and Bull admitted it. He couldn't find a way to deal with that delivery, but there was no way he wasn't going to play in our home summer.

Pakistan, like Sri Lanka the summer before, won the toss in Brisbane and chose to bat. It's always wise to do that, but you have to have the batters to cope with the seam and bounce which is most pronounced early in the game. It gets easier to bat as the Test goes on, in fact it can start getting easier after the first session, but you have to survive that tough early going. They did the brave thing but it cost them. Our seamers tore through their line-up and they were out for 240 just before stumps.

Day two and three were good for batting and our boys made the most if it. We were 1–222 when Joe Burns was out for 97. When Warner was out for 154 we were 2–351. Dave scored more runs and faced more balls in that innings than in the entire Ashes. That put to rest any question about his form and a few people had to eat their words.

Marnus had been brilliant in the Ashes but was yet to make a Test hundred. Now his time had come. He was in total control on his home ground and was 185 when he was finally dismissed. We posted 580 runs in our first innings to take a massive lead. Babar Azam, who is a great cricketer, got a century when they batted again but we won by an innings and five runs with a day to spare.

Bull was just warming up and when we batted first in Adelaide he smoked them again. He was 334 not out when I declared the innings closed at 3–589. Marnus got himself another century to add to the first one in Brisbane. Bull was reminding us how good he was, while Marnus was starting to show us how good he could be and was taking his game to the next level. Pakistan had nothing against our quicks. Mitch Starc took 6–66 and Pat Cummins picked up three wickets. Babar got 97 and Yasir Shah an entertaining century but I enforced the follow-on and we won by an innings again.

We'd won the series 2–0 and that was a nice way to start the summer.

When Pakistan left, New Zealand arrived amid a wave of publicity about how good they were going and how this was going to be a real contest. They'd only lost one of their past ten series and had just beaten England at home and were riding high, but I was confused by people saying they were going to be competitive, I couldn't see that. They were good at home and had thrived in the UK, which suits their bowling, but I didn't think they had the attack for Australian conditions, where you don't get that seam or swing. Man for man I thought we were a much better cricket team.

I told the team that all we had to do was match them in the things they do well, which is be disciplined and patient, and be absolutely team first. If we could match them, I said, they did not have the calibre of player to stay with us. The skill level and the pace in our attack is too much for them. Their bowlers are okay and have good plans, but if our batting group could remain patient in our conditions we'd clean them up. To me that was literally what the tour was about: check your ego at the door, be patient, be disciplined.

New Zealand were hoping we'd get arrogant and do something silly. Their Plan B was to drop short and put fielders back, all we had to do was ride that out.

The first Test was a day–night game at the Perth stadium which is pretty cool in the evening. We won the toss, Marnus peeled off another hundred, Travis got a half-century, a few others contributed and I wasn't unhappy with a total of 416. New Zealand withered at the first sight of our pace attack. Starcy got Tom Latham with the fifth ball of their innings and Josh got Jeet Raval next over. They were 2–1 and even though Josh limped off with a hamstring strain eight balls into his work, Starcy went on and took 5–52 to have them all out for 166. He backed up with four more wickets in their second innings to win the Test for us and the Man of the Match award.

Travis Head got the prize in Melbourne for a century in the first inning which set us up. Our attack was just too good for them and Pat's 5–28 kept New Zealand to 148 when they batted which let us declare five down and almost 500 in front. Blundell scored a hundred for them but this time James Pattinson and Nathan cleaned them up and we won by 247 runs.

In Sydney Marnus got his first Test 200, then Davey added another century in our second innings. We won the series 3–0. Marnus won player of the match for scores of 215 and 59 and player of the series for his 549 runs.

Apart from the form of our batters, the best thing about the series was Neil Wagner bowling at our bodies in an attempt to slow down our batters. He was brilliant. In the first Test Graeme Hick was saying, 'Just duck him for an hour and he won't come back,' but he just kept coming back. He was the one bloke who never gave up. His stamina was enormous. Bowling short is bloody hard work, but he did it ball after ball after ball. If he hit you he'd follow up with a few words, but it was all pretty respectful.

It was a great contest because all our batters were in good form. But Wagner just kept coming and he was so accurate, every delivery was aimed somewhere between your shoulder and your belly button. He couldn't be called for short bowling because he rarely got it above shoulder height. It slowed Smithy down, but it played into my hands because my favourite shot is the pull or hook and I much prefer blokes bowling short than aiming at my stumps. I was laughing between overs, saying to whoever was with me, 'If he pitches one up I'm gone here.'

Wagner and Wadey had a great battle, it was fun to watch and they're both pretty similar so they were right into it. Wadey was just wearing blows on the body, sometimes he was dropping his shoulder into the ball like he was playing footy, but you'd see them share a little glove punch at the end of overs. It was a case of two hard men sharing some respect.

We were playing high level cricket, our bowlers were on fire. If Pat Cummins or Mitch Starc didn't get you, Nathan Lyon or James Pattinson would. And to think that we had Josh Hazlewood injured on the sidelines. That's as good a bowling cartel as any in the world. When you think that guys of the calibre of Michael Neser, Jhye Richardson and Scott Boland – to name a few – couldn't get a start, you realise the depth we were developing.

Two years later in 2021 New Zealand beat India to win the inaugural World Test Championship. You couldn't begrudge them that, but it was a bit annoying that a side we'd beaten by 296, 247 and 275 runs took the trophy. We missed out on the final because match referee David Boon penalised us for our over rates against India at the MCG in 2020 in a game where it finished 13 overs into India's second innings on day four. We would have bowled Nathan Lyon the next two hours if necessary and made up the time, but they chased down the runs and the game was over. It should have been a fine, but it literally cost us a place in the World Test Championship final.

Our disappointment aside it was pretty cool that the Kiwis got the first trophy.

★

The year 2020 was frustrating for everybody and I was no exception. I'd nursed a busted finger through the prime of my cricketing years and now my second chance was on hold because of a pandemic. The world had changed overnight. The first game against New Zealand in the ODI series was playing in front of empty stands at the SCG and the next thing you knew everything shut down. I was turning 36, time was ticking by and like so many others I was doing nothing. At my age all I wanted to do was play. I was asked about this a lot in the media, but played it down in much the same way as most people, trying to put on a brave face while getting a grip on the situation we were in. After all, it was only cricket and things were a lot, lot worse for many.

It was a year of uncertainty and there was enormous relief when India finally arrived in Australia for the Border–Gavaskar Trophy series. There was a lot of conjecture about them coming and a lot of last-minute changes to their entry point as state governments got cold feet. For some reason there were only four Tests planned for the summer, but we were keen to make amends for the loss in 2018–19 and desperate to get out and play some bloody cricket.

We had a major problem at the start of the series with Dave Warner ruled unfit after hurting his groin during the white ball series in the lead-up. That was a significant blow and there was a lot of to and fro about who should open in his place. Joe Burns was in the squad and so was Will Pucovski but then Will got concussed in the tour game at Drummoyne and he was ruled out. Will would have played if he'd been fit so we were down two first-choice openers. Marcus Harris, who'd been part of a 486-run partnership with Will against South Australia, was brought into the squad but in the end we didn't play him.

It was decided that Travis Head would bat in the middle order along with the as-yet uncapped Cam Green as all-rounder so that meant we had to manufacture someone to hold the opening spot until Davey came good. At first we thought he'd only be out for one game so I would do the job as I had early in my first-class career, but then when it became likely he could be away for three matches it was decided opening was too much work for me and so they gave the job to Matthew Wade.

Cam Green was one of the most exciting prospects in Australian cricket. I remember watching his first Shield game against Tassie in February 2017. He was this hulking 17-year-old who bowled fast and got some serious bounce from his height. He took 5–24 in the first innings and we were stunned, but the kids in the side were telling us he could bat too, which got a few chortles from the old blokes who said nobody that big and that fast can hold a bat. At that point he was playing mainly as a bowler. Man, were we wrong. He is a serious talent and he proved it when he hurt his back later on and peeled off first-class

centuries playing as a specialist batsman. I played with him
in the Australia A game before the Test and was really
blown away by his temperament. He is measured, calm
and just looks like he belongs.

So we started in Adelaide with Matty Wade and Joe
Burns opening, Travis Head in the middle order and Cam
Green on debut. We blitzed them, but it was nowhere near
as easy as it looked on the scorecard. India were doing
well on the first day with Virat Kohli moving on to 74
and the score 3–188 when there was a mix-up and he was
run out. It was a huge wicket given the lights were on and
the new ball was due in a couple of overs. The hardest
thing to do in a day–nighter at Adelaide is face the new
ball. Mitch Starc took it when it became available and
knocked over Ajinkya Rahane who was also set and then
Josh Hazlewood, who'd run out Virat, got Hanuma Vihari.
They lost 7–56 and were all out for 244 when they could
have really made life hard for us.

On the previous tour India had shown up with a
top-class bowling line-up for what I thought was the first
time in the recent history of touring Australia. This time
they had an even better stable but we weren't to know how
deep it ran and how good they really were just yet. Their
seamers Umesh Yadav, Jasprit Bumrah and Mohammad
Shami were well supported by Ravi Ashwin in our first
innings and if I hadn't made 73 not out we would have
been in even more trouble than we were. They bowled us

out for 191 without needing any assistance from a second new ball.

I remember turning up to the third day and thinking we had a real fight on our hands to get back into this Test. Then we bowled them out for 36. We just had the perfect day. Josh took 5–8 from five overs and Pat Cummins 4–21. It was one of those days where the ball found the edge of the bat time and again. Sometimes the opposition play and miss all day, other times they get the edge and it falls short, or lands wide of the slips. Everything went right for us and wrong for them. Not one of their batsmen made double figures and we had chased down their total by the early afternoon. The Test was over with two and a bit days to spare.

It was a stunning turnaround. The bad thing for them was that Mohammad Sami had his arm broken in the second innings and he was on a plane for home. Joining him was Virat who was going back to India for the birth of his first child. People were writing them off, but I wasn't so sure, our batting had not been great and their second innings was so bad it was one of those aberrations that you can't take seriously.

So we went off to Melbourne but there was this annoying background noise that just wouldn't go away. We were playing in bubbles and there were all sorts of unknowns about how the tour would proceed and the whole issue seemed to be sucking a lot of attention away from the cricket.

With Virat gone, Ajinkya Rahane stepped up and it was interesting. The team seemed to respond to his leadership really well. From the outside it seems Virat can get really emotional, maybe he is calm with his teammates, but it looks like he gets caught up with the emotions of the game. Rahane has very calm body language and the side seemed to all step up a bit under his leadership – which isn't to say they weren't responding to Virat.

We batted first in Melbourne and were bowled for 195 which was very, very disappointing. Nobody got to 50, Jasprit Bumrah was all over us and then Rahane got a hundred when they batted and we were a long way behind. We got to 200 in the second innings which meant we had handed them the game and they won it in a canter. Our batting was disappointing and at points when our bowlers threatened to get us back into the game we put down catches, so it was all a bit deflating.

After Adelaide they'd brought in Ravi Jadeja and given debuts to batter Shubman Gill and seamer Mohammed Siraj, as well as replacing Wriddhiman Saha with Rishabh Pant. Siraj wasn't fast but he was seriously talented. He'd done well in the IPL, he had these subtle adjustments and could swing it both ways. He could bowl all day and he was always competitive. They were building up a good bank of quicks and had some real depth there which it turned out they needed. They kept getting injuries through the series but the blokes they brought in were ready to go.

As an aside, we couldn't believe it when they went with Wriddhi in the first Test when it seemed a no-brainer to give Rishabh a go with the gloves. As a batter he is one of those cricketers who can change a match in an hour. He didn't get going in Melbourne, but he is one of those players who is always a threat to the opposition.

Scoring runs was really hard work against their line-up. Ashwin bowled beautifully in Melbourne, he controlled one end and allowed their seamers to keep rotating at the other. Bumrah was always at you and even when our batters were getting starts they weren't going on because they were always being tested. The bowling was relentless. The year before, New Zealand and Pakistan's bowlers could test you but if you were patient you'd get on top of them eventually. We never got that second wind with India.

Christmas was a mess, some families flew in, some didn't. Bonnie and the kids went home early because they were scared of getting locked out of the state and everyone was in a fog of anxiety or confusion. The world was going through the same thing and a lot of people were separated from their loved ones at that time so we couldn't complain, but on reflection we let those things start to get to us. There was a constant background noise with all sorts of things floating around. State government regulations around borders and restrictions were changing all the time.

Some in the group became distracted by the uncertainty. Support staff were running around preparing for this contingency or that one. There were meetings going on all the time. We didn't know where we were going after Melbourne so we stayed there rather than go to Sydney. The Indians were putting it in the media that they didn't want to go to Brisbane or Sydney and we thought that was probably because they didn't want to play at the Gabba. There was talk we'd play back-to-back Tests in Melbourne and rumours that the Indians would go home if quarantine restrictions changed. Our executives and board were dealing with theirs to keep the series going. There was a lot of stuff going on that wasn't cricket.

So we just sat and waited until it got worked out. Their players were bending the rules and sometimes blatantly breaking them. You'd see people coming and going from the hotel, there were pictures of their players out at shopping centres, all sorts of things, which started to annoy us because we were the hosts and had to be on our best behaviour. We stayed locked on our floor and did the right thing while they seemed to do whatever they liked.

Eventually India conceded to playing at the SCG and the Gabba and so we finally left Melbourne.

In Sydney we allowed them to get under our skin even more and I was probably one of the worst culprits on that front. We dropped Joe Burns and Travis Head to bring in Dave Warner and Will Pucovski. We batted first and at least posted a score above 300 – thanks to our first century of the series courtesy of Steve Smith. Pucovski is a rare talent but injury and mental health problems had stopped him making that next step. His 62 at the top of the order confirmed he had the game for this level. Marnus got to 91, but we should have got a lot more runs. We kind of threw it away a bit when we were set.

Still, we made the running in that game and set them 407 to win with well over a day to play. With three hours left they were 5–272 and we just had to close the deal. They were trying to drag it out for a draw and are very good at bending the rules. If there was a Test match championship for time wasting, India would play every time. If someone got hit they'd stop play for five minutes, and lots of people got hit. They were always calling for new gloves, the magic spray and drinks. The physio was on the ground all day. The umpires just couldn't control the match. It became a total farce when Ashwin joined Vihari and the pair decided they'd swap chest guards at the end of each over. You can't tell me that there weren't two chest guards in the dressing rooms and even if there weren't, that's bad luck. It's not kid's cricket. At that point match officials have to take control of the game, but nobody did anything and they hung on for a draw.

Our biggest problem, however, was me. I grassed three catches in what was my worst day ever on the international stage. I let the team down, in particular Nathan Lyon, and I can only put it down to letting the situation get to me. By this point I was playing angry and I do not play my best cricket when I'm angry. When Ashwin had a go at me, I told him that at least my teammates didn't think I was a dickhead and another time I taunted him about playing in Brisbane because I knew he would not like our quicks up there. He didn't get there, but that's not the point. I shouldn't have been doing those things but I was doing it because I'd lost perspective. It was poor of me.

I walked off, thinking, 'I've cost us this game,' and that felt horrible. I was mentally cooked which was not good, but after a few hours I put it behind me and resolved to do better at the Gabba.

I thought we controlled most of the third Test and when we got to Brisbane I thought we controlled that game too, but they pulled one out of the bag. Again we batted well enough in the first innings, but we left runs out there and the same thing happened on day four. We batted well in our second innings and again we should have closed them out of the game. There was, however, the weather as a factor. We knew there was big storm coming so we were conscious of that when we were batting (and we did lose the whole last session). We wanted to take the risk to give us a chance to win the game and the series.

India had to make 328 to win and somehow they did it. On reflection we made a mistake by sticking with an unchanged pace attack in that Test. The seamers had all done well in the first three games and I reckon they still bowled well in the last too but an injection of fresh blood would have helped. In the bowlers' defence I have to admit that they were let down by our fielding. I think maybe if we had a fresh quick in that mix we might have created more chances, but no blame can be placed on any of the guys that played.

So we'd lost two Border–Gavaskar series and that felt horrible. The whole country was all over us, and the hardest thing for me was that we'd completely controlled the Sydney Test and then most of the Brisbane Test. To make matters worse, it was my fault that we hadn't won at the SCG. We should have won those last two matches. India kept hanging in which is the sign of a very good side when they are away from home. It was a hard loss to take. It's one thing to be beaten by a side that's significantly better than you, but we could have won that series. Should have. But didn't.

You move on and we were keen to get to South Africa for the next series as soon as we could but without us being consulted it was cancelled. That really hurt because I was itching to go and so were a lot of the players, but again COVID-19 had intervened and we were sent home to count off the days on the calendar until England arrived next summer. It was going to be a long wait, but this series was going to be very special.

Playing an Ashes at home would complete the cycle for me. I'd been called back in from the wilderness for the 2017–18 series, called up as captain by the time the 2019 series came around and now we were about to play at home again in 2021–22. Despite losing to India I knew this team was as good as any in the world and there is no greater honour than captaining your side in an Ashes series at home.

Australian cricket was entering a sweet spot and while I'd always said I was taking things one series at a time, I was in a really good place with my game. I still loved the job behind the stumps and despite a bad day in Sydney I was still at the top of my game with the gloves on. My batting was proving to be a bonus. I'd averaged 48 in that first Ashes at home, 43 against South Africa, 45 against Sri Lanka, 38 against New Zealand and 40 in the summer against India. More importantly I had worked out a method and rid myself of the demons that held me back during the bad years.

I said to people I might retire at the end of the Ashes but teased them by adding I was just as likely to keep going. I was in no hurry to give up this caper. It's all very well to walk away when you are on top if you have had a long fulfilling career, but I'd really only had a few years in the team. I was fit, I was performing and I had nothing else to do, so this party could go on forever.

THE PRICE PAID

We had had a rough loss against India, but I went into that winter hungry for another crack at England and determined to hold up that Ashes trophy on the dais.

13

UNDER PRESSURE

There are always recriminations when you lose and a lot of people had me squarely in their sights, but within the camp there was an unhappiness that just wouldn't go away no matter how hard I tried to work it out.

In the next twelve months Justin Langer would coach the team to World Cup and Ashes victories, but it still wasn't good enough for some and he left the job in sensational circumstances.

It was an extremely disappointing result.

I watched the lead-up to this in my last year as captain, no issue consumed me like this one did, and nobody will stop me believing JL was very, very poorly treated. Take the outcome out of it, that's not the point, the way that situation was managed was a disgrace, but not a surprise. A man tasked with rebuilding Australian cricket's reputation was hung out to dry.

I'll tell you two stories about JL to set the scene.

The first followed a chat I gave to the team after we'd been beaten by India in Brisbane and lost the series. We were all a bit burnt out by a stressful summer dodging the pandemic and were all feeling flat about the result I said to the boys, 'It has been a tough series and the bubble tested everyone, but we had a crack, it was disappointing because we had control in the last two Tests but couldn't get the result we were after.' At the end I said, 'We'll get another crack at it, so go home, dust yourselves off, have a bit of time out,' and then I added something like, 'At the end of the day it is not life or death, it's cricket, it's sport, it's a game.' Sometimes you have to remind yourself of that.

Later that night JL came over to me with those burning eyes and said, 'Don't you ever fucking say that again, it is not just a fucking game at this level.' I could feel the heat generating from him, it had been eating away at him. He was having none of it and he'd got himself really worked up over it. I said, 'Well, we are just going to have to learn to disagree, it is a game, that's what I think.'

He grumbled and cursed but we got on with it.

I love that side of him. He hated it if we had a loss and then blokes were having a laugh a few hours later, but that's the way it is these days. It annoys me sometimes at state cricket when young blokes don't seem to care about a loss as much I think they should, but you have to let it go and worry about getting them to play better cricket next game. Sulking and being in a shit mood is not going to help 90 per cent of the players so I am not going to do it.

The other story about JL was in November on the eve of the 2021–22 Ashes. JL and the T20 squad had arrived back from the World Cup and been locked up in quarantine for two weeks in Queensland. I'd stepped down from the captaincy soon after they arrived. As soon as JL finished quarantine, he got on a plane and flew to Hobart to see how I was.

He hadn't and wouldn't be home for months. He had an Ashes series to prepare for, he had not been able to get outside of the hotel for two weeks except for brief training sessions, but his highest priority was someone else in trouble. Me.

We snuck down to the corner of a local restaurant. I hid with my cap pulled down and my eyes rarely leaving our personal space. JL is such a passionate guy, he talks about 'people first' and he walks it too. He loves every one of his players whether they love him or not. He could be the grumpiest little bugger in the world at times, fuming over some minor matter, but the minute he knew you had problems he was there for you and his commitment was unconditional.

JL and I go way back. I remember playing against him in my first Shield matches in 2006. I looked and felt like a 12-year-old, he was this hardened professional who had a no-nonsense aura about him. I don't know if I have seen anyone take the game more seriously than he did. I respected him for that. It really mattered to him. Even then I looked up to him and tried to learn from him.

Later, when JL was batting coach, we got close when I was the back-up keeper to Brad Haddin. I'd do my gym with him in the morning, have breakfast with him and then he'd come to the ground to give me some batting practice so that I was out of the way by the time the team arrived. During the World Cup in India and Sri Lanka, JL and I would do our weights at 6 am and then get a car down to the ground to have a hit and be in the change rooms by the time the others arrived. After he went back to coach Western Australia we stayed in touch, because by then we'd forged a strong bond.

When he was appointed to the Australian job in 2018, it was easier for us because we had already connected. We both had to work on the captain and coach part, but the strong relationship we have means we could work things out when we had different opinions.

When I had my first go as captain in Tasmania, I tried to control everything and that was no good because it meant I couldn't have a good relationship with the players and it wore me out. I was doing things that would suit me or

I would get angry when blokes would do the wrong thing because I thought it made me look bad. When I became Australian captain, I wanted to do it completely differently, I wanted to have good relationships with the players, be inclusive, be open to other people's ideas and try to make the best decision for the team. Unlike my Tassie stint when I had no empathy for that sort of stuff, I wanted to make everything about the team.

I think the coach–captain dynamic worked pretty well for JL and me. If we disagreed on something, we would land somewhere in the middle and both support each other. We clashed occasionally but it was never anything major. Sometimes in that environment it doesn't have to be major for things to get a bit heated or lead to a few words, but we are pretty similar in that we let it go pretty quickly. Well, I move on quick, he holds on a bit longer before letting go. Things were usually settled by a civilised chat over coffee where we put our cases forward.

So JL took the lead when he was appointed coach and I concentrated on my own corner. I loved his disciplined, old-school approach to cricket. He was a hard taskmaster who expected a lot, but I respond well to those sorts of leaders.

A lot of people got the impression from watching the Amazon documentary about the team that he had a poor relationship with Usman Khawaja after they saw two exchanges, one at training and another after the

Melbourne Test. You can see JL is fuming as Usi gives it to him straight, he never liked hearing that stuff, but he'd get over it in a couple of hours, circle back to you as if to say that he had taken it on board and he respected you more for saying it.

I had a look at that exchange in the documentary the other day. It was at the MCG after we'd lost to India in 2018 and the players went off to one room to chat about what was going wrong. I was expected to bring some feedback to the coaches, you see me skirting around the topic a bit before I say, 'I know that you won't agree but they feel that they want just a little bit more positivity.' Pat Cummins says in an interview after the event that, 'The batsmen at times found it hard to relax,' and there was some truth to that. JL then gets us all together and Usman says, 'I think the boys are intimidated by you, Alf, walking on eggshells sort of thing . . . the boys are afraid to say it.'

He asked and Usman told him. For the record, Usi is one of the players fondest of JL.

I think the MCG meetings were a feeling out process, there was a bit of grumbling there, but that's not a bit deal, you have that all the time about any coach. The truth about that summer is that there was a lot of inexperience, it was not a strong team and we were trying to find a way.

Anyone who thinks every team is rosy is out of their minds. It is never the case, from club cricket to international cricket, there is never perfect harmony, there is always an issue, always something going on that needs to be dealt with. Ricky Ponting's team or Steve Waugh's team, those legendary sides that won all those games in a row, had issues. The difference often is that when you are winning it doesn't matter, but when you are losing everyone is looking for an excuse or a reason and we all want to blame someone else.

Another part of that episode of the documentary that was interesting was the talk about the media and the scrutiny. I honestly never let it bother me that much back then. A lot of others say that but don't mean it. At that time there was all this focus on us given it was the first time we'd played at home since the South African scandal. To add to the matter there were now two broadcasters covering the Test matches and three radio stations with rights. Then you had all the print media journos. The scrutiny and demands on our time were incredible. It also meant there were a hell of a lot of people ready to point the finger at this or that when things were going wrong, but when we won everything was fine.

It was no coincidence that when we won 2–0 against Pakistan and 3–0 against New Zealand there weren't any complaints about JL or his coaching method, but things got a bit prickly after we lost to India, again, in 2020–21.

Even before that the last day in London left a bit of a bad taste. As I said earlier, the coaches called a team meeting in the morning, kept us waiting then gave us a pretty harsh review. Most of us thought that was unnecessary. We'd retained the Ashes, no Australian team had done that since 2001, and it was not all doom and gloom which is what the coaches were saying.

There was a perception in the playing group that JL, our team manager Gavin Dovey and high performance boss Ben Oliver were too close and they would come into meetings or planning sessions with preformed ideas that they would push on us. I made them aware of it but they believed they weren't doing that. I tried to explain that whether or not it was true, the perception existed and we needed to find a way around it.

We won the first Test against India and everything was okay but then when we started losing, it felt like being in a pressure cooker.

We were a squad of 25 and we were in a bubble, we couldn't get out, everyone was on edge and someone always had the shits about something. People were starting to just look out for themselves, which happens when you are losing, but it was a difficult time and nobody in Australia had ever experienced cricket like that. The West Australians were locked out of their state and away from their families, and we had our problems with the borders in Tasmania. When the families did come up to Melbourne for Christmas, those that could, it was not a great time.

Bonnie and the kids had to go back early because we were worried they'd get locked out. Nobody was sure where the next Test would be. We were in our rooms for quarantine periods and only allowed out to train and then it was back onto your floor, no going out for dinner, no going to catch up with mates outside the game to decompress.

It was becoming obvious when the stories started dribbling out later that the boys still felt like they were on eggshells around JL and something had to be done about it. I started to spend quite a bit of time trying to make it work both ways. I saw it as my job as captain to be a go-between and sort things out, but it was getting hard to manage.

After the series JL asked me about why things were getting into the media. I told him that, yes, there were issues and I could see the problem, even though my thoughts on it didn't align with some of the other players.

It was no secret what the problems were – basically, it was just about his intensity, the boys wanted him to chill out a little bit, be less controlling. JL said, 'That's how I am,' and I replied, 'I know, but it's a bit much.'

On reflection, maybe I didn't spell it out strongly enough, but equally I thought it wasn't that big a deal. I told JL that I would speak to the Test players and tell them that he was going to work on this, but that we needed to start fresh and give him the respect to allow him to evolve. He'd come into the coaching role with a clear mandate to tidy the team up, to instil some discipline, and nobody had told him it was going too far or it was time to change. They were just whispering about it but now he knew.

After I spoke to the players I rang JL and said that they were on board, but looking back I don't think they all were.

Then there was an interview where JL said something about being himself and not changing, which didn't help things.

The team then headed off to Bangladesh and the West Indies for a limited-overs series in the middle of 2021 which most of the senior players skipped. There were stories that JL stepped right back and let the assistant coaches run training, which I think at first spooked everyone a little because he was sitting in the stands and they were all wondering what was going on. Still, he was demonstrating that he was willing to try and evolve.

However, people got uneasy around a report in the media of a blow-up which started with the team manager Gav Dovey having a go at a Cricket Australia journalist who was in the bubble with the team. JL apparently joined in to stand up for his mate, but it didn't sit too well with players who were watching and who liked this journo.

I wasn't around the group at this time but I knew there was trouble. Those blow-ups were one of the things the players didn't like.

There was real unrest among the playing group after the tour with people saying he was never going to change and I thought this was not going to end well, but out of nowhere Cricket Australia put out a media release endorsing their coach. I knew nothing about it and have to admit I was taken by surprise. Things were serious from where I was sitting but Cricket Australia just went and made a statement without speaking to us about it. You think they might have talked to us first and tried to find out what the concerns were.

That night the chief executive Nick Hockley and the chair Earl Eddings got me, Pat Cummins and Aaron Finch on the phone to talk about the situation. That was good because there was a feeling from the boys that the feedback to the board and the chief executive was not an accurate picture of what was going on. Gavin and the high performance manager Ben Oliver were very close to JL and they were the ones reporting up the line. That wasn't sitting well with the players.

Maybe the problem, too, was that I'd initially tried to take some of the sting out of the feedback to JL, but I was trying to mediate the situation. I had no problems with JL or the way he went about things, but I could see that others did and that had to be dealt with.

Maybe that shouldn't have been my job, there were other people in the organisation who could have or should have dealt with it, but I was the captain and good leaders take on jobs that others don't want to do.

I distinctly remember coming away from that phone meeting feeling that Cricket Australia was backing JL no matter what the players said. I think Earl Eddings had even started the conversation by saying something like, 'I can tell you one thing and that's that I won't be sacking the coach.' He and Nick Hockley insisted that we go back and tell JL the unvarnished truth about what the players thought.

The next phone call was the hard one. I lay awake that night sweating about it. I made notes about exactly what I had to say to JL. Then I made the call and laid it all on the table, in forensic detail, everything I had heard, what the boys were saying. I don't think I've ever given such frank and detailed criticism to anybody.

It was pretty confronting for him, I could hear that in his voice, and I braced myself for his comeback. Nine times out of ten in that situation, you'd expect the other person to be angry. But JL's reaction was to tell me, 'No one has ever spoken to me like this, nobody has ever been this honest,' and I remember him saying that it was like I'd given him a gift. The way he took it spoke volumes for the man.

After I spoke to him, Aaron and Pat called him as well and then when JL and the squad were in Adelaide in isolation after a limited-overs tour, some of the players started to have really open conversations with him. JL was genuinely shocked by what they said, he had no idea and it hurt him, but he appreciated the feedback. I thought we made some real ground after that, there was some honesty and people were owning it. I started to think that we'd got to a good place after all.

JL took it on board and applied himself twice as hard to what was being asked of him. I wasn't there, but from what I was hearing he was evolving, he was letting go, he was already giving his assistants more leeway to do their jobs, he had stepped back a little bit from the players, he wasn't overcoaching. I'm not saying he was perfect but he was evolving. It was an example that a coach doesn't have to be your best mate, there just has to be respect and honesty. I think in some instances both of those things had been missing.

The squad went to the World Cup and won, played the Ashes and won that too. Things were getting better, the complaints died down, winning makes everything sweet and I reckon JL was thinking that he'd found a new way to do his job that made it easier for him and everyone else. It was a win–win.

It's a results business and he got them.

I was hearing at the end of the summer that Cricket Australia was going to offer him a two-year contract extension or something like that. I was out of the picture by then, as was the chair Earl Eddings, who'd had JL's back.

And then the news came that they'd offered him a six-month contract.

What the fuck?

To add to the insult, it had been dragged out. Time was wasted. If Cricket Australia knew what they were going to do, they could have done it straight after the Ashes, the conversation had been going on for months, a year even, everyone knew his contract was up. I'll never back down from my opinion that it was poorly handled, embarrassing and unprofessional. I think they knew he wouldn't accept it and then they wouldn't have to sack him. It was the easy way out.

It was upsetting to see a man who cared so much treated like that. It hurt him deeply.

The bottom line in all of this is, whether he was kept on or not, he should have been treated better.

The silver lining was that every player in the group came out and supported him. They all said they respected or loved JL as a person.

14

RISING FROM THE DUST

I never did get to captain that Ashes series. The events of November 2017 finally became public and I was never to play another game of cricket for my country again. The nightmare that had haunted me in the background since the complaint in 2018 became a reality when I got a call from my manager James Henderson in November 2021 saying that a newspaper was on to the story.

I figured this was going to be bad, but I had no idea just how bad. I'd been cleared of any wrongdoing by Cricket Australia three years before and I'd addressed it with Bonnie, but dealing with the public shame was going to be tough for both of us.

James Henderson, my manager, went to work trying to deal with the crisis and the bigwigs at Cricket Australia did the same.

For the best part of ten days there was back-and-forth between them and the newspaper in an attempt to make the story go away. We told our version of the story and at times that seemed to satisfy them and at other times it didn't.

The paper had been told her version of events and gave an incomplete account of the exchange. They only had half the picture and it painted me in a bad light. Sorry, it painted me in a worse light.

Her court case was coming up again. It had dragged on over the years, with hearings and dates moving and mentions in the paper, but it was on again.

Some days the newspapers weren't going to print it, some days they were. It was nerve-racking, it was worse than four years before when the accusations were first made. Worse than any time it had popped up since. It just felt more serious.

Nick Hockley, the chief executive at Cricket Australia, and the acting chair Richard Freudenstein, were doing their bit to help, talking to the media group at the top level. James was doing the same.

I was a nervous wreck for that whole week. A few days into it James said that it looked likely the story was finally going to come out. I told Bonnie that it had all come back but this time it was more serious and it might not go away. She was not very happy, but we thought we'd dealt with it as a couple and I thought I'd dealt with it as far as cricket was concerned.

I was rehabbing from a pretty serious neck operation at the time. I've still got a big scar across my throat from the surgery which is appropriate in a macabre sort of way. I'd had a bad winter. There was a month there where I couldn't sleep because I had this excruciating pain shooting from my neck down my arms and I would lie awake all night. The only time I got any rest was when I was sitting on the couch and I would fall asleep from exhaustion, so I was pretty rundown from all that, but it was getting better and I was getting ready to return to cricket.

I had missed Tasmania's first four Sheffield Shield games of the summer, but I had a club game on the Saturday and then a Second XI game which should tune me up enough to play at least one Shield game before the Ashes.

On the Thursday I was in the change rooms with a couple of Tasmanian players including Jordan Silk and Peter Siddle. Sidds is a very close mate and one of the few people in the world I'd ever told about this shame that had dogged me for the past four years. In fact, I think that apart from Bonnie and James, he was the only person I'd told.

The phone rang, it was James and he said that the paper were going to run the story the next afternoon. My worst nightmare was coming true.

I was upset, but not devastated because I knew it was going to happen one day. I thought I knew how big and how difficult it was going to be. I never imagined it would have the consequences it did. At that point I still believed I had the support of my employer, there was a plan in place. I told the boys in the change rooms about it and headed out to face the world.

I went and saw Mum and Dad and told them. That was no fun. I'd let down so many people I loved. They were supportive, but I wasn't in the right headspace to listen, so I was in and out of there pretty quick and then went back home. There were endless phone calls back and forth with James as we worked out how to proceed and what to say when the news broke.

That night Cricket Australia had a board meeting and James rang and said that Nick Hockley and another guy wanted to talk to us. From memory it was quite late. Bonnie was upstairs in bed. We did a phone link which included this person they'd hired from a public relations firm who'd apparently given advice to the board in the past. He said that he'd been in the newspaper game for many years and this was going to be huge and would not go away. I found it very strange that this person, someone I'd never met and someone who did not work at Cricket Australia, took the lead in the call while Nick, the chief executive, took a back seat.

The consultant then said that the best way to get ahead of the story was if I stood down as captain.

I was stunned by that, so was James. Who was this guy? What did he know about the circumstances? That was the first time anyone had mentioned me resigning as captain. There was no way I was doing that. I knew what had happened. Cricket Australia knew what had happened and in my mind this guy didn't know, or worse than that, it was like he believed that I had sexually harassed her.

Then Nick chimed in, saying how experienced this guy was and how he thought I should listen to his advice.

I said, 'Do you want me to resign as Test captain, Nick?'

He couldn't give me a straight answer, or wouldn't. He kept talking around in circles.

And this guy said, 'If you resign as Test captain it will take the air out of it but if you stay on they are going to keep coming at you.' I think he said I wouldn't last until Monday and I replied that I would if they backed me in.

I said to Nick, 'You and the board know what's happened, you have an integrity report that clears me of any wrong-doing to anybody and that it was a personal matter.'

It was becoming obvious what Cricket Australia wanted me to do but they didn't have the courage to say it themselves, they were letting their hired consultant run the show.

When Nick asked me what I wanted to do, I said, 'Stick with the plans which we agreed to in the first place, nothing has changed, nothing has changed except it is going public and that is what we had the plans for.'

I think I finished the call by saying, 'I've had enough of this, I'm going to bed.'

James rang me back immediately.

'They're not going to back me in, I'm done,' I told him and then I lay awake the rest of the night. I was so disappointed by this. I hadn't seen it coming. It was obvious the board wanted me to resign and I had no option if they weren't going to back me.

I felt they were driven by the need to protect their image, they'd got in someone to look after them and he'd decided that I had to be sacrificed to save them, they were hanging me out to dry. The board had met that night and it was clear to me that they wanted to cut and run. I think that's why they got Nick and the consultant to call me. There was a feeling that if I didn't stand down, they'd stand me down.

In the morning I told Bonnie I was going to stand down as Test captain.

I rang Richard and Nick at Cricket Australia and said, 'I'm done,' and we drafted a letter. I had to say the words they wouldn't say. I couldn't go on without their support.

I was disappointed and I was tired of this. I was prepared to cop the flak for what I did, but in my mind Cricket Australia had abandoned me and made it look like they thought I'd sexually harassed someone and so everyone else would think that too. I felt like them flipping validated the story.

The thing that got me later was when Cricket Australia said that they would have handled it differently to the way it was done back in 2017, but for that seven days or whatever it was, they were doing their level best to stop the story coming out. When it got out, they seemed to change their tune about it.

I rang JL and I sent messages to the team telling them I was about to stand down as captain, and then I got into the car and drove to Bellerive for a hastily assembled media conference.

There were tears at my first media conference as Test captain when Darren Lehmann took to the microphone before me and resigned, and there were tears at this one, too. Strangely enough I'd been quite calm up until the time it came to read the statement:

Today I am announcing my decision to stand down as captain of the Australian men's cricket team. It's a difficult decision, but the right one for me, my family and cricket.

As a background on my decision, nearly four years ago, I was involved in a text exchange with a then-colleague. At the time, the exchange was the subject of a thorough Cricket Australia Integrity Unit investigation, throughout which I fully participated in and openly participated in. That investigation and a Cricket Tasmania HR investigation at the same time found that there had been no breach of the Cricket Australia Code of Conduct. Although exonerated, I deeply regretted this incident at the time, and still do today.

I spoke to my wife and family at the time and am enormously grateful for their forgiveness and support. We thought this incident was behind us and that I could focus entirely on the team, as I have done for the last three or four years. However, I recently became aware that this private text exchange was going to become public. On reflection, my actions in 2017 do not meet the standard of an Australian cricket captain, or the wider community. I'm deeply sorry for the hurt and pain that I have caused to my wife, my family, and to the other party.

I'm sorry for the damage that this does to the reputation of our sport. And I believe that it is the right decision for me to stand down as captain, effective immediately. I do not want this to become an unwelcome disruption to the team ahead of what is a huge Ashes series. I have loved my role as captain of the Australian cricket team. It's been the greatest privilege of my sporting life to lead the Australian men's Test team.

I'm grateful for the support of my teammates and proud of what we've been able to achieve together. To them, I ask for their understanding and forgiveness. To Australian cricket fans – I am deeply sorry that my past behaviour has impacted our game on the eve of the Ashes. For the disappointment I have caused to fans and the entire cricket community, I apologise. I've been blessed with a wonderful, loving and supportive family, and it breaks my heart to know how much I've let them down. They have always stood by me, been my most loyal fans, and I'm indebted to them for their support.

I will remain a committed member of the Australian cricket team, and look forward with anticipation to what is a huge Ashes tour. Thank you.

I was shaky all the way through but started to really lose it in that last bit about the support of family. I didn't take questions. I got up and walked out into a world that had changed.

My worst fears had come true.

Later, Cricket Australia put out a statement saying that they had accepted my resignation and would begin the process of picking a new captain for the team.

The statement went on to say, 'While the Board

337

acknowledges an investigation cleared Tim of any breach of the code of conduct regarding this matter some years ago, we respect his decision.'

Then they thanked me for my service as Australian cricket captain and mentioned that I could still be selected for the upcoming Ashes series.

Cricket Tasmania put out a statement too, saying that they had investigated and 'determined the interaction was consensual, private, occurred on the one occasion only, was between mature adults and was not repeated', and that they hadn't taken any further action.

I didn't turn on the radio in the car on the way home and I reckon it stayed off for the rest of the summer. When you are the news, you don't want to hear it. I kept my cap pulled down and made sure I didn't make eye contact with anyone as I drove.

I felt like a fugitive and I was going to live like that for a long time to come.

It was, as you can imagine, awful at home. I can't remember if Bonnie packed up and went to our beach place that day, but she was going to spend a lot of time there in the next few months and I couldn't blame her.

The following day I had to get up and play cricket for University, the club I'd been at since I was a teenager, because I needed to get some match practice in before the first Test. It was a nice day but the coach, my mate Damien Wright, rang me and said the pitch was wet and I should stay home as there was media everywhere.

An hour later, the club rang again and told me to come down because they'd be starting soon. I parked about a mile from the ground, they had opened a back fence for me, and I snuck in the back door of the change rooms with all the media waiting out the front. It was a total shock to see that many cameras and reporters there. It was a club game, but it felt like a siege. I didn't leave the change rooms for the whole day because they were everywhere. When Sidds came in the back gate to see me, the journos worked out how I'd got in and so they staked out my exit too. I was trapped.

The game was called off at about 2 pm because of weather and Scotty Barnes, the Hurricanes' general manager, pulled his car up as close to the change rooms as he could get but I still had to run the gauntlet like a criminal leaving a court case.

I'd never seen anything like the media scrum, they were pushing cameras into my face and every window of the car as we tried to navigate through. The journos weren't yelling or aggressive, they were people I knew, so they were asking me how I was feeling but they just wanted something, anything, for their stories.

When I got home there was media camped at the back and front of my house. They stayed there for the next week. Sometimes they'd come and knock on the door.

I was the centre of a full-blown media circus and that's not a good place to be. I can only imagine how many words were written in the newspapers, said on the television and radio about me that week.

On Saturday, Cricket Australia did a media conference. They didn't tell me they were going to do it and I could see why. That's when they said they would have handled it differently and all that stuff. The chairman Richard Freudenstein said that, 'Faced with the same circumstances and with the benefit of all the relevant information about this matter, Cricket Australia would not make the same decisions today'.

Really? Nothing had changed. Not one thing. They'd investigated me and cleared me.

The reality was they were happy to defend me and accept I hadn't breached their code of conduct as long as it was kept private. If the story hadn't run, I would still be captain and if Cricket Australia had handled it like they said they would I would still be playing for Australia.

For seven days they tried to quash the story and the only time it became different was when it was going to become public. I thought they could have dealt with the facts, they could have said, 'Here is what happened,' they could have got the integrity report and the interview with me and given it to the media, but they didn't. We asked them for those things around this time and they wouldn't give them to us. I have never received a copy of the integrity report.

The Second XI game at Lindisfarne started on the Monday. I tried to play it but I wasn't eating and I wasn't sleeping. I was physically and mentally exhausted. I kept really well behind the stumps. I got a stinking lbw decision when I batted, but I figured I deserved that. Then I hooked one to deep square in the second innings when we needed about ten to win.

Every day was worse than the one before and as the game continued I realised that I was fooling myself. At one point, while waiting to bat, I'd locked myself in the toilet cubicle and cried my eyes out. I was no good.

On the first morning of the game I'd pulled up in a little cafe near home to pick up a takeaway coffee. I got out of the car and took about six steps towards the shop and saw through the glass doors that there were people in there and immediately spun on my heels and got back in the car. There was no way I could face people. I don't know what I was thinking, stopping there. Maybe I was operating on muscle memory.

I went to the McDonalds drive-through and got coffee. Over the next couple of months that was where I'd get any food I ate, which was not much, and any coffee I drank, which was not great. I don't reckon I'd eaten fast food since I was a kid, but it was the only thing I could stomach and as time went on I started to lose a lot of weight.

I left that Second XI game and went to Cricket Tasmania and sat down with our high performance manager Simon Insley and chief executive Dom Baker and said, 'I think I'm out.' I couldn't play the one-day game that week. I told my manager Hendo. They all advised me to sleep on it, and I did, but confirmed it with them the next day.

You know, I was someone who was a little cynical about mental health issues and sport. Sometimes when people pulled out of games citing mental health, it confused me because I'd be spending time with these people but they seemed fine, then when it happens to you . . .

I couldn't control my thoughts, it was shocking. No matter how many times I tried to pull myself together, my mind just fell apart.

There was no way I could play Test cricket.

I rang JL and said I wasn't coming up to Brisbane. I told him I had to concentrate on my marriage, that I couldn't think about cricket. He understood. JL's very family-oriented, cricket might appear to be the most important thing in the world to him but he knows that family is more important.

I became really strange around this time. I couldn't listen to music because something I heard would trigger my anxiety. I switched my phone to 'do not disturb' and it stayed like that for months. Obviously I was not listening to the radio or looking at the television or social media.

Things went from bad to worse at home.

Bonnie was coming and going over the following days, she'd go down to the beach shack while I looked after the kids. It was suffocating for her. Horrible. She'd done nothing wrong and I can't blame her for trying to get away from it all, but mostly get away from me.

I wished I could do the same.

Our beach place wasn't far away and one day Bonnie was there with a few mates and these paparazzi had anchored a boat about 15 metres from our back deck and sat there with cameras. I found that staggering. That was shit and it was my fault. She was innocent but she was being publicly shamed because of me. They took photos of me and the kids, too, which was just horrible.

Bonnie shut down and then the day came when she told me that our marriage was over. There was absolutely no emotion in her voice. She was so clear, calculated and calm. It was chilling. Devastating. But understandable.

The situation had just gone from bad to worst.

In the days up to then I would look at the kids and think about how badly I'd let them down, but now it had gotten worse because they were going to have to live with their mum and dad separated. I didn't want that for them, but above all I wanted to be with Bonnie. When I thought the marriage was over I would look at the kids and see her, particularly with Milla. It broke my heart to look at these tiny people who had no idea what was going on. They were ours, but I'd screwed it all up.

I was a mess. An absolute mess. I was crying all the time. I would sit at home by myself and cry. Sometimes I would cry in front of Bonnie but tried not to because I didn't want her to see me feeling sorry for myself.

I was struggling to look after myself, let alone the kids. There were times I'd call Bonnie and say, 'You're going to have to pick them up, I have no idea what I'm going to do in the next ten minutes, I can't cope.' It was self-indulgent, I guess, but the fact was I couldn't get it together for more than a few minutes and I knew it was no good for the kids.

Thousands of people contacted me. I couldn't begin to tell you how many phone calls, texts and emails were there when I finally looked at my phone. They were all supportive but that didn't help. I still feel tainted as someone who would sexually harass women, someone who would send unsolicited sexual texts. That doesn't sit well with me.

I had some horrendous thoughts in that period. Like maybe it would be easier for people if I wasn't here. I genuinely thought that at times. I felt so ashamed about what I was putting Bonnie, my family and other people through that I thought it would be better. I knew I'd never do anything too dramatic, but just having that thought in my head freaked me out.

About two weeks in I went and saw the Cricket Tasmania team doctor and he lined me up with a psychiatrist. I was worried about the thoughts running through my head but he said he would be surprised if I didn't have that response given what I'd experienced – was experiencing. The bottom had fallen out of my world and I was in freefall. I didn't want to take any medication partly because I thought I deserved to feel the way I felt, but I needed to find a way to cope with it.

That was partly why I turned to running.

It just happened, strangely enough, on the first morning of the first Test in Brisbane. I went out and played golf that morning. I never play golf, I don't even like golf, I was just trying to find a way out of the pit I was in, looking for distraction. Then I got home and even though the television was off I knew what was going on there. There's no feeling like the first day of a big series. The anthems, the huddles, the anticipation . . .

I put my shoes on and went for a run. I'd never done that before. I never ran long distances. In fact, I despised running and the longest I'd ever done was the two-kilometre time trials at training camps.

That day I ran 15 kilometres. I just headed out and kept going. It's pretty hilly around my house and it hurt. But I kept pushing myself.

Every day after that day I ran. It was one of the only times I could go outside. I'd put on my hat and sunnies and avoid crowds or anywhere I thought people might see me. I wouldn't wear headphones, I thought that was a cop-out. A couple of times I thought I'd put them in and then I'd say to myself, 'No you won't, you don't fucking deserve it, get out there and suffer, you are a piece of shit and you should run with that pain in your head.'

It's strange but that self-loathing taught me what I was physically capable of. I had no plan but if I saw a hill I headed up it. If I started to slow down on a hill or think I should stop, I would push on, telling myself that I didn't deserve to stop, that I should keep going until I had a heart attack or collapsed.

People would say, 'It's good he's getting into his running.' They thought it was a positive sign, but it was a long way from that.

I was trying to hurt myself, I was punishing myself. It was working. Weight started to fall off me and I noticed my clothes doing the same. I lost close to ten kilos because I wasn't eating properly and I was flogging myself every day on the hills of Hobart. I hadn't been inside a gym since all this went down. Obviously I couldn't face people in that situation. The irony here is that I'm a partner in a gym chain and had been a regular presence up until then. So, I was losing muscle as well. Even I could see how drawn I looked in the mirror.

It's funny that once the Ashes started, it wasn't that I missed playing the game, it was the little things, being with the boys in the change rooms, staff members like Frankie the security guy, the rituals around our morning coffees in different towns, the huddles – I loved the huddles before play – all those unique moments you can't replace. I missed the privilege of being in that environment with that group.

As the summer progressed I'd try to watch the Ashes on the television but after two balls I would have to turn it off. It was a layer of anguish I didn't need.

I could only speak to a handful of people. Peter Siddle was strong for me. We had shared a lot of stuff over the past 12 months. He'd been going through his own problems with his marriage ending when we were in the Adelaide hub to play Shield cricket the season before. He did a remarkable job to play those games when he was not in a good place. I was rooming with him and I think that's when I first told him about my troubles.

I ended up leaning on Sidds a lot. He would drop by and we had countless coffees. He's a good man. We're both the same age, we had been through all the highs and lows of international cricket careers together, and we were tight. When my marriage was falling apart, I asked him how to get through it, because by then he was almost flourishing, he was as happy as I'd ever seen him. He told me that he was fucked for a long time but he was hiding it, he would go to work, do his job with a grin on his face and then go home and fall apart.

Sidds told me it would get better, I'm not sure I believed it would but it was good to know that he'd come through. He was right, though, and things started to improve slowly. Bonnie didn't leave and we worked hard to try and make things as right as they could ever be.

After the summer, a business mentor I had said to me that next time I went out running, I should head down to Salamanca, run where people were, rather than going up the hill where nobody was.

At first I thought that wasn't a good idea, I wasn't ready to face the world, but then I figured I had nothing to lose. I ran into town and it wasn't as bad as I thought. Nobody stopped me or abused me. Eventually I started returning to my old routines, I was pretty tentative at first but everyone was kind and encouraging. They were kinder to me than I had been to myself.

EPILOGUE

I think there was an expectation I would retire after the 2021–22 Ashes but I hadn't made that decision. I was comfortable with the idea of cricket finishing, but if I was still going okay I would push myself to get through the next series. That's how I'd been since I was picked after the Adelaide Test to finish those Ashes four years before.

If I was fit and my form was good it would be silly to hang up the gloves. The tour of Pakistan after the Ashes was a tantalising prospect and I'd talked to the selectors about that when we'd done our planning. Shane Warne said before the Ashes that I'd had a shocker as a captain and couldn't get a run in the last two series. He sent me a message later, saying it wasn't personal and that he hoped I knew it was part of his job. I was fine with him having an opinion on my captaincy or whatever, but I pulled him up on the batting part. I'd averaged 38 and 40 in the last two series. Against India I had the third-highest average behind Marnus Labuschagne and Steve Smith.

The point here isn't the argument with Shane but that even though I was 37, my game was in good order. In fact my batting was getting better every series. Not that any of that matters now, but in terms of what I would do and when I would do it, had things not turned out the way they did, I think my options were open.

I hadn't really thought seriously about what I'd do when I was finished but I knew there was always a media gig out there for a retired Australian captain. That's the cushy one. You get paid more than you would in coaching but the best thing about it is that there'd be no accountability and less stress, and that would have been enticing. Coming off the captain's job and with the scrutiny you are under as a player, I think I would have liked going into media where there's no scorecard. In coaching there's still results, still wins and losses, it is still high performance. I wanted out of that.

I think I was looking forward to getting out of cricket but I was in no rush.

I'd started doing some morning radio with Jack Riewoldt in Tasmania on SEN in the winter and I loved that. I liked getting started at 4.30 am. I enjoyed putting on my track pants, grabbing a coffee and going into a studio to talk about sport three mornings a week. That's a good gig and it's done by 9 am and you still had the opportunity to spend the rest of the day doing other things.

At the moment I don't miss international cricket. But I miss the big moments, like walking around Headingley or Lord's. You can't describe the first day of an Ashes series, that's a feeling not many people know.

You know, I think I was a bit scared to find out what I was without cricket because from the age of about 13 that was what defined me and that was how I related to the world and why people related to me. I started to think that if cricket wasn't there, all those relationships were gone. Everything in my life had cricket at its centre.

I was upset about having that taken away from me in the first instance, but that was nothing compared to having Bonnie leave me. When that happened, I just wanted her to come back and I have never wanted anything more badly.

Sure, I am disappointed not to have played the Ashes or whatever, to have it taken away from me the way it was – that was shameful and embarrassing. I'm upset and I'm angry, I have cost myself and I feel I've been let down by Cricket Australia, but I'd much rather have been through that than not have my family.

In the middle of the year my mate and the coach at University took me down the nets for a hit and it triggered something, so I started thinking about getting out and just playing cricket for fun again at that level. I don't know where it will lead, but we've found our feet at home and everyone seems really keen on the idea.

I am a better person now, a good person. We've all made mistakes, but the husband and father I've started to become is worlds away from the one I was. I've redirected all the energy I put into captaining my country and getting the best out of myself into my personal life.

This has opened my eyes. Cricket's important but it is not as important as that.

One of the few benefits of what's happened to me is that I am completely the opposite to the self-centred person I was before. I get a huge kick out of doing things for the kids and Bonnie. I said to Bonnie a few months ago that I'd never done anything for anyone else in my life. Now I get up in the morning and make her coffee or breakfast and I make the kids breakfast, just little things that they find really helpful.

It's addictive. I feel like a puppy and when they thank me I want to do more, I want to do it again.

I love it. I genuinely get a kick out of doing things for other people, particularly the ones I care the most about. Who would have thought?

I made Bonnie's life harder for ten years and now I'm trying to make it easier. It's not a big deal or earth-shattering stuff, I guess, to just be a reasonable person, but it's a long way from where I came from. These days I'm making her lunch and I'm picking her up from work and she is a bit unsettled by it. She's finding it strange, almost like 'Who is this?', and she says I am a completely different person. I don't think I am, I've just redirected my energy and focus, and the person I am now at home with her and the kids has always been there but hidden behind a heap of shit that's been scraped away.

The psych says that I was wired the wrong way. I was in high performance set-ups since I was 13 where the priority was me and being the best sportsman I could be. Anything else was a distraction. He said that I was wired to be all these things and now I need to re-wire.

The running and going to the gym is my game. I've backed off the running now and put weight back on. I lost about ten kilos in the initial aftermath, but I've built back up and exercising has become my physical outlet. It replaced cricket in a way.

There's another thing that seems strange to admit. Part of the reason I was addicted to cricket is that I was amazed I got to do what I did or be with who I got to be with. I was a battler from Lauderdale, I couldn't believe that I got to be friends with guys like Steve Smith or David Warner, let alone play for Australia and captain the team. Those people were my teammates and my friends, never in my life did I dream that would happen.

I miss that and I miss putting the tracksuit on, believe it or not. I loved the Aussie emblem and the sponsor logos. I actually wore it to the gym one day in the middle of the year and George Bailey laughed at me and said, 'Back are you?' Every time I put it on, I felt like a kid at Christmas who'd got a new cricket bat. Every single time.

When everything fell to pieces, I threw away all my gear including the precious tracksuits. I realise I shouldn't have done it, but I also understand I had to find something else to give me that feeling, I had to let go.

At times it makes me smile and at times it makes me really sad.

The team got together and gave me this kind of mural thing that's a series of photos of my Test career. It was a gift they left for me in Hobart after the last Ashes Test.

You'd have to think the game was mocking me, wouldn't you? There'd never been an Ashes Test in Hobart but in that summer they made the last Test of the series at my home ground. Not far from Nan's house.

JL and Pat Cummins and all the boys had told me I could drop in anytime during the summer. They were really keen to have me there in the Hobart Test. Cricket Australia wanted me to come too.

I wanted to be in the change rooms, I wanted to be there at the ground and I wanted to see everyone, but I couldn't do it, I reckon I would have cried.

You know, in my head I'd planned my retirement and I wasn't going to tell anyone. I didn't know when it was going to come, but I wanted to go out the way I came in. I was not a Warne or a Gilchrist. I didn't want attention. In my plan I was just going to ring the selectors and the coach before a tour and say, 'I'm not going,' and they'd put out the squad without my name in it.

Some people expect me to play state cricket next summer but we'll have to see how that goes.

In the end, when the Ashes came to Hobart I was miles away. I'd left town and I'd left the game and it was all too much, too soon. I don't know if I'll ever be able to walk back into the dressing rooms again but I miss my mates and I miss all the things I left behind.

It's funny how your mind works. When I was on those long runs around Hobart, most times when it was getting hard I would do it to punish myself, but sometimes this old thought would come in that I had to keep going because there was a tour coming up and I had to be right for it. That would get me up another hill, but it was a stupid thought, a fantasy that I didn't seriously contemplate.

Shane Warne had sent me another text when everything blew up, saying he was happy to talk if it would help and that he'd been through similar situations. It was good of him to reach out and demonstrates the sort of bloke he was. A couple of months later I was checking into a hotel in Brisbane to escape Hobart and the last Ashes Test when

Andrew Symonds called. He said that he, too, had been
through his share of public drama and if I needed anyone
to chat with, he was there. It was classic Symmo.

Then both of them were gone and I still can't get used
to that.

In the last text exchange I had with Shane, he'd said,
'At the end of the day family is the most important thing,
fuck everything else.' Whatever I end up doing, I'll live
by that.

ACKNOWLEDGEMENTS

Thanks to Mum and Dad for all their support and the love. My siblings Nick, Madeline and Meagan. My Nan, who was at every single early game armed with sandwiches and a smile.

To the coaches who have helped me to the next level at every step of the game: Enrico Di Venuto, Tim Coyle, who had an enormous influence on me, Jeff Vaughan and Justin Langer, who schooled me in the game and became lifelong friends. To University of Tasmania Cricket and Cricket Tasmania, which became like second homes.

To James Henderson, my manager and mate, who has guided me through every part of this journey.

To Ricky Ponting, who inspired me when I was young and rescued my career when everyone thought it was done.

To Pan Macmillan for publishing my story, and Peter Lalor for help with the wordsmithing.

And to Bonnie, Milla and Charlie, my family, thank you.

INDEX

INDEX

INDEX

INDEX

INDEX

INDEX

INDEX

INDEX